WHITMAN COLLEGE LIBRAR
Latin American Politics

D0040093

Translations from Latin America Series
Institute of Latin American Studies
University of Texas at Austin

WHITMAN COLLEGE LIBRAR

LATIN AMERICAN POLITICS
A Theoretical Framework

By Torcuato S. Di Tella

Withdrawn by
Whitman College Library

 University of Texas Press, Austin

JL
966
.D513
1990

This book is a revised version, translated by the author, of *Sociología de los procesos políticos: una perspectiva latinoamericana* (Buenos Aires: Grupo Editorial Latinoamericano, 1985; reprinted by Editorial Universitaria de Buenos Aires, 1987).

Parts of chapters 8 and 9 were published previously in English as an article "Working Class Organization and Politics in Argentina," *Latin American Research Review* 16, No. 2 (1981), pp. 33–56.

Copyright © 1990 by the University of Texas Press
All rights reserved
Printed in the United States of America

First Edition, 1990

Requests for permission to reproduce material from this work should be sent to Permissions, University of Texas Press, P.O. Box 7819, Austin, Texas 78713-7819

The paper used in this publication meets the minimum requirements of American National Standard for Information Sciences—Permanence of Paper for Printed Library Materials, ANSI Z39.48–1984. ∞

Library of Congress Cataloging-in-Publication Data

Di Tella, Torcuato S., 1929–
      [Sociología de los procesos políticos. English]
      Latin American politics: a theoretical framework / Torcuato S. Di Tella
            p.   cm. — (Translations from Latin America Series)
      Translation of: Sociología de los procesos políticos.
      Includes bibliographical references.
      ISBN 0-292-74661-X. — ISBN 0-292-74664-4 (pbk.)
      1. Latin America—Politics and government—1948– 2. Political
science—Latin America. 3. Political sociology. I. Title.
II. Series.
JL966.D513 1990   89-37497
320.98—dc20   CIP

PENROSE MEMORIAL LIBRARY
RECEIVED

APR 16 1990
90-6589m
ACQUISITIONS DEP'T
DEC 17 1990

For Tamara, who is a bit responsible

PENROSE MEMORIAL LIBRARY
RECEIVED

APR 1 6 2020

ACQUISITIONS DEPT

Contents

Preface and Acknowledgments

This book is the result of a long journey in which I have tried to integrate different intellectual traditions and research strategies. I owe a great deal to the very stimulating atmosphere created by Gino Germani in the Sociology Department and José Luis Romero in the Institute of Social History of the University of Buenos Aires during the late fifties and early sixties. The search for universally valid truth, which was promoted there, has persisted, though enriched by the necessary adaptation to a local perspective. I remain committed to the scientific approach, which distinguishes between the study of reality and the attempt to change it, however much both tasks are connected in practice. I also believe in the need to formalize and quantify the description and study of that reality by reducing it to clearly defined variables and hypotheses.

But it would be naïve to think that that is the end of the story. National characteristics, to a large extent shared throughout Latin America, require an adaptation of the above-mentioned intellectual package, although without going to the extremes of the xenophobic nationalist reaction that gripped intellectual circles in the University of Buenos Aires and other parts of Argentina and the continent as a reaction to the eclipse of democracy by the mid sixties. Even if in an early essay I had written about the *homo peripheriae* as typical of the Latin American condition, I must admit that it took some time before I came to appreciate fully the need for understanding our own history and valuing our political and intellectual experiences as a way of correcting distortions in perspective.

On my journey of discovery I met politicians like Víctor Raúl Haya de la Torre and spoke, sometimes heatedly, with others like Raúl Ampuero and Clodomiro Almeyda, typical practitioners of that wonder that was the Chilean political system. Their influence and example were stronger than they may have realized, as were those of others more academically oriented, like Hélio Jaguaribe, Fernando Henrique Cardoso, and Raúl Prebisch. My work experience in Chile and Brazil and—in a more imaginary dimension—in Mexico contributed to my itinerary. I came to consider as contemporaries—and members of a developing nationality—such figures as Túpac Amaru or Toussaint Louverture and I came to appreciate, in spite of some excesses in their romantic phraseology, our nineteenth-century thinkers, beginning with Simón Bolívar. I persist in rejecting hagiography, but I consider essential a familiarity with what has been going on for almost two centuries in terms of political experience and analysis as seen from the participants' perspective. That is why in this book theoretical elaboration is intimately connected with an examination of historical events, mostly those that took place in the area, although, of course, without forgetting a wider comparative reference. The Latin American conterednooo io nooeooary if only to oomponoate the moro uoual poropootivo, whioh, as a result of cultural dependency, sees things from the outside.

It is obvious that in this effort the sociologist must establish an intense dialogue with the historian, often resistant to formalizations and generalizations. In this sense I benefited from a prolonged stay in Great Britain, at the Universities of London and Oxford, citadels of the most diffident empiricism in these matters. If I survived the experience, coming to appreciate much of what that approach has of validity, and emerged still holding to my sociological beliefs, it was only after profound soul searching. Tulio Halperín Donghi, Herbert Klein, and Luis González y González have performed an important role in this dialogue. My conclusion is that it is necessary to disaggregate the empirical material offered by a society as much as possible. To make sociological generalizations or hypotheses about societies in general may be interesting as a sensitizing device, but often does not lead to valid results. It is necessary to get to smaller units of observation—social classes, institutions, or other types of groups—and then to reconstitute their interactions as the stuff of politics. Sociological laws should, preferably, apply to the behavior of those component parts, not to society as a whole, which is much more unpredictable in its behavior.

I undertook a theoretical revision of the literature and a reinterpretation of events in Latin American history around 1964, in collaboration with Oscar Cornblit and Ezequiel Gallo and with some prodding from Gino Germani. The intent was to see to what extent Latin American experience exemplified, validated, or forced corrections of existing theories. The aim was somewhat excessive, but it produced a formalized model, which, after several revisions and adaptations, has been a guide to my thinking in the planning and writing of this book.

From a methodological and epistemological point of view, I had the benefit of going for advice to Gregorio Klimovsky and Thomas Moro Simpson. The study of authoritarianism owes a lot to conversations with Carlos Strasser, José Nun, Wanderley Guilherme dos Santos, and Guillermo O'Donnell. On the subject of populism and socialism I am indebted to Leôncio Martins Rodrigues, Manuel Mora y Araujo, Miguel Murmis, Juan Carlos Portantiero, Eugenio Kvaternik, Juan Carlos Torre, and the late Jorge Barría.

The economic explorations of Arturo O'Connell and Javier Villanueva, concerned as they are with the Argentine riddle, were also very helpful, as were the Economic Commission for Latin America and Raúl Prebisch. To all of them I must express my recognition without pretending to shield myself behind their authority, although I do use some of their recipes in my own theoretical kitchen.

In the approach here adopted, the sociological study of political processes must keep as close as possible to short-term and detailed events, rather than attempting generalizations about broader themes, such as modernization, transition to socialism, or redemocratization. Not that these are not valid, even essential, subjects of study, but they must be approached by breaking them down into their constituent elements. Sociological hypotheses and generalizations will then apply to those elementary components, not to the processes as a whole, which are the outcome of a complex interaction, with many contingent factors and unforeseen singular events. This being so, prophecy is impossible, quite apart from being desirable or not.

Marxism has been one of the main attempts at establishing long-range forecasts of historical paths, combining as it does factual with evaluative statements. This has proved to be scientifically invalid, although it has been successful in creating a universal religion, which today is as difficult to judge as was Christianity in the time of Torquemada. At any rate, despite ideological and political distortions, Marx is responsible, with Darwin and Freud, for the Copernican revolution in the image humanity has of itself. Successful application of the relevant theory needs a total break with self-styled orthodoxies or reductionisms, however.

In this book the presupposition is accepted that the study of society must be started with a consideration of the social class structure. But this is coupled with the determination to use as many "superstructural" variables, even as independent factors, as necessary, an approach today quite current among Marxist scholars. More controversial, in this theoretical tradition, is the perception of the impossibility, given present and foreseeable technological characteristics, of a classless society. This has important consequences for the analysis of socialist societies—which I prefer to call bureaucratic-collectivist—and for the determination of the social groups more likely to favor transitions toward that type of system.

Two theoretical and practical concerns dominate the book: the prerequisites for democracy, and the role of the popular classes in social change. Democracy is first of all a concept about which some debate may legitimately exist; this is referred to in the first chapter and taken up again several times. The importance of the class structure as the source of conflicts and tensions is seen in chapter 2, and chapter 3 introduces the main contenders in the political game, the social actors. Various aspects of the concentration or fragmentation of power are seen in chapter 4, followed by a treatment of violence and revolution in chapter 5 and military intervention in chapter 6. The last four chapters, 7 to 10, are an extended commentary on the predicament of the popular classes, especially under conditions of relative underdevelopment, given a theoretical vision that no longer sees them as necessarily associated with the establishment of a socialist order via the revolutionary collapse of capitalism. Leaving aside millenarian hopes, the objective of a socialist society is still a valid subject for study or for practical commitment. The last four chapters are dedicated to a better understanding of this matter and consider alternative courses of action and the role of intellectuals in the process.

Finally, in the appendix I doff my sociologist-cum-historian hat to don the more ferocious headgear of a modelist. The appearance is strictly limited to the confines of the appendix, however, so that sensitive readers can avoid it altogether or else enter it as consenting adults.

This book is a revised version of *Sociología de los procesos políticos: una perspectiva latinoamericana* (Buenos Aires: Grupo Editorial Latinoamericano, 1985; reissued by Editorial Universitaria de Buenos Aires, 1987). I undertook the revision and translation during an extended stay at the University of Texas at Austin during the academic year 1987–1988, with the sponsorship of the Institute of Latin American Studies and the C. B. Smith, Sr. Centennial Chair in U.S.-Mexico Relations and a travel grant from the Fulbright Commission. Professors Richard N. Adams and Bryan Roberts, of the sponsoring institutions, were particularly helpful as interlocutors in this last important stage of my project. So too were many other members of the university (too many to enumerate) and the graduate students with whom I came in contact, always ready to poke the weaker spots of one's armor. To all of them, my thanks.

1. The Study of Latin American Politics

Writing in 1853, Juan Bautista Alberdi, the noted Argentine political thinker, argued that the trouble with the Spanish American republics was that they had gone through too many "democratic revolutions." He was involved at the time in a violent polemic with Domingo Faustino Sarmiento, compatriot in exile in Chile, about how to handle the situation after the recent demise of Juan Manual de Rosas' long dictatorship. Sarmiento favored a radical rejection of all elements associated with the deposed regime, including the rival *caudillo* who had overthrown it and who had been its supporter for many years. Alberdi thought it necessary to make more concessions to the existing structure of power, so as to bend it in favor of a possibilistic version of social change. He inveighed against the earlier, rigidly ideological generation of liberals, who had allowed power to slip from their hands and had refused to "establish a government with some Asiatic traits, akin to those of the land of its application." Alberdi reproached Sarmiento for not drawing the logical conclusions from his own analysis in *Facundo*, where he had described those "Asiatic" characteristics. "It is not *resistance,* Señor Sarmiento," he added, "that good writers should teach our rebellious Spanish America, but rather *obedience.* Resistance will not give us freedom; it will only jeopardize the establishment of *authority*, which South America has sought since the inception of its revolution as the basis and fountainhead of its political existence."[1]

One may wonder what conception of "democracy" could lead one to say that Latin America had had too much of, in the middle of the nineteenth century. In fact, it was a hallowed traditional interpretation, beginning with Aristotle, who condemned *mere* democracy, equating it with power of the popular sectors, or prevalence of popular pressure, and contrasted it with *politeia*, or mixed government. In a *politeia* channels were also provided for the expression of the interests of the middle and upper sectors. Balanced government required an element of aristocracy, or of what today we would call "technocracy."

But was there any truth in Alberdi's contention that there had been a lot of, if not democracy, at least popular pressure in the Latin American political experience? Duly interpreted, he was right. From early times, mass rebellions had punctuated the continent's history, notably those initiated by Túpac Amaru in 1780 in Peru, the

Haitian slave rebellion at the time of the French Revolution, and the Mexican insurgents of 1810, all of which involved vast masses in extremely violent confrontation with the dominant powers. The fear of mass rebellion interfering with elite-controlled emancipation bedeviled the independence era. The prospect of a conventional separatist war degenerating into "caste war" was present almost everywhere. In a subsequent period, many *caudillos* enjoyed considerable popular support, expressed in street agitation or militia participation. In some instances the resulting rule was socially progressive, in others regressive and conservative. In either case, popular support was not simply a decorative feature of these regimes, but an important element in their acquisition and retention of power. They could be considered, then, from an Aristotelian point of view, as in some way democratic. But very often they did not respect due process and they lacked the other component of a democratic government, a balance of powers.

The mixture required for mixed government, however, had to be different in Spanish or Portuguese America than in Europe or the United States. According to Alberdi, it was necessary to incorporate not only elements of aristocracy but of monarchy, that is, strong presidentialism, able to influence elections so as not to be unduly dependent on the vagaries of public opinion, which might produce civil war rather than peaceful alternations in office. It is easy today to scorn Alberdi's insistence on authority, equating it with the more recent twentieth-century authoritarian arguments of the military dictators and their civilian advisers. The difference is basic, however, because modern authoritarianism—not to speak of totalitarianism—is not concerned with the balance of power, and it enforces state terrorism and systematic violation of human rights—this as much in the capitalist as in the socialist areas. While condemning the *caudillista* exercise of popular power, Alberdi was not rejecting an approximation to constitutional democracy, a regime, however, that in those days existed in a precious few countries in the world. What can be validly retained from his approach is that to consolidate democracy, it is necessary to pay attention to the legitimate formation of authority in the state and to ensure adequate conditions for the exercise of technocratic and managerial functions in the sphere of production.

It should be noticed, in this context, that in the present state of liberalization in Latin America, many a civilian government is turning out to be a strong government, stronger, as a matter of fact, than some of the military dictatorships that they replaced. In a sense, these new democracies are doing what Alberdi thought was necessary: to consolidate authority, which is not the same as authoritarianism, but which has definite requirements. Those requirements do not consist simply of the expansion of basic freedoms; they also involve the strengthening of bureaucratic, technocratic, administrative, scientific, and teaching structures, that is, the "aristocratic" component in a truly Aristotelian *politeia*. To combine this component with the other one, involving distribution, participation, sectoral demands, in short, egalitarianism, is no easy matter, particularly under straitened economic conditions. Any society that does not provide adequate institutions for the expression of those contradictory requisites can easily degenerate into a war of all against all.

On the other hand, the revolutionary socialist experience has reproduced, in a different context, many of the problems that bedeviled Western capitalist countries during the early stages of industrialization. The Leninist ideology argued the case for a "democratic dictatorship," or unobstructed proletarian rule. The passage of time showed that this was no temporary expedient, but tended to consolidate and generate strong vested interests for its continuation. However, there is also a need here to recognize the requirements of authority and management of complex structures. The genuine democratization of socialist regimes requires something more than the creation of areas of freedom and grass-roots participation. A *glasnost*, to prevail, must also provide adequate guarantees to the bureaucracy.

In Latin America the prospects for democracy depend also on an adequate equilibrium of power between the forces of the Right and those of the Left or of the popular parties. Popular movements, already significant in some countries before the Second World War, experienced a new surge as a result of the increased pace of rural urban migration and industrialization. The lack of previous political experience and the difficulty of establishing autonomous class organizations resulted in the spread of a new form of *caudillismo*, often of an authoritarian nature. Gino Germani observed this process in the early fifties and created the term *"nacionalismo popular"* to describe it. In contrast with those who believed it was only a form of fascism, he pointed to what may be called the "democratic" nature—in the Aristotelian sense of the term—of those phenomena. He believed that the difficulty *nacionalismo popular* had in adopting modern liberal democratic features lay in the semirural, traditional, mobilized but not yet organized character of the mass of its supporters. To this were added the authoritarian preferences of some of the anti–status quo elites that joined the movement and generally provided the leadership and the entourage of the *caudillo*. It was foreseeable that with the passage of time and with a greater experience of urban life, there would be a reconciliation of the popular majority with the requisites of a division of power and a respect for minorities. The result would be an *integration* of the masses in a pluralist political system, with a capitalist basis though with important elements of state property, planning, and social welfare.[2]

The Fall and Rise of Democracy

Beginning in the sixties an increasing malaise was felt toward this view, as it became clear that many countries in the area were not developing fast enough, and democratization, far from consolidating, suffered serious setbacks. The military coups of the decade, including those in countries that might be considered similar from many points of view, like Greece or Turkey, led observers to believe that a new phenomenon was in the offing, not a mere temporary downturn in an otherwise ascending curve. The evolutionist perspective implicit in the previous paradigm was questioned, and a basic difference between central and peripheral countries was posited as a result of dependency. Some economists, like Celso Furtado, forecast a stoppage of development, which would naturally stimulate violent confrontations, dictatorship, and, as a reaction, social revolution. Others, like Fernando Henrique Cardoso, Hélio Jaguaribe, and Osvaldo Sunkel, accepted the existence of alternatives, arguing that economic development might continue, though under conditions of transnational domination and dependency, which set limits to the social consequences of growth and made the consolidation of democracy as its result more unlikely.[3] Both the prospect of dependency with stagnation, or heavily dependent development, converged into catastrophic scenarios. An increase in revolutionary tensions was forecast, as exemplified by the Cuban case. The repression, in Chile, of one of the more important democratic alternatives confirmed the diagnosis, polarizing opinion in intellectual and political circles.

Another line of thought was growing parallel to these, mostly in the North, which attempted to reconcile itself to the inevitable, that is, to authoritarianism by exploring the positive aspects it might have. The term "modernizing autocracy" was created to distinguish some of the new regimes from traditional barracks dictatorships. A modernizing autocracy might be necessary as a step in the construction of a productive apparatus. It was seen as a sort of capitalist Stalinism or, to use more proximate examples, an updated version of the regime of Porfirio Díaz in Mexico, whose developmental traits were being rediscovered. It was thought that conditions under early industrialization did not allow for a wider sharing of power between groups or classes, not even a restricted version of a balanced *politeia*.[4]

From a Latin American perspective, Guillermo O'Donnell tried to interpret these tendencies, coining the term "bureaucratic-authoritarian" to describe the emerging regimes. He rejected the stagnationist forecast and argued that, rather, this type of modern authoritarianism was a response to the needs for deepening industrialization in a context of dependency. The vested interests created around the new industries pressed for a repressive government to maintain discipline in the workplace and stop redistributive efforts so as to protect capital accumulation. This was not intended as a justification of the supposedly functional traits of those regimes. On the contrary, their hypothesized need to appeal to dictatorship became the basis for their condemnation. It was implicitly assumed that under some new form of socialism there would be no need for such repressive apparatuses.

In O'Donnell's vision another aspect was added to this analysis about the pressures emanating from the requirements of intensified industrialization: the concept of popular menace toward the existing system of domination, that is, toward private property of the means of production. In the more simplistic evolutionist scheme the working class was seen as passing through a period of violent radicalization at a relatively early stage of development, only to become eventually integrated into the system via reforms and acquisition of social citizenship. Germani had made some alterations to that sequence and emphasized the greater duration, in the countries of the periphery, of the transitory period of nonintegration of the masses. The result was the abundance of "available masses," whose heavy load of traditionalism mixed with frustration, mobilization, and authoritarianism made them easily amenable to alliances with disgruntled sectors of the elites. Economic conditions in the periphery, on the other hand, induced anti–status quo attitudes among some sectors of the upper or middle strata, thus providing the bases for coalitions between social actors located in widely separated parts of the social pyramid. But despite this, in the long run, Germani did forecast a progressive integration of the working class in the capitalist system, reproducing with some delay events in the Northern Hemisphere.

O'Donnell attempted to break what he considered an unwarranted and optimistic unilinearity. He maintained that a capitalist regime burdened with dependency and the requirements of intensified industrialization would not be able to afford the integration of the working class. He recognized that populism had attempted, though under somewhat authoritarian conditions, to incorporate those masses and distribute some of the benefits of growth; but due to economic astringency, the dominant sectors would inevitably appeal to the armed forces for a noninclusive, repressive regime. This would generate a vicious circle, because the excluded masses would become ever angrier and more menacing. Any attempted democratization might give rise to renewed activity of a threatening kind, and thus generate demands for a return to the more repressive features of the bureaucratic authoritarian regime. It was unclear, in this view, which would be the final outcome. One possibility is that after two or three decades of successful accumulation conditions would change, and the system liberalize slowly without mishaps, opening a *"tiempo político"* made possible by the larger size of the cake. The other alternative was that eventually the bureaucratic authoritarian regime would lose control, despite repression, inaugurating an era of revolution and radical transformation.[5]

Eventually, during the decade of the eighties it became necessary to introduce changes into this analysis. It was apparent that several authoritarian regimes were in the process of democratization, not necessarily as a result of successful accumulation, and that the outcome would not be the creation of an excessively menacing popular force. To understand the new scenario, it became necessary to distinguish sectors within the government and in the opposition (the *duros* and the *blandos*, or hawks and doves, intransigents and negotiators, and so forth). The somewhat deterministic and rigid outlines of the previous scheme gave place to almost its opposite, a flexible description of events, alliances, and strategic decisions of participants.[6] The evolution is welcome, making theoretical analysis more human, more adaptable to the fluid character of reality. With the diffusion of democratization in Latin America by the late eighties, it is evident that the resulting mood of the masses and the anti–status quo elites does not follow a rigid pattern, but rather varies according to each country's social structure and political traditions. Each process should be studied as a special case, tracking down the effects and mutual interactions of a host of variables, according to the historian's craft. But it is not necessary to give up theory as the price of factual accuracy.

Sociological Laws and Historical Processes

The sociological approach involves establishing relationships between variables, which apply *other things being equal*. A confirmed and widely accepted relationship can be termed a law; more modestly, while it does not yet have enough evidence behind it, it is a hypothesis. The problem, of course, is that the impossibility of holding experiments and keeping "other things constant" makes the task extremely difficult and often unrewarding. To add confusion, there is free will or human volition, the analysis of which has produced and will go on producing endless volumes. The combination of all these considerations should make us tread with great care before offering sociological laws, or even hypotheses, for consideration.[7] At any rate, it is highly unlikely that any concrete historical event or process (like democratization, or its breakdown) could be explained by just a couple of hypotheses, even by approximation. On the other hand, though, if a large number of variables, running into the dozens, are required, explanation may become unwieldy, or look excessively like mere description. Common language itself is not designed for handling so many variables in interaction at a time. It should be replaced by a mathematical or formal logical treatment, a system of equations, leading to a model. But this is not realistic either, because of the impossibility of measuring the variables concerned.

As a result of these difficulties, the dominant attitude among historians is to stick to the exact and painstaking description of what actually happened, establishing causal connections between singular facts or events. These connections are established without attempting to derive them from a more general law. The refusal to explore the existence of general laws can derive from practical or epistemological grounds. Historians are in a stronger position when they say that, in practice, it is extremely difficult, and unrewarding, to look for those general laws. They are in a weaker position, however, if they argue that because of the "peculiarities of the situation," or the "nonreproducibility of historical events," no lawlike statements can be ascertained.[8]

While recognizing the strength of the practical historian's arguments, in this book the sociological approach is maintained, though with great respect for the complexities of each situation. Human curiosity being boundless, a search for generalizing hypotheses is irrepressible. Even the most classical historians use them, however implicitly. The sociologist's contribution to a better knowledge of man and society is to look explicitly for systems of scientific, that is, general, hypotheses, which can apply to more than one case.

A central problem in the establishment of sociological theory is the definition of the variables that are going to be related to each other. They may be very concrete or highly abstract; they may incorporate very heterogeneous empirical contents or they may be more selective in one dimension. Let us analyze, from this point of view, a statement by the nineteenth-century Mexican historian and politician Lucas Alamán: "[Our political convulsions are erroneously attributed] to our inexperience, to the inclinations of our military officers, to the fickleness of our opinions, to the violence of parties. . . . There is another more effective cause: the contradiction between our form of government and our national reality."[9] Here several hypotheses are denied, and one is asserted. In the latter, two very abstract variables are used, which incorporate multiple meanings: *form of government* and *national reality.* The relationship that is stated to hold between them (contradiction) may be interpreted as meaning that there are marked differences between the distribution of power deriving from constitutional provisions and that which is rooted in other aspects of civil society. As a result of this relationship, it is argued, a state of convulsion arises, that is, a predisposition to violent and constant changes of government, which seriously affect the economic and social situation of individuals. It can be seen that the variables employed are highly abstract and multidimensional and incorporate many different meanings, in many directions. Statements that include such variables may be valid, as surely Alamán's is. But, in fact, they do not help very much to understand concrete events, except by reference to a much more general situation, or as illustrations of a condition that includes them. Let us suppose that we want to know why Pres. Antonio López de Santa Anna was overthrown in 1844. Can we apply Alamán's law? In fact, this law only predicts that any government is likely to be overthrown violently, with serious consequences for daily civilian life. The stated law explains the recurrence of a large number of events (the many social and political alterations of Mexico at that time), each one of them being simply an indicator of the variable used (political "convulsions"). But if we wish to deepen the study of a given event, like the downfall of Santa Anna in 1844, we need a different type of variable and hypothesis, a type that would allow us to draw conclusions from some of the singular events that happened during that year or some of the preceding ones.

Let us now take an opposite example, one in which excessively specific variables are used to understand a historical event. Ian Christie, describing the American War of Independence, says,

> The British had lost. But competent historians have expressed their view that in the early stages at least they might have won. . . . The seizure of New York in 1776 gave the British an important strategic advantage. . . . During the next eighteen months errors of execution rather than an utter lack of resources for the task were the main reasons for defeat. The two more fatal were . . . the failure . . . to force Washington into pitched battle on unfavourable terms . . . and the failure to take only ground that could be held and to hold ground once taken.[10]

Of course, it is very difficult to discuss the various points made in the text, particularly when stated in such a contrafactual form. But few people would feel convinced that the historical outcome can depend on such "mistakes." It is not necessary to subscribe to a totally deterministic interpretation of history to believe that if the United States had not got its independence, or had had to wait a couple of generations to achieve it, it would have been due to more weighty reasons than those referred to in the above text. In other words, there must have been some very solid factors making it difficult for the British to obtain a victory, so that the moment they committed a mistake, its consequences easily proved fatal, although the opposite was not true for their enemies.

A first-hand knowledge of history does have the advantage, at any rate, of sensitizing us to the plurality of causes and mechanisms present in any concrete historical process. Simplification is legitimate in formulating a general hypothesis *relating variables* to each other; but, when the task is the description of a *historical process*, which is a succession of singular events, the wisest thing is to accept that there is a whole array of relevant general hypotheses that, combined with a plethora of initial conditions, will result in a very labyrinthine path. It is not convenient, and probably not possible, to establish a causal connection between the actual path (which is a succession of singular events) and the variables that are supposed to be explanatory.[11] In a society, at any given moment, a multitude of causes are in operation, so it will never be possible to explain the total outcome in terms of just one hypothesis. It is necessary to employ many hypotheses and to consider a large number of initial conditions, or exogenous factors, to obtain finally the actual historical result.

Good historical research provides an excellent basis for establishing the level of abstraction at which concepts should be constructed, and the degree of detail necessary for realistic description. Let us take as an example an article by Tulio Halperín Donghi on the rise of the *caudillos* in the Río de la Plata region, to see at what point sociological analysis can make its contribution.[12] Halperín Donghi takes four cases, roughly within the first two revolutionary decades (1810–1830): Martín Güemes in Salta, Francisco Ramírez in Entre Ríos, Felipe Ibarra in Santiago del Estero, and Facundo Quiroga in La Rioja. We shall see (table 1), beginning with the Salta case, how the author's argument can be outlined, singling out the main factual statements and marking the causal relationships, of which some are numbered to comment on them later on.

In this scheme one of the more important sequences goes from the intensity of the war of independence (singular fact B) to the recruitment of militia at a provincial rather than a purely local level (singular fact G) and thence to the mobilization of the rural population in such a way that it erodes traditional local loyalties (fact J). This causal mechanism is the one that provides the available mass for a mobilizational experience. If to it we add the existence of strong antagonisms between classes (fact H), we get the basic etiology of the type of populism led by Güemes in Salta, in the north of Argentina. It is also important to note that, given the existence of deep divisions within the Salta upper class, some of its members having gone over to the royalist side, a policy of requisitions and confiscations against them became easier. This had an impact on the political system as a whole, increasing the need to mobilize the militia (E to F to J). We should also note the sequence (from

Table 1. The Emergence of the *Caudillo* System in the Province of Salta, Argentina, under Güemes (ca. 1810–1830)

Singular Facts	Causal Lines	Singular Facts	Causal Lines	Singular Facts
A. From 1810 commercial circuits to Upper Peru are broken because of war	→	E. Salta's upper class suffers economic deterioration and splits between patriots and royalists		
B. War in Salta is very intense and is made with local resources	→ (1)	F. Requisitions and confiscations of upper class property are made to finance the war effort	(2)	
		G. New militia are recruited on provincial basis, superseding old locally manned ones	→	J. High mobilization of rural population, which no longer recognizes local leadership
C. In Salta there is great social rigidity and distance between classes	→	H. Antagonisms between upper and popular classes are very high	(4) (3)	
D. Güemes is a marginal member of Salta's upper class	→	I. Güemes adopts attitudes opposed to those common in his social class	→ (5)	K. A radicalized populist regime with *caudillo* leadership emerges

D to I) that indicates that Güemes' being a marginal member of the local upper class facilitated his adoption of anti–status quo policies.

All of these causal connections are stated as though they were so many other singular facts. This is partly due to the degree of detail in which the historical process is described, subdivided into its component parts, so that the connections stated are almost considered to be common sense. The emphasis, therefore, is put on the research necessary to ascertain the facts, letting them, so to say, speak for themselves. Two causal chains stand out as particularly important. The first is the already-mentioned sequence relative to the mobilization of the rural population, indicated with numbers 1 and 2 over the relevant arrows in table 1. The second is the process (marked 3, 4, 5) by which the coexistence of a mobilized mass, strong social antagonisms and a leadership drawn from the upper classes, generates a radicalized variety of populism. The first sequence (1–2) we can call the *mobilization process*. The second (3–4–5) is the *formation of a populist coalition*.

We may contrast the situation in Salta with that in Santiago del Estero, a less prosperous and more central province, where the war of independence had only marginal effects. Table 2 gives a scheme formally similar to the one for Salta, so as to make comparison easier.

Now we are confronted with a much more reduced process of mobilization, due to a weaker war pressure and to the absence of requisitions against the upper classes. This lower level of mobilization could also be linked to other factors, for example, the form of aggregation of the urban and rural popular strata in productive enterprises, the stability of their occupational situation and land tenure, or their migratory patterns, though these factors do not appear in the above scheme. On the other hand, if we examine the form in which the populist coalition was formed and compare it with the Salta case, it is reasonable to expect that the Santiago type of *caudillismo* will be more conservative and regionalist. The main conflict, which in Salta runs across a *horizontal* line separating upper from lower strata, is replaced by another one grouping sectors on each side of a *vertical* line, separating regions from each other, or the whole province from the rest of the nation.

Similar schemes could be established for Entre Ríos and La Rioja. The accumulation of these types of sequences should allow us to try some generalizations, as well as to suggest other cases worth investigating for the purpose of building a system of hypotheses applicable to various historical instances. In some cases, the author proposes explicit general hypotheses. This happens when he observes that in agricultural zones *caudillo* leaders do not emerge, though there may be local violence (p. 146). He establishes the following causal sequence: (1) where there is large property, authoritarian relationships dominate the scene; (2) large property produces social homogeneity, simplifying the class structure; (3) even when the *caudillo* is not himself a large property holder, he uses to his advantage the existing system of authoritarian relationships; and (4) the fact of having performed police or judicial roles, delegated from the old viceregal center, allows the potential *caudillo* to achieve wider positions of leadership, thus consolidating his position, provided the other three factors are present (pp. 142–147).

Another case of the use of a general hypothesis is Halperín's analysis of the "democratic" impact of *caudillo*-led militarization, at a time when one man meant one gun. Here also a general hypothesis is being assumed, and the concept of democratization is used in the sense employed at the beginning of this chapter. The author is no doubt conscious of this, when he indicates that there is a complex interaction between the *caudillo*'s popularity, which makes him to some extent a representative of his followers, and his exercise of command, which converts him into an unquestioned and authoritarian superior, associated to a structure of large landed property, and therefore socially quite conservative.

The contribution that a sociological analysis can make to this type of interpretation consists mainly in a careful examination of the causal connections. Let us consider, for example, the two sequences that we have called *mobilization process* and *formation of the populist coalition*. The process of mobilization need not coincide always with the formation of militia with local resources. Even given the formation of militia, these can be subjected to a greater or lesser degree of social control, according to the characteristics of the popular mass, or to the presence of certain constellations in the class structure. The latter must be taken into account in order to understand the alliance of various sectors that often is the base of the populist coalition. In Mexico, for a period approximately equivalent to the one here considered, violence was much greater than in Argentina, and equally so social mobilization, for reasons not only due to that violence. The *caudillo* types emerging in that country were, on the other hand, different from those of the Río de la Plata, except in a few areas. Maybe the explanation lies in the different density of population, its urban condition, or the prevalence of insecure and downwardly mobile middle sectors in Mexico. At a national level, there was a *caudillo*, Santa Anna, comparable to Rosas, but he lacked stability. Political expressions of a popular character were mostly based on the urban mass of the capital city. There were local chiefs, and civil wars, but these were decided more quickly than in Argentina with the victory of one side, or else they were transformed into total wars, like the one started in 1858 and ending only in 1867, after foreign intervention. Taking into account the four cases mentioned in Argentina, and considering that the more radical one was Güemes', based on the more rigidly stratified province (similar in that sense to Mexico), we might extrapolate and consider Mexican *caudillismo* as a more radical version of the Argentine. This may be so in a first approximation, but a more adequate understanding requires a deeper comparative analysis, and an increase in the number of explanatory variables. The same happens if we make incursions in time rather than in space, examining more recent phenomena in terms of what they have in common with those of the past. In so doing, we pass from historical interpretation to sociological analysis, built on the comparative study of a large number of cases.[13]

Table 2. The Emergence of the *Caudillo* System in the Province of Santiago del Estero, Argentina, under Ibarra (ca. 1810–1830)

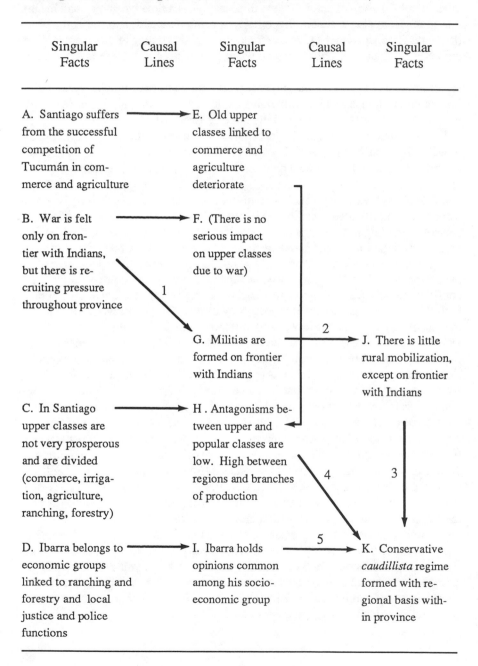

Singular Facts	Causal Lines	Singular Facts	Causal Lines	Singular Facts
A. Santiago suffers from the successful competition of Tucumán in commerce and agriculture	→	E. Old upper classes linked to commerce and agriculture deteriorate		
B. War is felt only on frontier with Indians, but there is recruiting pressure throughout province	→ 1	F. (There is no serious impact on upper classes due to war)		
		G. Militias are formed on frontier with Indians	2 →	J. There is little rural mobilization, except on frontier with Indians
C. In Santiago upper classes are not very prosperous and are divided (commerce, irrigation, agriculture, ranching, forestry)	→	H. Antagonisms between upper and popular classes are low. High between regions and branches of production	4	3
D. Ibarra belongs to economic groups linked to ranching and forestry and local justice and police functions	→	I. Ibarra holds opinions common among his socioeconomic group	5 →	K. Conservative *caudillista* regime formed with regional basis within province

Sociological Models

The Achilles' heel of sociological analysis is conceptual abstraction, which establishes what there is in common between various concrete phenomena. If we limit ourselves to abstracting what there is in common between those phenomena we call *caudillista*, we will probably not arrive at interesting explanatory hypotheses. The concept "*caudillismo*" is too broad, with too many dimensions and components. Too many different realities are included; therefore, it is not likely that they will all have the same etiology. What is necessary is to subdivide the concept into several simpler ones, which will be its dimensions and which may appear in different combinations. For example, we may call one of its dimensions "mobilizationism," which consists of a certain manner of establishing relationships between leaders and followers, but this can happen in such different concrete cases as Hidalgo's hosts and the Rosas regime. The hypotheses to be established must state universal connections between certain *variables*, and not between them and the *total phenomenon* under consideration, of which mobilizationism is just one dimension. In the search for comparative material, it may be necessary to look at situations that have nothing to do with *caudillismo*, but that throw light on some of the links between the variables under scrutiny. Thus, we will have hypotheses about mobilization, about the formation of coalitions, or regarding the emergence within a sector of a class of ideas antagonistic to those dominant in that same class. There will not be, strictly speaking, general hypotheses about the emergence of *caudillismo*, because each *caudillismo* is a different, singular phenomenon, which may have grown as a result of a great variety of events. The sociology of *caudillismo*, then, will consist of a selection of hypotheses relevant to the variables that interest us. It must be accompanied by the study of cases where, by interaction of initial conditions with sociological laws, global phenomena that we may call "*caudillista*" have taken place.

The purpose of this volume is to explore this area of middle-range theories, building a system of hypotheses connecting clearly defined and eventually measurable variables. In other words, a *theoretical model*, a concept, however, that also requires some caveats, as it is used in several ways.

To begin with the most common, the term "model" refers to a specific series of singular events capable of being reproduced—even if only approximately—in different places. Thus, we may speak of the Japanese model of development or the Russian model of social revolution. The model, in this sense of the term, is a rather rigid structure. It consists of various parts that, though interrelated, are fixed and result from the selection of the most relevant events or components of a historical process. If for a given country under study the model is not applicable, either because the required conditions are not present or because, for one reason or another, certain causes are not followed by the expected consequences, the model will be discarded as inappropriate and another one, more adaptable to the circumstances, will be looked for. Thus, if we study the processes that led to the downfall of the dictatorial regimes of Marcos Pérez Jiménez in Venezuela, Gustavo Rojas Pinilla in Colombia, and Manual Odría in Peru (between 1956 and 1958), it may be possible to formulate a model of redemocratization. This model could then be found applicable to the cases of the first government of Gen. Carlos Ibáñez in Chile (1927–1931) or to the fall of the Greek colonels (1975), but not to the liberalization that has taken place more recently in Brazil. The latter would rather resemble the Spanish process. Different, again, would be the Portuguese case, which may lead to formulating yet another model, encompassing the Peruvian revolution of 1968, the "military socialism" of Cols. Germán Busch and David Toro in the Bolivia of the 1930s, and other cases of radical nationalist revolutions in the Arab world. This is the sense in which the term "model" is more commonly used in the social sciences, in journalism, and in everyday speech.[14] It helps categorize and systematize available information, though it results in rather rigid groupings. If the historical phenomenon under consideration would in any way depart from the model, the dynamics of change in that case become unpredictable. Perhaps there will be a tendency to shift to another model, but if this is the case, then the model is not an explanatory tool but only a descriptive one. It lacks the capacity to grasp original patterns of development. It may be useful as a first sensitizing instrument, but it yields diminishing results for the understanding of actual events in any detail.

It is necessary, then, to explore an alternative concept of "model," which can be better described by thinking of a flight simulator. The pilot who is being trained is faced with a panel of instruments similar to those found in a real plane and, by means of a computer, alterations of certain values are introduced, whose consequences are calculated through the general laws of aerodynamics, combined with the specific characteristics of the shape of the airplane, wind speed turbulences, and so forth. In this case, the model does not describe a concrete sequence of events, but rather consists of the formulae representing the laws that have been taken into account, and whose effects are calculated and measured by various instruments. For all pilots, for all styles of planes, for all temporal sequences of flying events, the model remains the same. This is the kind of model that will be used as the basis for theoretical integration in this volume. However, in order not to alarm the reader, it must be said that not much use will be made of complex formalizations. We shall simply take, as a frame of reference, the construction of a simulation model of political processes, potentially to be expressed with mathematical symbols, but stated only in its barest outlines.[15]

Ideally, the model would consist of formulae relating variables to each other. For each application to a concrete situation initial data describing the characteristics of the case to be analyzed should be provided: social stratification, group organization, social psychology, type of government, and so forth. Some changes in "exogenous" variables can also be provided (e.g., fall of export prices, increase in the organizational capacity of the popular classes, penetration of multinationals). The equations of the model should indicate how the rest of the "endogenous" variables are affected (e.g., spread of authoritarian attitudes in the upper classes, politicization of the armed forces, radicalization of the middle sectors).[16] It is important to recall that the model does not represent a particular type of historical evolution (consolidation of the bureaucratic-authoritarian regime in the Chilean case, democratization in the Spanish example, revolution in the Cuban experience) but, rather, a group of explanatory hypotheses and their interrelationships. Thus, the above-mentioned three "cases" must result from the use of the same group of sociological hypotheses that constitute the theoretical model, though applied to different initial conditions.

The Program to Be Developed

The principal objective of this book is the development of a theoretical body of knowledge to enable us to better understand political processes in Latin America. Throughout I try to combine eclectically elements of classical sociology and political science while giving priority to the theoretical assimilation of the historical experiences of that region. Both political science and sociology, having been elaborated overwhelmingly in Europe and North America, present us with a picture that is not always adequate. I am not here suggesting a radical relativism but simply pointing out that culturally based distortions do exist. This is the reason why it is important to include as much as possible the analysis of Latin America's past and present political events as sources of useful hypotheses.

The subject matter treated here is divided into four parts, which roughly refer to social stratification and definition of social actors (chapters 2 and 3), concentration and fragmentation of power (chapter 4), the generation of violence and repression (chapters 5 and 6), and the organization of the popular classes with attendant ideological phenomena (chapters 7, 8, 9, and 10).

The study of social stratification is based on the conception of the social pyramid as a representation of hierarchically stratified social space. Within it the various social actors (classes, sectors or fragments of classes, ethnic or religious groups, foreign interests, institutions such as churches or the military) are located, their interaction making up the political game. The size of the middle sectors determines the shape of the pyramid and influences, together with other factors, the type and intensity of antagonisms between classes. Two concepts that mainly apply to the popular strata are here developed: social mobilization and organization. On the other hand, mobilizationism, a particular form of connection between followers and leaders, is here defined and analyzed.

The problem of concentration and fragmentation of power is then taken up, referring first to the European and North American experiences, which led to the theoretical and ideological formulations of liberalism, and later contrasting them with their Latin American applications. The evolution from a restricted to a wider participation in the political process is also considered, as well as the contrast between what may be called the associationist and the mobilizationist modes of participation.

Various approaches to the study of the cycle of violence are then reviewed, including the traditionally endemic trait of military interventionism. Special emphasis is put on the concept of *menace*, especially that which has its origins in the popular sectors and threatens the upper echelons of the social pyramid. The experiences of Argentina, Brazil, Chile, and Mexico are systematically compared, both during the last century and in more recent times.

The final chapters focus on the problems of the organization and ideology of the popular classes, especially trade unions and political parties, and their relevance for the consolidation of a democratic regime. The Argentine case is covered in more detail, contrasting the early anarchist and socialist period with the Peronist stage, still dominant. The possible causes of the weakness of the expression of conservative or entrepreneurial interests in the political arena in this country are also explored.

An appendix is included, which summarizes some of the main findings and outlines a theoretical model capable of simulating and interpreting political processes. It has been kept separate from the text because of the more tentative nature of the formalizations involved and to emphasize their experimental character.

2. Tensions in the Class Structure

Karl Marx's was the more radical attempt at envisioning a society free of hierarchical differences. Not only did he believe it possible to do away with private property of the means of production, but he also thought that modern technology, properly managed, did not require a division of labor between managerial, supervisory, skilled manual, and unskilled positions. Given this perception of what industrialization had in store for the future, it was possible to conceive of a short transitory period when a proletarian dictatorship might finish off the destruction of the old society. In its place no new edifice of privilege could possibly emerge, but only a classless society, free of the division between mental and manual labor. Of course, this utopia, whatever the possibilities of its realization in the very distant future may be, is not at all realistic for the foreseeable time span that concerns political action.[1]

If the working class is not to be the creator of a New Jerusalem, but simply one more pressure group in society, it becomes necessary to reconsider its role in the political arena. The experience shows that the working class and, generally, the popular strata, do not always perform a "progressive" role, in whichever way this word is defined. Marx was already conscious of this, and he tried to cope with the problem by introducing the concept of class consciousness. He knew that the popular mass had often been the support of conservative or Caesaristic regimes. Of the latter, Napoleon III was the more recent example, to which he dedicated one of his more famous works. But his theory permitted him to forecast a tendency toward the consolidation of class consciousness. Mental emancipation and the acquisition of organizational capacity were necessary results of the work environment demanded by high technology. The elimination or drastic reduction of the middle layers would do away with their classical moderating function. Under these conditions the working class would be ready and prepared to confront not only the existing but any other system of domination. But if the Marxist hypothesis about the liberating effects of modern technology is abandoned, the political behavior of labor, seen now as an actor struggling for power within the social pyramid, becomes more variable. Manual workers are condemned to the unending task of confronting those in command of the productive apparatus, without being able to take their place except by delegation. The working class, in fact, cannot occupy en masse the higher parts of society, because someone has to go on performing the necessary mechanical jobs. In this it is differentiated from the bourgeoisie, which, when pitted against the previously dominant classes, can dislodge them totally and occupy their positions. It also differs from the bureaucracy, which in this sense is similar to the bourgeoisie, being capable of destroying the propertied classes and replacing them.

The Social Pyramid

In this chapter some characteristics of the social stratification pyramid will be considered, especially to ascertain their effects on the middle and lower strata. Some of the early experiences of mobilization of those popular strata in Latin America will also be considered. Marx's theoretical scheme will be contrasted with what actually took place in the industrially developed countries and with events in the Third World. Though several Latin American countries are in an intermediate position, as they do not clearly belong in the Third World nor do they possess the traits of the industrialized ones, a study of the polar cases will help to understand the social pressures at work.

The social stratification pyramid can be divided into three main levels: upper, middle, and lower. The upper level includes the bigger entrepreneurs and the top bureaucrats and administrators, public or private. They are the dominant group in any society, but would not be able to exert their hegemony if they did not have some support among the next level, the middle classes, urban and rural small shopkeepers, officials, middle-ranking white collar employees, salespeople, foremen, overseers, independent artisans, and farmers. Finally, the lower tier is formed by the urban and rural working class, peasants and poor artisans, some of the self-employed, and various types of marginals. Many white collar employees and salespeople are very near this level.

The limits between the lower tier and the middle strata are not clearly defined. The former in most parts of the world live at subsistence levels (subsistence, however, being defined in a flexible way so as to include some commonly accepted minimums). As for the middle sectors, the imprecise nature of their limits and their heterogeneity have robbed them of a class character in most Marxist-inspired analyses. Actually, this is a Byzantine question. Whether the term "class" or "stratum" or "layer" is preferred, the attitudes, beliefs, and types of political action of those groups must be determined empirically. For quite a few of them, their differentiation from the mass of manual workers is rather small, if it exists at all. As is well known, often in industrial societies white collar employees earn less than skilled manual workers, to give only the better-known example. From a certain point of view, that part of the middle sector who have only a few elements of status, education, or self-image to separate them from the rest of labor might be considered as part of the working class. If this were done, the result would be an enormously expanded "popular" class, including the large majority of any country. But this would be more an ethical than a sociological classification. If that way of cutting the social pyramid were politically valid, the result would be an extreme weakness of the dominant classes. In general, this is not the case, because (1) in preindustrial, or Third World, societies, where the middle sector is quite small, the mass of the population is not organized and is very heterogeneous, particularly its urban and rural components; and (2) in more developed societies, middle strata proliferate, often on the basis of emphasizing small differences, which are enough to generate among those who benefit from them an attitude of acceptance of the dominant social order. Though advanced industrialization obliterates some of these differences, it generates others in the technical and service areas.[2]

It should not be expected, however, that the middle strata are always more conservative than the popular ones. This is so in most cases, but there are numerous exceptions, in social milieus where intense frustration is originated by the lack of gratification of expectations. This frustration, no doubt, exists at all stratification levels, but at the higher ones achievements compensate for shortcomings. At working-class and peasant levels, by contrast, low education, family atmosphere, and the deadening effects of the division of labor cut the wings of ambition. It is among the middle classes that the chasm between aspirations and gratifications is wider, so much so that it might seem that the middle ought to be more dissatisfied and therefore more radicalized than the working class. This generally does not happen, because the prevalence of aspirations for social mobility, even if thwarted, keeps a large part of the middle class trying harder. The final answer in each case, of course, can only be learned through empirical evidence.

The historical evolution of the pyramid's profile indicates the type of social conflicts that are present. Here it is necessary to contrast Marx's predictions with the pattern prevailing in the more economically advanced countries and with that typical of less-developed nations.

In Marx's conception the following sequence was supposed to take place:

(a) Industrialization, urbanization, technological progress, and allied cultural effects would proceed at great speed, but without raising the standard of living of the working class. This class would acquire a solid organizational and associative experience and a corresponding level of education, formal and informal. Workers would become more capable of defending their own interests, including the ability to control their leaders.

(b) Middle classes would become proletarianized as a result of the comparative advantage of large versus small or medium enterprises. With the waning of the middle classes, their moderating influence would disappear and the numerical support for the dominant sectors would melt away. Erstwhile members of the middle classes would join the proletariat, without performing any special leadership role in their new social position.

(c) As a result of these factors, the social domination system would break down without being replaced by another one, because, according to this conception the working class would be sufficiently mature and capacitated to perform managerial roles.[3]

It should be noted that if points (a) and (b) were to occur, that is, if high industrialization were accompanied by a low standard of living and proletarianization, the production of a successful popular revolution would be quite reasonable. But let us see what actually happened in highly developed countries, mostly in Western Europe, where what we may call the "social democratic" sequence prevailed:

(a) Technological, urban, industrial, and cultural development occasioned an increase in the standard of living. Manual workers became autonomously organized, with strong associationist traits and a considerable degree of control over their leaders. Political parties based on the support of, and financed by, the urban working class were formed.

(b) The middle classes did not become proletarianized, except in special episodes, but, rather, increased in number and prospered economically. In the few cases when they were seriously menaced by massive downward mobility, they turned to the extreme right rather than to the left. Generally, they became the electoral basis of the moderate Right and Center. Social mobility was quite high.

(c) As a result of the interplay of the two above points, the working class adopted reformist attitudes, with socialist ideological components capable of being channeled in a constitutional system. The North American case, though it did not produce a labor party, is similar to the European one, as far as the reformist attitudes of the working class are concerned.

Let us now look at the situation in Third World countries to the extent that it is possible to generalize in this matter. In those countries, the following alterations of the previous sequences can be observed:

(a) Urbanization and industrialization are low, and the same happens with the technical training of the working class. The latter is, in some cases, concentrated in large units of production (mining, agribusiness, railways, some other foreign-owned industries), forming enclaves, far from the main urban centers and coexisting with ample artisan sectors and a peasant majority. The standard of living is low, and organization is deficient. What organization exists is mostly not based on intense associationist experiences but depends on personalist leadership mingled with spontaneity and communal or ethnic solidarity as well as with other elements of a preindustrial mentality. It becomes necessary for the working class and peasant movements to have the support and the leadership of elements drawn from other social classes, to a far greater degree than in the social democratic pattern.[4]

(b) The middle classes, in these early industrializing societies, are weak economically, menaced by foreign competition and by the growth of an internal modern sector. Their living conditions are poor, not only as a result of the scarcity of resources at their command, but because of their level of aspirations, increased by demonstration effects of all types, among them the one resulting from the expansion of higher education beyond the occupational opportunities afforded by the system. Unemployment at the intellectual, professional, and semiprofessional levels also affects students, generating an attitude of rebellion against the status quo. "Youth" (of the middle class) becomes a political category, denoting a situation of class transition and a process of resocialization at the schools and universities.

(c) As a result of the above points, the typical Third World society generates two storm fronts against the dominant system. On one hand, peasants and workers accumulate antagonisms, but without much autonomous organizational experience and with a tendency to volcanic, occasional, and violent action. On the other hand, at the middle or even upper levels, radicalized elites are formed, based on groups threatened with downward social mobility. It is quite likely that the two factors operate at the same time; that is, a revolutionary elite is formed while a mass following becomes available. The result can range from developmental nationalism (Mexico, Egypt) , to fundamentalist revolution (Iran), to radical anti-imperialism (Peru, Algeria), to different forms of populism (Bolivia, Brazil) or collectivism (Russia, China, Cuba).

In the social democratic pattern generally there is a two-party or two-coalition system. On one side there is a party or alliance rooted in the organized working class, with some following among the lower middle classes, particularly their intellectual sectors. On the other side there is a conservative party or alliance whose main support and financing come from high up in the social pyramid but which is capable of winning elections, for which it needs the votes of most of the middle classes and even of a sector of the urban workers, particularly the nonunionized ones.

The typical situation in the Third World, if superficially analyzed, looks more like fulfilling Marx's prophecy than the social democratic one does, because it includes a certain proletarianization of the middle classes and it leads to violent outbursts and political takeovers by popular movements. The differences, however, are very great. The most important element, autonomous class organization, is absent, though, numerically, this may not seem to be so. Often the presence of masses of workers or peasants in the streets, in gatherings and celebrations, does not express real participation but simply a ritualized support for those in power. As for the middle classes, rather than disappearing, they are first weakened and later transformed, and often reborn from their ashes as leaders of the political process. They form the new bureaucracy, the postrevolutionary dominant class.[5]

Of particular importance is the relationship between the worker or peasant component and the middle or upper stratum involved in the coalition. There are many reasons why a middle or upper sector can turn against the system of domination, or against its present beneficiaries. Ruined aristocrats, industrialists in trouble, students without job prospects, military without weapons, marginalized clergy, all are candidates. The processes through which the structural conditions affecting these groups can cause the spread of certain psychological and ideological attitudes among them must be studied with care.

Social Mobilization and Mobilizationism

The integration of broad popular masses with a leadership drawn from other strata is such a typical phenomenon in Latin America that it can be argued that it is the main form of expression of the interests and political capacities of the popular classes. In the remainder of this chapter, the two allied concepts of social mobilization and mobilizationism will be defined, and the Latin American and Southern European historical experiences will be searched for early forms of the phenomena these concepts refer to. (Chapter 7 will be dedicated to a study of more recent instances, which generally go by the name of "populism," an all-encompassing term under which different realities are included.)

For the alliance between a mobilized mass and a leader of the *caudillo* type to materialize, it is necessary that a middle or upper status group should exist that shares anti–status quo attitudes convergent with those prevalent, for totally different reasons, among the popular sectors. Social psychological convergences also help in producing the coalition, which is not usually the result of a conscious calculation on the part of the involved actors. What leads to the alliance is a whole array of causes, some economic, short or long run, some emotional, some ideological. Leadership mechanisms are essential in this matter, and here the role of individuals should be considered. There is no doubt that, in many historical processes, prominent leaders have had a very important role. However, once this fact is noted, it is convenient to explore the social conditions that might have fostered the emergence of such personalities.

Let us take, for example, the phenomenon of charisma. This is not a trait of the leader, but of the relationship. Its emergence can be subdivided into two processes. At the mass level, a certain form of aggregation of the popular sectors, their life chances, organizational experience or lack of it, mobilization, and migration, generate a *demand*. At middle or upper levels, social tensions may push a certain number of groups or individuals out of the usual ways of thinking and acting of their class. Under conditions of dissatisfaction or frustration, the pressures toward homogeneity of opinions diminish or disappear and new, risky strategies flourish, including the espousal of a popular alliance. These tensions among the middle and upper layers create what may be called a *supply* of leadership. The conjunction of demand and supply facilitates the formation of a mobilizationist movement that, because of the strange alliances on which it is based, and the potential uncontrollability of the masses it involves, has a Protean nature. It can be of the Right or the Left, popular or aristocratic, reactionary or progressive.

In current political language, the concept of "mobilization" designates a movement with high organization and consciousness of its aims. Political leaders, when they say that they are preparing a mobilization, have in mind a concerted effort, with a considerable structure and clarity of aims. Several dimensions are thus taken as being present at the same time, when in reality they can appear separately. It is preferable to distinguish between *social* and *political* mobilization. The concept *political mobilization* may be reserved to refer to its current meaning. By contrast, *social mobilization* will be employed to describe a deeper phenomenon affecting the social structure, following, to a large extent, Karl Deutsch and Gino Germani. It implies the massive rejection of the traditional system of norms, prestige criteria, and leadership roles, breaking with paternalism. It is associated with a greater concern about national events. New solutions, new forms of relating to others are sought, but still with little perceptual clarity about the fields of politics and ideology and little capacity for autonomous organization, which is supplanted by loyalty to a charismatic leader or *caudillo*. The person undergoing this process enters into a state of availability, having rejected or often simply lost his or her old world and not yet comfortably adapted to the new surroundings.[6]

The concept of social mobilization is useful to describe the passage from a rural to an urban setting, or other geographical migrations. However, the only factor causing social mobilization is not migration. The change may occur within a rural zone, under the impact of technological or economic forces, or as a result of political agitations. On the other hand, in large cities it is also possible to find groups submerged in the utmost political and social indifferentism, groups that in response to political events or alterations in the system of mass communications acquire greater awareness, thereby experiencing social mobilization.

A political movement that incorporates masses with a high degree of social mobilization but little autonomous organization can be called "mobilizationist." Though distinct from more complex forms based on voluntary associations, it does require quite considerable readiness for political action and thus differs from the more traditional forms of political clientelism. Mobilizationism often overflows the existing institutional channels, given the highly violent potential of a mass that is limited by neither traditional restrictions nor by complex organizational requirements.

Social Mobilization in the Colonial Period

Social mobilization in Latin American colonial society was in some cases quite high and the source, in moments of crisis, of political phenomena that cannot be described as merely based on the actions of elites; rather, they involved a special kind of popular participation. Even in moments when the system was not in crisis, the presence of masses with a high degree of social mobilization required a system of control adapted to their manipulation. The more typical cases of high social mobilization were found in the larger cities, with their masses of marginals; in the mining centers, with a fluctuating population following the cycles of prosperity and decadence; and finally in some Indian sectors torn from their traditional communities and forced into the salaried labor market of haciendas and *obrajes*.

The more outstanding example of an urban concentration with dangerous masses of marginals was the City of Mexico, with more than 100,000 inhabitants toward the end of the eighteenth century, when New York and Philadelphia hovered around

20,000. In the North American economy, cities were highly specialized centers of administrative, artisan, commercial, and transport activity. In the larger cities of Latin America, by contrast, the Spanish colonial system generated large population concentrations with high indices of unemployment or underemployment. The coexistence of extremes of riches and poverty stimulated social tensions, and occupational instability implied the continued possibility of violence. The migratory origin of a great part of the marginals, separated from their traditional rural milieus and families, must also be taken into account. These marginals were called "*léperos*" in Mexico and were equated by international travelers to Naples' *lazzari*. The large marginal element in Naples, like that in other southern European and Latin American cities, was combined with a numerous but unstable artisan class, creating a social and political powder keg that was responsible for many a political agitation of the nineteenth century.

Mining concentrations, which also had their greatest expression in Mexico, grouped considerable human masses. In Guanajuato the largest mining concern employed over three thousand persons by the end of the eighteenth century. On a somewhat lesser scale, this situation was reproduced in other areas of New Spain, in Peru, and in what is today Bolivia. Violence could easily take hold in those places. Something similar happened in the woolen textile *obrajes*, employing up to a hundred workers, many of them recruited among convicts.

As for the indigenous population, to a large extent it was integrated in the traditional communities, or *pueblos*, many of which still possessed sizable amounts of land. Within those communities a whole social pyramid existed, differentiating the *principales* (nobles) from the rest and expressing itself most forcefully in the competition for posts of *alcaldes*, *regidores*, and other functions in Indian *cabildos* and religious *cofradías*, involving not only prestige but the more concrete privilege of exemption from forced labor (*repartimiento* and *mita*). These *pueblos* can be considered as having a low degree of social mobilization. They were integrated through the extended family, which fixed the individual into a network of loyalties and hierarchies. The situation was very different for those Indians who abandoned this microcosm, whether seeking employment in Spanish haciendas or remaining "loose" after some stint of forced labor in faraway places.

The social characteristics of the zone of Guanajuato and Querétaro, where the Mexican independence struggle of 1810 was nurtured, should be looked at from this point of view. Several types of highly mobilized population were combined in that area. To begin with, nominally free but indebted Indians—*laborios*—predominated, separated from their traditional communities and ready to join any focus of social agitation. In the outskirts of the city of Guanajuato the principal mining concentrations of the times existed, with a population equally prone to violence and with few or weak family ties. Querétaro, the other urban center of the area, had many *obrajes* and other small-scale textile manufacturing activities, adding more combustible material. If the dissatisfaction of middle-class sectors (provincial clergy, like Miguel Hidalgo, and low-ranking military officers, like Ignacio Allende) is also taken into account, the insurgency explosion is easier to explain. Started by an alienated elite, in a zone affected by arbitrary economic measures coming from the metropolis, the smallest spark could produce a conflagration of incalculable proportions. The whole first half of the nineteenth-century social and political history of Mexico was marked by the consequences of these events. Right, Center, and Left, from Iturbide to Gómez Farías, including Santa Anna, tried to reconstruct some form of alliance between dissatisfied elites and the people.[7]

In other large Latin American towns of the time, like Rio de Janeiro or Havana, free lumpen proletarians were replaced by slaves. These were, of course, much more controlled than the former, as potentially they represented an even greater threat in case of rebellion, which was not a mere paranoid fear, as the Haiti slave insurrection had proved.

Preindustrial Mobilizationism and Its Mutations

In a preindustrial situation the menace represented by the masses for the established order (conservative or reformist) was of a magnitude not easy to appreciate today, when we are likely to consider it a modern phenomenon. The potential presence of the masses in the political scene was occasionally very high. On the other hand, it could take place in alliance with the most unexpected groups, generally subsectors of the elite.

Of particular interest, and taken into account by Latin American contemporary actors, was the case of Naples. Toward the end of the eighteenth century this was one of the more populous and poverty-stricken cities of Europe. In its streets a multitude of unemployed, marginals, day laborers, and fishermen congregated, the so-called *lazzari*. Already in the days of Spanish domination viceroys were forced to pay special attention to the control of this human mass, which had rebelled in 1647, threatening royal authority. Obviously, the *lazzari* constituted a serious menace to the calm of the city, though they could be controlled using some skill. But, in the eyes of the upper classes, they were a danger to be handled by experts.

At the end of 1798 an open conflict with France erupted. After a short campaign Neapolitan troops had to retreat, though in the provinces a popular resistance started, not too different from the Spanish one a few years later. The king and his court abandoned the capital, leaving it to the care of the royal representative, who decided to mobilize the *lazzari*, inciting them against the more secularized city nobility and the bourgeoisie, who were thought to sympathize with the invaders. The royal representative gave the control of the military fortress defending the city to the *lazzari* militia and allowed them to select their leaders. Two noblemen, who hoped to moderate the militia, accepted. Tumults and pillage could no longer be contained, despite the archbishop's efforts to pacify his flock. After a few days, a Jacobin plot was successful in surrendering the fortress to the invaders; after a protracted struggle the French occupied the city, and the Neapolitan Republic was established.

Meanwhile, the Bourbon insurrection in the provinces was spreading, supported by sea by the British and with secret support in the capital. From Sicily Cardinal Fabrizio Ruffo took over the command of the war and finally entered the city, where "another more cruel and obscene war started. . . . The victors ran after the vanquished: whoever was not a warrior of the Holy Faith, or a plebeian, when found out, was killed . . . streets were deserted or full of tumults; lazzari, servants, enemies and false friends denounced to the plebeians the houses of the rebels. . . . Prisoners were carried naked in the streets . . . people of any age, any sex, old magistrates, egregious ladies, were subjected to these tortures."[8]

Thus, Pietro Colletta, chronicler and participant as a moderate liberal on the side of the French, describes the events. But let us see how these are seen by Mikhail Bakunin seventy years later. He was writing in 1870, after the defeat of Napoleon III, but before the Commune, when in Paris a provisional government was at a loss about what to do to resist the German occupation. It was necessary, according to him, to mobilize the French rural masses against the invader, so as to radicalize the situation. The examples of the French Revolution were no doubt present in the consciousness of all Frenchmen; but Bakunin appealed to no other than Cardinal Ruffo, the chief of the Bourbon restoration in Naples. In a brochure titled *Letters to a Frenchman* he refers to the peasants, sympathizers of the fallen Napoleon III, arguing that they could be mobilized against the Germans if they were incited before against the local notables. He added, in support of his thesis:

> It is not the first time that a government exploits the natural hatred of the peasants against the rich property owners and the rich bourgeois. Thus at the end of the last century Cardinal Ruffo, of blood-stained memory, raised the Calabrian peasants against the liberals of the Kingdom of Naples who had established a republic under the flag of France. At bottom, the revolt led by Ruffo was a socialist movement. The Calabrian peasants started looting the castles, and once in the city they looted the houses of the bourgeoisie but did not touch the people.[9]

Bakunin, obviously, had a mobilizationist model of political action in mind. He believed that the resentments that exist latently among the people, which were used in Naples by the clergy and a sector of the Bourbon aristocracy against the rest of that aristocracy and the bourgeoisie, could well be used for other purposes by different hands. This strategy whereby an absolutist government agitates the masses against its aristocratic or bourgeois enemies is as old as the world, but it requires some preconditions to be successful. It may fail, particularly when the system of social control is not consolidated enough because of the intensity of class or ethnic antagonisms, favoring revolutionary transmutations. A classic example occurred in Haiti at the time of the French Revolution.

The island, then known as Saint Domingue, was the richest French colony and could compare with any of the American states in wealth and population. Slaves composed an overwhelming proportion (over 85 percent) of the population and about two-thirds of them had been born in Africa as a result of high mortality rates in the island and the expansion of production in recent decades. With the convocation of the Estates General in France, agitation started in the colony, which had its Cahiers de Doléances, its local assemblies, and representatives in Paris. The conflicts between the various factions of white planters, and between them and the mulattoes, ended in armed confrontations. As a result, the slave population was also affected and took the opportunity offered by the loosening of social controls to start a rebellion by mid-1791. Initially it was quite circumscribed, though very violent. The blacks received support from the neighboring Spanish part of the island, where emigré monarchist leaders were stationed. For the first three years the insurgents used the royalist insignia and in their correspondence with the governmental authorities styled themselves as representatives of the kings of France, Spain, and the Congo, descendants of the Magi of Bethlehem.

The strength of the rebellion increased because it was used as a possible source of support by the warring French and mulatto factions. The apparently monarchical nature of the symbols of the rebels and the structure of their early alliances led many observers at the time to speak of a "Black Vendée." In 1794 the beleaguered representatives of the French revolutionary government finally appealed to the insurgents to join them in overcoming the local white planters, nominally republican but tending toward separation from the mother country. After several efforts, the rebels joined the French authorities, who had been led to promise the abolition of slavery, a measure that was finally approved by the Convention. The freed slaves, under Toussaint Louverture, became the main military force on the island, defending it against a British invasion. After a brief attempt by Napoleon to regain full control of the island and reestablish slavery, a new rebellion finally succeeded in attaining independence in 1804. By this time most of the white population had either been expelled or killed, the sugar economy nearly destroyed, and a return to subsistence agriculture under way. The efforts of the various sectors of the dominant classes to use the rebels as a source of support that could be controlled had misfired.[10]

The example of the horrors of the Haitian war were to remain engraved in the memory of several generations of political leaders in all parts of the Americas, especially in those countries that had a large slave population, like the U.S. South, Cuba, the rest of the Caribbean, Venezuela, and Brazil. In most cases it induced moderation and quiescence among the white element, which considered it too risky to adopt an aggressive policy in seeking independence. But in Venezuela another "experiment" took place, similar in some ways to the Haitian one, though, because the black population made a much smaller percentage of the population, conditions were no so explosive.

The independent government of Venezuela, established in 1810, succumbed in 1812 to the Spanish reconquest. Already in that early period Venezuela had had to confront slave revolts, although they were not very consequential. In 1813 Bolívar, acting from New Granada (Colombia), liberated the country, defeating the regular Spanish troops. Royalists then took to a different sort of war, led by José Tomás Boves, a former Spanish navy petty officer who had established himself as a merchant in the midst of the *llanos*, the flat southern part of the country, bordering on the Orinoco River. The social conditions of the *llanos* were very special. Frontier lands, with an abundance of cattle, they were a less fertile version of the Río de la Plata pampas. They sheltered a floating population, with an irregular property structure, where cattle were a more important source of wealth than land. There Boves' leadership started. He soon became the chief of improvised militia, inciting them to raid and to destroy the hated white Creoles, the main property owners and enemies of the local mixed society of small traders, adventurers, and seminomadic workers of the *llanos*. In Juan Uslar Pietri's words, "Boves was the caudillo those masses full of hate were expecting . . . the first mass conductor, the first leader of Venezuelan democracy."[11]

Looting and indiscriminate massacre of whites, sanctioned by royal authority, soon became the normal form of action of these irregular troops, though they acted independently from the Spanish army, led in those days by Juan Manuel de Cajigal. The latter, in his memoirs, mentions that "after each victory, which was the occasion of looting, killing, and violence, a good third [of the troop] disappeared, but this did not matter to the chief; immediately they were replaced by [people prepared] to enrich themselves at the next attack."[12] In fact, pillage, terror, and the liquidation of the civilian enemy were already practiced in Venezuela by both sides, but Boves added the radical mobilization of the *llaneros*, slaves, and other elements of the popular classes. As his enemies represented the most important part of the propertied white population, they could not compete, at first, with him. The second Venezuelan Republic succumbed before the prospect of a general annihilation of its white population, except those closely related to the Spaniards. Bolívar as a last resort attempted to appeal to the British, pointing out, "our enemies have not spared any means, however infamous and horrible, to succeed in their projects. They have liberated our peaceful slaves and agitated the less cultured classes of our people, inciting them to the assassination of our women and our tender children. . . . The fatal example of the slaves and the hate of the coloured man for the white, stimulated and fanned by our enemies, are soon going to infect all British colonies, unless they take the part they must in attacking such disorders."[13]

Finally, in 1814, the royalists entered Caracas, already abandoned by most of its white population. Boves inaugurated a brief reign of the people of color. However, when new troops arrived from the metropolis, a new social order, more in accord with the standards of the time, was imposed. Boves retired to the *llanos* and soon afterward died in battle against the patriots. Even so, the independence of Venezuela was delayed for seven more years.

Once power was recovered by the Spaniards, the mobilization of the *llaneros* was no longer necessary and was relegated to a secondary position by the authorities. This, plus the death of Boves, weakened the alliance between the Spanish government and the *llanero* masses. The patriot forces, prepared to try any method, started agitating the same people who had been the main support of their enemies. Gen. José A. Páez, himself of humble *llanero* origin and future president of the country, was the artificer of this transformation. After several years, the *llaneros*, now with Páez as their chief, were integrated into the new independent regime, which was very different from that of the First and Second republics.

Once Páez established order and became consolidated as ruler of Venezuela, he did not lose his following, as one might hypothesize. Lack of clear enemies, greater stability, and time to consolidate the new system of *caudillista* domination kept Páez's following intact. However, when decades later, other conflicts erupted in what is known as the Federal War, the *llaneros* again formed the mass support of those who were the "outsiders" of the political system.

Two Conceptions of Democracy

Liberal political theory was developed in times like those just described. Experience produced a serious preoccupation about the role of the masses in the public arena. They were seen more as a menace than as a support, though they could be separated into *people* and *plebs*, the one positive, the other negative. What was required to pass from plebs to people was education, family organization, a stable occupation, preferably in small-scale activity, and limits to the influence of the clergy. Land colonization, trans-Atlantic migration, and economic development were the main instruments for avoiding urban preindustrial concentrations like that in Naples. The vote should be given only to those who had promoted themselves to the category of "people," showing some skill in the management of their own interests.

There was always, though, a radical or populist sector of liberalism, which favored a more widespread participation in politics. The Spanish Constitution of 1812 had incorporated most of those radical principles, inspired in the French texts of 1791, and established the predominance of the legislative over the executive and granted the vote to all the adult male population. This constitution became the paradigm of progressivism for the Mediterranean and Latin worlds, though it also encountered strong criticism from moderate liberals. Thus, José M. L. Mora, a noted Mexican writer and politician of the liberal school, in many of his essays and articles condemned the practice of places like "Spain, Portugal, Naples, and all the new republics of America, which adopting the principles of the Spanish constitution extending to non–property owners the exercise of public rights, have uninterruptedly moved from one revolution to another." He contrasted this with the example of the more advanced nations, which almost without exception (he was writing in 1827) limited the right to vote. In Latin America, by contrast, "the times of elections have always been a public calamity for the nation," because of the disorder and agitation accompanying them.[14]

In the Río de la Plata the moderate-liberal governments of the first years of independence soon were replaced by a host of provincial *caudillista* regimes with a capacity for popular mobilization, of which the most solid was that of Juan Manuel de Rosas in Buenos Aires.[15] The authoritarian and at the same time popular nature of most of these regimes was a permanent source of concern for intellectuals and liberal politicians. It could not be argued that any government, once installed, could manipulate public opinion so as to obtain popular support and the presence of the masses in the streets or in the irregular militia. A special type of leadership, a peculiar form of distribution of benefits or defense of sectoral interests was necessary to obtain those results. And the required policies were generally at loggerheads with the established canons of economic development or balance of powers and individual guarantees. This is why Esteban Echeverría, Argentine liberal thinker of the early nineteenth century, maintained that representation should be granted to the "people's reason" and not to the "people" as such. He argued that when the moderate-liberal Unitario party had granted universal suffrage, it had dug its own grave as the weapon had been turned against the party.[16]

In fact, when that legislation had been enacted in the province of Buenos Aires in 1821, the governing group led by Bernardino Rivadavia believed that it could rely on the support of the landed *estancieros* and thereby on the almost automatic vote of the labor force. That vote was seen as counterbalancing the possible adverse results of urban elections, always somewhat freer or more unpredictable. Eventually, the *estancieros* turned against the ruling Unitarios—a local version of the American Federalists—whose policy of centralization was proving to be too costly, and supported Rosas, who could control the popular sectors.[17]

In a later generation, it is worth examining the way José M. Estrada, a liberal Catholic, conceived of the political spectrum in Argentina in the early nineteenth century. After describing the Unitario party as aristocratic, he considered the Federal party as

> not abundant in towering personalities. It was more political than doctrinaire; it believed less in abstractions, and analyzed better the realities of social life. It avoided French doctrines of government and preferred the Anglo American school. . . . The Federal party, because of its composition and nature was a popular party; and as such it had to compromise with the caudillos who held sway over those masses.

He went on to say that the collapse in 1820 of the central government was the "hour of democratic victory," but that "democracy succumbed because it was not organized. . . . Democracy is not equivalent to the election of the rulers, or to 'popular sovereignty,' which is the domination of sheer numbers, a multiform and uncontrollable Caesarism. It consists in the solidarity of the people in the exercise of the law."[18]

Bartolomé Mitre, the Argentine liberal historian and politician, also saw the *caudillo*-dominated Federal party as "democratic," and its opponents as "oligarchical."[19] Sarmiento, who felt that without education the people would always vote for a Rosas, and Alberdi, who believed Spanish America had witnessed too many "democratic revolutions," were particularly concerned with the way a genuine democracy would be established in this part of the world.

From the use of the word in the above texts, two conceptions of democracy emerge. For one, a political party with popular support is democratic. This argument is represented in its extreme form by Juan Uslar Pietri when he so characterizes Boves, but it is shared by Mitre. The other conception of democracy bases it on a balance of powers and respect for minorities, which include the privileged ones with interests opposed to the popular majority. That this majority may express itself genuinely and at the same time spare those "aristocratic" interests it opposes is the difficult equilibrium that the democracies that really function have achieved.

This equilibrium is possible only through a system of political parties, preferably including one that expresses the needs of the popular classes and another, those of the dominant classes. Not that any democratic system must have a two-party (or two-coalition) system, but it is no mere coincidence that most democratic regimes share this trait. From this situation two issues emerge in the study of Latin American politics: the problem of the party of the Right, and the problem of the popular party. In the Latin American experience, the popular party is generally populist, that is, a combination of minorities from the elites with the popular sectors, highly mobilized but with little autonomous organization. Populism, with its charismatic leadership and apparently personalized relationship between leader and follower, rarely accepts being the representative of just *one* sector, not the whole nation. From this to defining as antinational all opponents there is only one step. On the other hand, mobilizationism, as seen by the historical examples considered here, is highly Protean in its capacity to shift to the Right or the Left. However, under a given type of leadership, it may become quite a conservative if unstable form of social control. Of the cases described in this chapter, some are clearly classifiable as being on the Right (e.g., the Bourbon reaction in Naples or Boves' royalist campaign in Venezuela). Others are on the Left (the Mexican insurgency and the Haitian slave revolt, in spite of the manipulatory efforts of the Right in the latter case). Between these extremes lie early populist systems like that of Artigas in Uruguay or Güemes in Salta, and the conservative but also popular regimes of Rosas and Páez. The organizational weakness of these movements makes them particularly attractive to minorities of any ideological sign, intent on getting on the bandwagon. This, so notorious in recent cases like Peronism, was already present a century and a half ago in Iturbide's entourage in Mexico.[20] Organizational weakness—as long as it lasts—makes it difficult for populism to perform a more positive role in the consolidation of democracy. The instability of the policies adopted, the dependence on the charismatic figure of a leader, the ever-present possibility of internal *coups de main* and sudden changes of position, all convert populism into a difficult participant in the democratic process. However, democracy does require popular participation, which cannot be restricted as it was during the last century in the countries that are today examples of democracy. Hence our predicament: with scarce associative and organizational experience and with a socially mobilized popular mass, it is necessary to build a balance between powers that are seriously unbalanced. The Right is strong in economic and military terms, but in most cases has not yet been able to co-opt the middle classes. The popular party, in contrast, has a large numerical force but is weak in associationist experience, intermediate responsible leadership, and pluralist participation.

3. Actors and Coalitions

In the theoretical perspective here adopted the political process results from the interaction between several actors who try to impose their interests and opinions on society. For this purpose, they form coalitions, the stronger one of which occupies the government. A historical sequence can be seen as the trace of successive coalitions that have left their mark on society. The search for sociological laws should be built around this process and hypotheses formulated so as to understand this basic scheme. The process includes the following:

(1) individualization of actors, who must be sufficiently homogeneous to support the role of elementary participants in the political game;

(2) characterization of each actor, according to its place in social space, its economic and social psychological attributes, its ideology, and its attitudes toward specific issues;

(3) hypotheses about how changes in these actors' characteristics occur;

(4) hypotheses about coalition formation between actors;

It could be argued that this is an excessively voluntaristic and individualist perspective that sees the historical process as based on the volitions (opinions, interests, attitudes) of actors instead of resulting from the operation of social forces. However, the aim of explaining the social by the social—to use Durkheim's words—is not abandoned. Actors are social groups, not individuals, and their attitudes must be seen as to a large extent generated by the social context.

The most obvious way to subdivide society into actors, if the validity of the basic Marxist theory is accepted, is to take classes or their fragments as elements. We shall start the search for social actors by introducing enough subdivisions to obtain homogeneous units. Of course, social groups are rarely completely homogeneous. If, no matter how minutely subdivided, we never found homogeneity in an actor, then the entire strategy of analyzing the political process in terms of interactions between social actors would be invalidated. For each issue, in each crisis, the crystallization of society into homogeneous groups would be different and therefore actors would dissolve. We would simply divide the total population in different ways according to the issue being considered. The strategy here adopted is based on the assumption that, for a given society and a not exceedingly long period (a decade or two), it makes sense to begin by subdividing the population into a number of groups defined by stratification, groups that are homogeneous enough to maintain individuality and be considered the basic elements in coalition formation. The fact that they maintain their individuality does not mean that they do not change their economic, social psychological, political, and ideological traits through time. But using actors as units requires selecting some variables to define actors, while others will be taken as changing attributes of those actors.

Let us suppose that the issues of private versus state education, the role of foreign investment, and the functions of trade unions successively come into the limelight. We could define actors by grouping individuals first according to their attitudes toward education, then according to their opinions about foreign enterprise, and finally on the basis of their favorability to trade unions. This, though feasible and perhaps more closely connected to the empirical base, is not the strategy here adopted. That type of empiricism would be too radical, too unaware of the latent structures causing political phenomena. In a case like the above, homogeneous actors will be identified on the basis of their stratification characteristics. Their attitudes toward education, foreign investment, and trade unions would then be attributes, variable through time, of those actors.

For this approach to be useful, the gamut of opinions about contentious issues among individual members of each social actor should not be too wide. This is a rather stiff requirement, and it certainly involves subdividing social classes into a considerable number of actors. The usefulness of the approach can only be justified by its results.

In some cases, however, it may be impossible or impractical to define homogeneous actors using only stratification variables, because subdivision would have to be extreme and would therefore increase the number of actors beyond manageable limits, or because of a lack of data. Thus, in Lebanon actors would have to be divided along religious lines. Perhaps religious affiliation is the result of a myriad of economic and class factors operating along the last eight or nine centuries of the history of that country. To unravel that yarn is surely beyond anyone's strength; even the most rigid theoretician would have to introduce new, nonstratificational variables, such as religion, ethnicity, or nationality, to define social actors. Of course, if only those other variables were adopted, leaving aside class-based ones, the theoretical approach here adopted would be questioned.

When a social class is taken as an actor, its main organizations are included, such as corporations (national or foreign) or professional associations. Foreign business, or multinationals, must be considered as social actors in the local political game, though their strength derives from beyond the borders. Often it will be necessary to include an actor representing the foreign interests of another country, powerful enough to become a participant in the internal political system. This actor need not coincide in its interests and attitudes with the business sector of that same national origin. The actor *foreign country* represents the general economic, strategic, and international policy interests of that country, usually expressed by its government.

Eventually, it might be necessary even to subdivide that actor (Pentagon versus State Department, Party versus Foreign Ministry), but usually it will be enough to adjudicate to the *foreign country actor* the attitudes of the changing groups that control it.

Church and Armed Forces: Effective and Potential Noninvolvement

Of particular importance is the treatment of the type of participation in the political system of such actors as the church and the armed forces. Though their members belong to some social class, their identity is very strongly marked by their institutional roles. This also happens to some degree to individuals in other social positions. Thus a worker reacts to political events not only in his or her condition as such but also as a member of a trade union. However, a trade union can be considered as simply an organization of the working class. But what class is represented by the church (or churches) or the armed forces? Are they simply expressions of the dominant classes, specializing in ideological or coercive tasks? Though this hypothesis has enjoyed its period of popularity, it cannot be taken very seriously today. This is not to deny the very strong functional connections often existing between these "guardian" institutions and the existing dominant order. But they are far from operating always in the same manner, and sometimes they are dysfunctional. For these reasons, we must consider these institutions, and some others, as social actors and eventually we must subdivide them. Thus, for example, we may include high or low clergy, the army and navy separately (vertically or horizontally divided), the state itself or the government bureaucracy. All of them must be taken as institutional bodies, different in their effects from what would result from the simple sum of their members' opinions, because of their hierarchical composition. In each case, we must decide whether the inclusion of some or all of these actors is required; at the very least we must take into consideration the armed forces, even if they do not have the habit of intervening in politics. Their presence, even behind the scenes, is always central as the last resort guarantors of the system of domination through their control of violence. They exert influence in indirect ways and they have the capacity to assume a more direct role under changed circumstances, although in the more democratic countries they generally are not involved in the political game. But experience shows that, if for any reason they feel threatened, they react by entering the political arena—whether in Sweden or in Argentina. In France the armed forces participated in de Gaulle's coup in 1958 when faced with the intractable problem of Algeria, though the solidity of the institutional system caused them to withdraw to their traditional position of noninvolvement soon enough. The armed forces' presence in the French political scene cannot be denied, however, and has always been a factor when considering the eventuality of a Communist electoral victory or even a socialist one (if of a radical nature). Their presence is equally obvious in Italy and Spain. In Great Britain, Sweden, or the United States the withdrawal of the armed forces to noninvolved roles is much more solid. It is sometimes argued that this is rooted in culture, but this explanation is not sufficient. Without denying the presence of a political culture with a certain weight of its own, its operation is more likely to consist in the consolidation of mechanisms that have operated for a long period. Noninvolvement is not mainly based on tradition, but it has to be won and reaffirmed every day. In those countries the social and political system is such that practically never do the armed forces or actors close to them feel seriously threatened by other actors.

Noninvolvement can be potential or effective. It can be hypothesized that certain actors, in a given type of institutional or cultural evolution, are *potentially noninvolved*, even if they are not always actually noninvolved.[1] This statement about the potential noninvolvement of the armed forces apparently clashes with everyday observation if applied to Latin America. The more dominant assumption is that, because of the rigidity of the ruling classes, imperialist dependency, or their own authoritarianism, the armed forces, far from potentially noninvolved, are permanently ready to throw themselves on the defenseless players of politics. The evidence lends this pessimistic hypothesis much credibility. I believe, however, that it is mistaken.

The norm of professionalism, often expressed by the armed forces, is not merely a cover for other intentions. Professionalism has a weight of its own, and in some Latin American countries effective, not only potential, noninvolvement is the rule. What is observed is effective noninvolvement, that is, the armed forces' actual abstention from politics, as in Venezuela for the last couple of decades, or in Mexico for an even longer period. On the other hand, "potential noninvolvement" cannot be observed, as it is a theoretical term, a predisposition that cannot be shown to exist except by a theoretical calculus based on it.

Let us now summarize the argument about the role of the armed forces. In the first place, even in countries with a democratic tradition, the armed forces are a political actor, with interests and opinions in most areas, though more intensely expressed in security matters. They are noninvolved in the actual formation of government, that is, in the alliances that lead to party formation or other political coalitions, but they can be activated more easily than the public suspects. If they are not activated, it is not mainly due to their traditions but to the functioning of the political system, which does not menace them. Their opinions are taken into account by the more direct participants in the political arena, who avoid antagonizing excessively the armed forces on sensitive subjects.

Second, in most of Latin America the armed forces, even if often actually intervening in the exercise of power and the formation of ruling coalitions, still can be considered analytically as forming a social actor that is potentially noninvolved, in contrast with what was the rule in such polities as the Ottoman Empire (and also in a minority of Latin American situations). It is, admittedly, legitimate to doubt the validity of this conceptual differentiation. What would be its use if most of the time, say, in the past forty or fifty years, the armed forces were considered to be at the same time potentially noninvolved and actually involved? The answer is, precisely, to help differentiate most Latin American societies from those like the Ottoman Empire. In the latter, tradition, culture, and the whole institutional development caused the armed forces (and the clergy) to be permanently and directly involved in politics. This was also so at earlier periods of Latin American or southern European history, but not so now. The general evolution of these societies, which influences all of their members, sets for the armed forces an ideal norm of nonintervention (potential noninvolvement). Transgressions are due to peculiar constellations that, admittedly, are quite endemic. In this, Latin America differs from France, where only a brief episode of direct military intervention took place in 1958. However, even if in Latin America those activating constellations have been recurrent, they need not be permanent, or only eradicable through a revolutionary transformation of society. Much less are they changeable via a sudden conversion or change of heart on the part of the military, or a purge of its worst elements. All of this is helpful, but not enough.

On the other hand, the armed forces' withdrawal from direct intervention in politics is occasionally due to some episode that has weakened them radically or robbed them of their prestige, as in Argentina in 1983. If only this factor were present, they would soon return to their traditional ways, as they did in that same country in 1976, a mere three years after the downfall of the Onganía-Levingston-Lanusse regime What really would control them more permanently would be the unity and moderation of the other sectors of society, political parties, pressure groups, and the like. The problem is that often among these there are some who feel menaced by popular majorities and who appeal to the barracks, thus activating the mechanism of military intervention.

This problem leads us to the subject of the party of the Right and to the argument that the economic Right should have legitimate ways of defending its interests because, otherwise, its indefensibility makes it aggressive. Of course, there are many who argue that if it is defenseless, so much the better, as this offers the opportunity to liquidate it. But this is not so simple, and generally the economic Right manages quite well to survive, with the help of its friends in the armed forces, whose own feelings of menace must also be studied to forecast their behavior.

These are, then, the peculiarities of political participation by certain institutional actors. Even if not explicitly participating in the formation of political coalitions, they are always taken into account in the calculations of political parties and pressure groups. But their institutional peculiarities are such that their participation in coalition building is different from that of other political actors. Even when actually involved, they must be considered as potentially noninvolved. This subject will be treated further in chapter 6.

The State as an Autonomous Actor

The problem of adequately analyzing the behavior of the state approximates that of analyzing the military. This is especially fertile ground for worn-out Marxist statements ("administrative committee of the ruling classes") whose irritating simplemindedness has led many to consider the state as an autonomous actor and to view political conflict not as a result of class conflict, but as a fight between political elites for control of the state. Once a group is in control of the state, according to this perspective, it could manage to remain in it independent of the social interests it represents; it might represent nobody but itself, deriving its power not from class representation but from control of the state apparatus. The ruling group, then, would confront other social actors, classes, or institutions as rivals for power, not as sources of its power. This scheme owes a lot to attempts at interpreting what happens in countries with a "socialist economy," where social classes are not easy to discern, and therefore there is a tendency to overemphasize the quota of power that mere control of the machinery of state can give to a political group.

This is a necessary corrective to more simplistic interpretations, but it threatens to lose more than it gains in its revision of the central role of class analysis. Though the state may wield some elements of autonomous power, it operates like the armed forces. It has a certain weight, greater in some societies, but not overly dominant if compared to the weight of civil sectors. To understand "socialist economies," it is necessary, before assigning excessive weight to the state, to consider class composition. If we accept that apart from workers and peasants other social classes exist, then a distribution of power where the popular sectors have the worst part can be explained without recourse to the omnipotence of the state. Power resides, rather, in such social classes as the bureaucracy. The state, although far from negligible, has less weight than the bureaucracy taken as a social class.

The state, then, may be taken, if the evidence requires it, as a separate actor, but without an excessively predominant weight. In a consolidated democracy, the fact that a party comes to office does not give it much more weight than it would have otherwise. Where civil service neutrality is established, this is particularly so. In most Third World cases, though, the state does have a greater weight, but not comparable to that of all other social actors taken together. It is particularly important, as already suggested, not to confuse the state with the bureaucratic class.[2]

Intellectuals and Political Elites

Intellectuals are another group needing special treatment. Though not very numerous, their long-range influence can be very important, as generators and transmitters of ideology. The complexity of their motivational mechanisms forces us to take more variables into consideration when studying their attitudes than when considering those of class-defined actors. In this they share some traits with those other superstructural specialists, the armed forces and the clergy. On the other hand, it is not clear where their limits lie. In some analyses all those who do intellectual work, whether of a professional or managerial kind, are taken to be intellectuals, thus increasing their numbers and their heterogeneity. It is better to restrict the term to include specialists in the elaboration of ideas, writers, artists, university professors, journalists of a certain standing, and the like. Students to some extent belong temporarily to this group, but most of them soon enter the middle and upper classes as professionals. Another definition that must be distinguished from the one here adopted is Gramsci's. For him, intellectuals are those who think autonomously and who have a consciousness of historical processes, that is, the active members of the party of the working class.[3]

Intellectuals, in some cases, must be subdivided into two or more groups, according to their ideology. But if the majority lean toward a certain ideological position not much is lost by taking only one social actor to represent them. The others, because of their small weight, or their close connection with some other actor—the bourgeoisie, for example, if right-wing intellectuals are considered— need not appear as a separate actor. In this, as in other cases, the increase in the number of actors helps reflect society more accurately, but it complicates its analysis.

Often, in the Marxist tradition (in the same way as the armed forces and the clergy are not taken to be autonomous actors) intellectuals are also considered capable only of representing other social classes. Karl Kautsky, however, took an important step in the study of this subject when he pointed out that class consciousness emerges as the interaction between two elements: labor struggles, and the ideas of intellectuals (often of bourgeois origin). Lenin adopted this conception and expanded it into his vision of the proletarian party as a party of professional revolutionaries, that is, individuals of whatever social extraction, presumably in their majority "intellectuals."

Neither for Kautsky nor for Lenin did the non-working-class origin of this elite matter, which is surprising in a Marxist analysis. This is particularly so in Lenin's case, because for him the revolutionary party performed a much more central role than the intellectuals did for Kautsky. Lenin engages in a veritable logomachy in his use of the words *intellectuals, revolutionary party,* and *proletariat,* treated as equivalent to and representative of each other. Far from this being so, it is more sensible to consider intellectuals as advanced representatives of the bureaucratic class.

According to Marxist theory, a class can only achieve power when it has fully matured within the existing mode of production. In czarist Russia it was evident that the working class was far from having done so, but it was equally obvious that the regime faced serious survival problems. Practically all Marxist observers— including Lenin—agreed that the impending revolution could only be of a capitalist nature, that is, that private capitalists were going to manage production after the event. As the political weakness of the bourgeoisie also appeared evident to those observers, it was not clear who would actually succeed the czar. Lenin's answer, very creative but not quite Marxist, was that, though capitalists would continue to run the productive apparatus, political power—and social domination—would be exercised by the proletariat (that is, the Social Democratic party). History took its revenge on this infringement of Marxist doctrine.

In Russia the bourgeoisie had matured economically to a considerable extent; under more peaceful conditions it would probably have taken over after the czarist regime's demise. But together with the bourgeoisie another social class was maturing, namely, the bureaucracy, with its numerous dissatisfied aspirants who were not all intellectuals. Marx did not foresee a situation of this type. It so happened that, given the critical circumstances of a lost war accompanied by social upheaval, the new class was the best prepared to replace the czarist regime. Lenin's political party was one of the expressions of that superiority. The members were recruited among the same sectors, generally undergoing rapid transformations, that fed the bureaucracy: the provincial nobility unable to readapt to life in the capital, the rural gentry in the process of becoming professionals or officials, the impoverished small businessmen forced to maintain their status by shifting to salaried activities, students, technicians, and other college graduates seeking positions congruent with their qualifications. When Lenin, in *What Is to Be Done?* (1902),[4] said that toward the end of the last century "all" Russian youths were converted to Marxism, he was referring to the youth of these social strata.

The social alchemy by which these elements of the old society became a basic component of the new one was very different in Russia than in the West. In Western Europe and the United States, the salaried middle class expanded enough to integrate most aspirants into its ranks. The new public or private bureaucratic sector was formed in a manner completely compatible with the existing order, of which it became a solid support. Bourgeoisie and bureaucracy, in those countries, were fully intermingled. Not so in Russia, where economic limitations and the war crisis made the peaceful absorption of enough new elements impossible. A large number of individuals remained as frustrated candidates to become part of the new social stratum required by a modern and industrial economy. The Russian Social Democratic party, despite its ostensibly working-class ideology, ended up representing that transitional social sector that may be called, for brevity, a bureaucracy-in-the-making. The party became the pivot of a class alliance, much stronger than any the bourgeoisie could place in the field.

To analyze the Russian prerevolutionary situation in terms of social actors, it is necessary to subdivide the social pyramid to reflect adequately the process described above. The bureaucracy-in-the-making must be included, but we should not consider the intellectuals or sectors of the petty bourgeoisie as representing it, because the majority of neither of them was pro-Bolshevik, even though they formed the main sociological niche from which the party recruited its adherents. Another concept is necessary here: *elite*. An elite is a human group of diverse origins, selected through some special social mechanism, that in many ways acts as a single body. It is not a social stratum nor a class sector nor an institution like the armed forces or the clergy. It constitutes an independent actor. The Bolshevik party was a coalition, or fusion, formed by that elite, the working class of the larger cities, and sectors of the lower middle classes and the intelligentsia. In the social convulsion induced by the military defeat, this group proved capable of integrating the mobilized masses of soldiers, most of them peasants. The elite played a central role in this coalition—as Lenin saw very well—but it did not act as a mere spark. Rather, it was the moving force in the process, remaining in the scene and taking over in the construction of a new system of domination.

The formation of elites at odds with their class of origin is a central subject in the study of Third World countries, where economic and social conditions create a chasm between aspirations and gratifications. Apart from the great national social pyramid, numerous other small pyramids exist in towns and villages, valuable and relevant to their inhabitants however oppressive and asphyxiating they may look to the external observer.[5] The impact of the world market on self-contained local economic circuits, the rapid increase of education over and above the sluggish occupational structure, the demographic explosion, all tend to produce dissatisfied elites at middle levels of stratification. The same result is produced often by the economic unification of a country, with its strengthening of channels of communication and homogenization of attitudes. In these cases, many traditional artisan groups, commercial and service operators, even clergy and educators, suddenly lose their status as local notables, coming to be seen by others and by themselves as rejected and marginalized by the national culture. If to this some economic deterioration is added, plus internal migration to larger cities where groups of relevant others disappear or become marginal, the effects in terms of loss of self-esteem and resentment can be abysmal. What comes as a surprise to many observers is then more understandable: rapid and efficient economic development can increase rather than moderate social tensions. Often the place where those tensions accumulate and breed revolutionary elites is not the working class, nor even the lower peasantry, but some middle sectors.

Coalitions

Different sorts of actors have been mentioned as being the essential components of the political game: classes; strata or class fragments; ethnic, religious, or national groups; intellectuals; foreign interests; institutions like the church, the armed forces, or the state; and political elites of assorted origin, often nucleated around a personality. From this perspective, parties are the result of alliances or coalitions (explicit or implicit, conscious or not) between those actors. It should be possible, then, to describe a political party as being formed by several of the actors present. If this proves too difficult or impossible, political parties might be taken as individual actors rather than as coalitions. In general, though, it should be feasible to reduce a political party to a coalition between more elementary actors.

In the formation of coalitions, actors are guided by their similarity in economic interests, political attitudes, and ideologies. Between any two actors, this similarity defines a certain affinity, or an antagonism, which may be conceived of as negative affinity. Though a fully developed simulation model would include methods of calculating these variables, here we shall only look at some qualitative aspects of the structure of coalitions.

In entering a coalition each actor contributes its own political weight, which is the quota of power the actor can command. Political power, or weight, is a magnitude that can change with time. It depends on many elements, among them the actor's economic resources, numbers, degree of organization, and strategic centrality of the functions performed. But as a first approximation, at any given moment the actor's political weight is a constant magnitude, whatever coalition it enters. A ruling coalition can take measures that benefit its member actors and increase their weight, though the effects are generally not immediate. Thus, under the Popular Front government in France in 1936, trade union organization was favored; something similar, though in a more authoritarian context, happened in Argentina under the influence of the then-colonel Perón starting in 1943. Inversely, if a government exercises repression against its opponents, weakening their organization (one of the main determinants of political weight), important changes in the relative power of social groups will occur. In countries with little or no repression or violence, actors' political weights do not change very much in the short run. What does change is the structure of coalitions, whose total political weight is the sum of the weights of their members. The breakup and recomposition of coalitions is a central political process under both democratic and dictatorial regimes. In this process, it is also necessary to take into account those actors that, in the national context, are potentially noninvolved. In some cases, as we have seen, these actors enter the field of politics directly. But even when they do not, they continue to play a political role, due to the ever-present possibility of their reentering the scene and joining in the process of coalition formation.

As an example of the structure of coalitions, let us take Argentina at the beginning of the 1970s, when the *"revolución argentina"* military government (1966–1973) was still solidly in the saddle, with conservative support, and facing the opposition of the Peronists, the Radical party, and various sectors of the Left. Violence, however, was becoming generalized, and youth groups dedicated to armed struggle were forming, like the Montoneros and the Ejército Revolucionario del Pueblo (see figure 1).

Only some of the affinities and antagonisms are represented. The size of the circles is proportional to actors' political weight. The position in space represents social status. The rectangles incorporate actors forming a coalition. Arrows between actors or coalitions indicate antagonisms. An actor that is not associated with others forms its own coalition.

The church (CH) and the armed forces (AF), according to our previous analysis, should be considered potentially noninvolved actors, but only the church is effectively out of the partisan game. The military is allied with an actor representing the business and upper middle class sectors of the country (BG, bourgeoisie). There are four actors forming—at this level of disaggregation—the Peronist coalition.

Actor P is a political elite symbolized by General Perón, whose power is reflected

Figure 1. Political Coalitions, Argentina in the Early 1970s

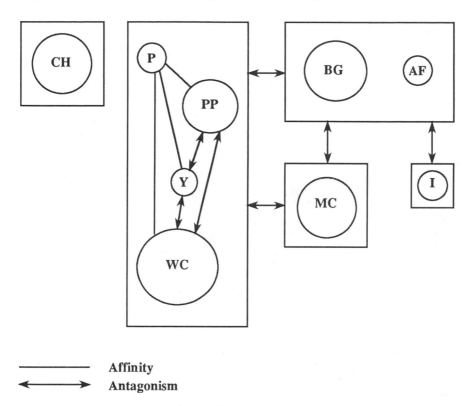

—————— Affinity

◄——————► Antagonism

in the prestige of its leader. The working class (WC) has a strong organization and a high affinity with Perón. Actor PP is the provincial politicians of Peronism, mostly from peripheral provinces, with a following among local middle classes and popular strata. Actor PP is also strongly attached to the leader, though somewhat antagonized by the trade unions. The Juventud Peronista (Y), including the guerrilla formations, is linked positively with Perón (perhaps only tactically) and strongly antagonized by the other components of the alliance, notably, the trade unionists. These disparate elements are brought together by the elite symbolized by General Perón. The intensity with which the working-class component rejects the other two is not strong enough to expel them from the coalition, because "Perón" keeps them united. Between the whole of this coalition and the military government there is a strong antagonism, marked by the arrows separating them. The middle classes (MC) are alone, forming the basis of the Radical party. The intellectuals (I) have little political weight, reject any coalition, and support several small leftist parties. If at a later date the Peronist elite (P) breaks with the youth (guerrilla) sector of the movement, the latter is irremediably expelled from the alliance. If the political elite

Figure 2. Typical Coalitions in Social Democratic Processes

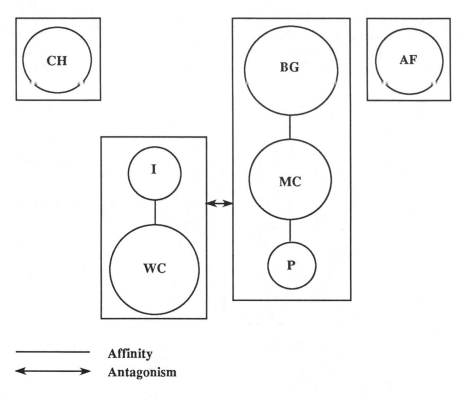

———————— Affinity

◄————————► Antagonism

of Peronism becomes disorganized through the death of its leader or changes some of its attitudes, the alliance enters a period of crisis, losing some of its provincial elements. Modifications in the relative weights of actors or in their affinities and antagonisms might reconsolidate the alliance. If a tactical understanding (a subject to which we shall return) is established between this Peronist constellation and radicalism, the military government remains in a difficult predicament.

But to produce a genuine understanding between two social actors is no easy matter. It is not equivalent to signing a joint declaration, because it must reflect the whole structure of opinions and affinities, which do not depend on the leadership alone, but are rooted in collective feelings. On the other hand, the military governing coalition is more complex than here represented. To depict it more faithfully requires establishing subdivisions among sectors of the business community, as well as of the upper middle classes, not to mention the armed forces themselves.

Figure 2 represents a situation typical of the social democratic processes referred to in chapter 2. The church and the military are considered to be effectively noninvolved. The conservative party is interpreted as a coalition between the business or upper middle class actor (BG), the bulk of the middle class (MC), and the peasants or farmers (P). The popular party is formed by an alliance between the organized working class (WC) and the socialist intellectuals (I).

This is, of course, a simplification, valid only as a first approximation. We must keep in mind that several elements are being left out of this scheme:

(1) The conservative party (or party coalition) actually obtains votes from a sector of the working class, which has not been represented as it is not very relevant in terms of its political weight (it should be taken into account, however, if a more accurate representation is required).

(2) Social democracy, on the other hand, gets votes from the middle classes, which for similar reasons have not been considered as a separate actor but should be in a more exact rendering of the situation.

The degree of subdivision introduced in the schemes depends on the object of the exercise. It should be kept in mind that these schemes do not aim at reflecting the distribution of the electorate, but only the *latent structure* existing in the country and responsible for the prevalent social equilibrium. The political weights of both coalitions are approximately the same, so that alternations in government are not too significant (in most cases) because the party in office is scarcely stronger than the opposition, which retains a high veto power.

The mass of "marginal voters," or fluctuating, independent electorate, is not represented in this figure. To take it into account, one or more actors should be introduced, defined by their attitudes, because it would be difficult to define them by their stratificational characteristics. Between both coalitions, then, at least another actor, F (fluctuating) should be imagined, whose affinities and antagonisms would oscillate, determining its alliances with the other parties. If only those actors represented in figure 2 are used, changes should be registered by altering their respective weights. When there are many actors, this method is preferable to the former for avoiding unnecessary detail that hinders the understanding of the processes involved. Actually, any party, apart from the actors that are its main support, always gets some adherents from the other side of the fence; there is always some social democrat businessman or peasant, and it is not impossible to find a conservative intellectual. But this is no reason to proliferate social actors, unless it were the only way to reflect reality. Therefore, the figures representing actors and coalitions do not purport to be exact reproductions of public opinion in all its shades. They are only schemes designed to express the main aspects of the latent structures affecting the processes of party formation.

In these schemes the political weight of an actor at a given moment has been considered as a fixed magnitude, which is added to that of its allies. However, in some cases the political weight added to a coalition by an actor does not follow such a simple rule, particularly so in the case of mobilizational coalitions, one of whose components is a mass with a low degree of autonomous organization. If that mass is socially mobilized, it will add to the coalition more strength than the amount it has when acting in isolation. The weight of the coalition, then, will be greater than the sum of the individual weights of its components. This multiplication of the loaves is based on the alchemy of social mobilization and mobilizationism.

Mobilizational Coalitions

For actors with low organization but high social mobilization, we shall define the concept of "mobilization weight." In much the same way as the political weight is considered to be a function of organization, the mobilization weight of an actor with low organization but high social mobilization depends on its social mobilization. For an actor with high organization and high mobilization, for example, the working class of an industrialized country, political and mobilization weights are approximately equal. By contrast, in situations of high mobilization and low organization, as in Boves' following in Venezuela or for many a Latin American *caudillo*, the political weight of the popular sector taken by itself is small, but its mobilization component is very high. If a mobilizationist coalition is formed, it will benefit from the mobilization weights of its components. That is, a mobilizationist coalition has the secret of converting available into actual political power.

For a mobilizational coalition to be formed, there must be at least one social actor capable of exerting leadership functions in such a context. An individual, according to the hypothesis here adopted, is not enough without the support of what we have called an elite. The individual may be its symbol and organizer, the visible part of the iceberg. This elite must compensate for the organizational shortcomings of the mass; it must of course also be attitudinally in favor of the mobilizational mode of social participation. This is not overly easy to achieve. There will probably always be some individuals prepared to act as leaders for such a movement. But the existence of a somewhat ampler social group, with the required characteristics to be the nurturing environment or entourage of the individual leader, depends on social tensions of a peculiar kind being at work in society. To perform its role, the mobilizational leader must be an actor of relatively high social status (from middle class up, including military and clergy), or else compensate by having a high organization. High status provides connections, resources, and prestige, all helping to perform a nucleating role in a mobilizational coalition, hence the variable nature of these coalitions, as the masses (with interests and attitudes potentially opposed to the dominant order) become associated with an elite that can range from very conservative to highly antagonistic to the status quo.

Though in most cases the leader actor must have high status, it might be a highly organized sector of the lower strata. However, the short social distances between leaders and followers would make this event highly problematic. It is not easy for a low-status actor to assume the role of mobilizational leader. If it has emerged from the condition of low organization of the majority of the members of its class and become a separate actor, it is still too close to its origin to provide mobilizational leadership, in the sense used here. This requires a greater social distance between leaders and led and the existence of mechanisms of prestige that will give to that elite the rather regimented and monolithic support of the unorganized mass. That type of mass is not likely to be stimulated by an elite of its own status into a mobilizational mode of participation.

For the mobilizational coalition to come into existence yet another condition is required: there must be affinity between its member actors. It is not necessary that there be coincidence in all economic interests, political attitudes, or ideology, but only in a majority. Some issues will be more relevant than others, depending on the degree of conflict about each one. Thus, in many cases the difference in ideology is not very important, because it has low relevance for the stronger social actors. As for economic interests, it is reasonable to suppose that there must be enough convergence in this area for a coalition to be formed. However, for actors with little education or political experience, there may be a lack of clear perception of their interests. Social psychological convergence, or the shared preference for the mobilizational mode of political participation, can overcome some differences in economic interests.

An extreme example of this possibility—one that has stimulated a host of studies of mass psychology—is the Nazi movement. The existence of a mobilizationist elite is clear enough there, as is the economic affinity with upper- and middle-class sectors, some of them downwardly mobile or insecure as a result of the protracted economic crisis. But it is difficult to deny that there was also a social psychological component, rooted in the economic and class characteristics of the groups involved, but not identical to them. This allows political fusions of a much more unexpected kind than would be the case if only coincidence of economic interests or simple deceit based on misinformation were involved.[6]

Latin American *caudillismo* is usually also based on a mobilizationist coalition, but this need not always be so. Of the cases in chapter 1 (tables 1 and 2), Güemes' leadership in Salta was more obviously mobilizationist and anti–status quo, based on a peasant mass mobilized by the needs of irregular warfare. In the less-agitated province of Santiago del Estero, by contrast, Ibarra's leadership had few or no components of mobilizationism, nor was he so clearly antagonized by the local dominant classes as was Güemes.[7]

The mobilizationist mode requires a mass that, on the one hand, must be active (it is socially mobilized) but, on the other, depends on an authoritarian chief, which explains the contradictory nature of these experiences. Not all forms of *caudillismo*, or *caciquismo*, must be mobilizational, however. Conservative parties need to rely partly on a local leadership capable of recruiting more popular elements, without necessarily adopting a mobilizational pattern. Often in describing these conservative *caudillista* structures, the word *populism* is used, but it is better to preserve the concept for those movements that encompass a socially mobilized but not autonomously organized mass, with an anti–status quo leadership capable of establishing a charismatic relationship with the former and favoring a mobilizational mode of participation.[8] Argentine conservatives have had, in figures like Avellaneda's mayor Alberto Barceló, *caudillos* with some popular following built on a mixture of favors, menaces, and shared social psychological traits—something similar to the "machine" described by Robert Merton when referring to the corrupt Tammany Hall–type of municipal structures in the United States, generally associated with the Democratic party.[9] However, none of these cases is mobilizational. It is also argued that the provincial components of Peronism (especially in the more backward areas) have a lot of similarities with the old conservatism and form what Manuel Mora y Araujo calls "populist potential." This provincial Peronism is based on local elites with a following of peasants, rural laborers, small-town workers, and marginals with little or no autonomous organization. This electorate, according to Mora y Araujo, would have some tendency to become reincorporated into a more natural expression of a conservative type. By contrast, in the more prosperous and urban parts of the country Peronism, dominated by its trade union sector, would tend to adopt a "labor" form.[10] Nationwide, then, the party would have two components: the unionized working class in the industrial areas, and the mobilized but unorganized popular strata that, associated with local middle sectors, predominate in the economically less developed parts. Many of the equivalents of those who vote for Peronism in the interior provinces of Argentina vote for the Right or Center-Right in other Latin American countries with strong conservative parties, like Brazil, Chile, or Colombia. It is thus reasonable to think that—given a prudent time span— they might show a similar inclination in Argentina. However, before that happens, the mobilizationist scheme into which they are incorporated would have to change into a nonmobilizationist one. This subject will be taken up further in chapters 9 and 10.

4. Authority and the Fragmentation of Power

In times of crisis and violence there is a search for the consolidation of authority so as to "order" society above the wills of individuals. Comtean positivism clearly shared this concern, as did Spencer's evolutionism, even though in both cases a lot of faith was placed in automatic market mechanisms to regulate some areas of social conflict. A radical economic liberalism can coexist with considerable doses of authoritarianism in political, cultural, or ideological areas. The main lines of Comtean theory were adopted by Latin American thinkers preoccupied by the waste of resources stemming from endemic civil wars. In Venezuela during the early part of this century Laureano Vallenilla Lanz was one of the more forceful exponents of this point of view, basing himself on the theoretical elaborations of the sociology of his times, which, "undertaking the study of society with the precepts of evolution and determinism, definitely condemn[ed] anarchy and revolution." In *Cesarismo democrático* (1919), taking as an instance Venezuela under Páez, he argued that the latter's authority, like that "of all Spanish American caudillos, was based on the *unconscious suggestion* of the majority. Our people . . . then and even now are at some intermediate stage between mechanical and organic solidarity, the latter being the characteristic of *legitimate and stable* societies." The transition must be overseen by "the Great Egoist, the Dictator, the Caesar or Caesarion, who dominates all other rival egoisms by organizing and disciplining them, founding like Juan Manuel de Rosas a despotic state, which in all times has been the basis of nationality." This necessary dictator, as Francisco García Calderón, a Peruvian writer akin to Vallenilla Lanz, called him, is seen—paradoxically—as representing democracy, understood, of course, in a very peculiar manner. Páez was "a legitimate son of our egalitarian democracy, violently propelled by ethnic and geographic reasons towards a regime of political and social mobility without selection."[1] Again, democracy is understood as a combination of popular support, close relations between leader and people, and a special type of social mobility "without selection," capable of generating social groups supportive of the new system of political domination.

Without going to the lengths of Vallenilla Lanz, politically identified with practical versions of authoritarianism (he was civil adviser to Venezuelan dictator

Juan Vicente Gómez), other students of Latin American reality have also pointed to the permanence of the authoritarian and personalist tradition in societies of a Hispanic origin.[2] This inheritance would be at the source of the repeated failures to establish a democratic or liberal regime. Latin patrimonialist and corporative traditions, in contrast with the more capitalist and associationist ones of the North, are in this view taken to be a central datum of public life. It follows that it is necessary to pay some homage to these *idola fori* to establish a more civilized and free type of polity.

The problem is not only Latin American, as in all societies the requirements of authority and of the construction of a nationality with a minimum of internal solidarity set limits on liberal demands. In fact, liberalism is a basically divisive ideology: individual against society, region against center, voluntary association against state, small producer against monopolist. For a country to prosper and become independent, it must have a minimum of consensus, its central power must dominate the regions, and the state must show its capacity to set the rules. If it takes the capitalist path, it must allow the development of large-scale corporations and even tolerate if not foment some monopolies. If it takes the socialist road, it will have to feed the state even more, at least in the early stages of development. In other words, a centralizing and overtowering power, generating consensus and overseeing the accumulation of capital, has been present practically everywhere in the formation of nationalities, from Louis XIV to Mao Tse-tung. It is not a Hispanic American peculiarity. The problem of authority versus freedom is universal, and so is the need to appease to some extent the monster so as not to be devoured by it. In the American North and in Europe it has created as many victims as elsewhere. The difference is that in those privileged areas the process has taken more time to unfold. A strong state has centralized, consolidated, and capitalized those societies since an early date, and the advances of liberalism have been made without endangering the national identities or capital accumulations already achieved.

In Latin America, given the deficient civic culture, not only the Right, associated with the military regimes, invokes the need for authority. The Left uses a similar argument, accepting the lack of genuine elections in countries like revolutionary Cuba or the Peru of General Velasco Alvarado (1968–1975). Both sides argue, not without some logic, that the construction of a new society in conditions of intense underdevelopment and the need to resist destabilizing pressures from abroad justify a concentration of power in the top authorities. This authoritarian reasoning is not always explicit; often it is argued that the system represents "true" democracy, based on confidence in the leader, untrammeled by complex checks and balances.[3] With a different dress and a more modern language, this is not too different from Vallenilla Lanz's conceptual scheme: democratic Caesarism, not now to justify Gómez but to legitimate Fidel Castro, Velasco Alvarado, or the Perón of the fifties.

Caesarism—popular or not—implies the maximization of three dimensions of social control associated with the exercise of authority: centralization, executive predominance over a weak or nonexistent legislature, and repression of independent organizational forms. These three dimensions are conceptually independent, though often they go together. It is possible to conceive a centralist and quite "executivistic" regime that is not repressive, like the French Fifth Republic. On the other hand, there can be a federal and not very executivistic system, as under the Old Republic in Brazil (1889–1930), accompanied by strong occasional repression of opponents.

Social Structure and Authority in North and South America

The social structure in Spanish and Portuguese America favored the establishment of alliances between a "Caesar" and "the people," which so seriously preoccupied liberal theoreticians. One of the main attempts to find an original institutional solution was elaborated by Simón Bolívar. In 1813 in an address to the citizens of New Granada he summarized his interpretation of the failure of the First Venezuelan Republic (1810–1812) as being the result of the "system of toleration." Typical had been the reaction of the government against the city of Coro, which supported the royalists. Caracas authorities declined to repress it on "principles of ill understood humanity, which did not permit any government to use force to free those stupid people who do not know the value of their rights." Because of toleration, or political weakness, "to every conspiracy a pardon followed, and to each pardon a conspiracy." For similar philosophical reasons, veteran troops were not given priority, because "republics, so our statesmen thought, do not need paid men in order to maintain their freedom." The decentralizing federal system was applied, "fomenting an acute rivalry between cities and minor towns against the capital, which congressmen ambitious to dominate in their districts accused of sucking life out of the state." The spirit of party dominated everything, taking advantage of "popular elections made by the rustics from the countryside and the scheming dwellers of the cities ... who convert everything into faction, so that never did Venezuela witness a free and wise election. ... Our division, not Spanish arms, returned us to slavery."[4] In other words, the enemy was anarchy. The word was widely used in those days, and it reflected the difficulty of establishing in revolutionary or postrevolutionary circumstances a solid and stable government.

Hispanic American social structure included among other things an excessive development of cities and, therefore, of an urban bourgeoisie and middle class, given the existing level of economic development. The Spanish crown, perhaps because of the necessity of managing an economy to a large extent based on mining and on tribute-paying Indian labor, had to organize a sprawling administration. This included the church, which with its complex structure of monastic orders, bishops, ecclesiastical chapters, canons, chaplains, and curates of diverse magnitude, was a source of headaches for any viceroy that far surpassed those confronted by North American colonial governors. The fact that the clerics were not very democratic did not diminish their bellicosity, particularly when *odium teologicum* was fired by meager sustenance, which was at the base of disorderly conduct and adversary politics. The Hispanic American peculiarity (shared to a lesser extent by Brazil and some zones of Southern Europe) consisted of (1) large urban centers, both in absolute numbers and as a proportion of the population under their jurisdiction; (2) proliferation of an urban bourgeoisie and middle class, with weak economic bases due to the underdeveloped state of manufacturing, commercial agriculture, and family farming; and (3) high administrative, ecclesiastical, and university composition of that middle class, by comparison to its North American counterparts.[5] In contrast to the usual perception of this Hispanic American middle class, the emphasis here is not on its insecure and rachitic economic status—an obvious fact— but on its relatively large size in the urban areas and the centrality of its functions within the existing system of social control. The peculiarities of this class are behind the swelling numbers of "*aspirantes*" and their tendency to become "anarchist." This is also linked to the role of the clergy. Nothing was easier than for a friar or curate to become a hot-headed liberal doctrinaire. North American colonies were not so burdened with this insecure, status incongruent social group, and what existed was better integrated into the system. Probably this is at the source of the greater legitimacy conservative ideas had in the United States. Not that conservatism had no strength in Spanish America, but its ideological influence was more concentrated in peripheral, backward, and peasant areas.

In the United States conservatism was much more solidly rooted in modern sectors and performed a very central role in the formation of the nation. The Federalist party of Washington and Hamilton (which was relatively centralist) was able to unify the country, converting it from a confederation to a federation, and to govern in a rather conservative way until 1801 by overcoming the resistance of its rivals in the states, the so-called Antifederalists. These Antifederalists were the equivalent of Latin America's *federales*, that is, those who sought the greater autonomy of the parts as opposed to the whole. Vanquished in their efforts to obstruct the federal (that is, centralizing, anticonfederate) constitution finally approved in 1789, they went into a period of latency, only to reemerge as the popular party, under the leadership of Thomas Jefferson (who had broken with his Federalist allies).[6] The combination of political, economic, and ideological forces that directed the struggle for independence and unification in North America was strong enough to overcome separatism and created a centralist, plutocratic, and somewhat authoritarian tradition.

Events in Spanish America were an approximation of what would have happened in the north if the Antifederalists had won. The thirteen colonies had no centralist tradition equivalent to the Hispanic American one. Unification was largely the work of a plutocratic consolidation, whose artificer was Alexander Hamilton. Plutocracy in the United States was the functional equivalent of authoritarianism. National and international economic conditions permitted its growth and expansion. That unifying force allowed the country to pass through its first democratizing challenge: the peaceful transfer of power to the opposition popular party, dangerously tainted with pro-French ideas, in 1801.[7]

The Political Project of Simón Bolívar

In 1815, two years after his address to the citizens of New Granada, Bolívar again analyzed the experience he had been through. His fortunes had fluctuated violently in those two years: victorious return to Venezuela in 1813 as liberator; defeat in 1814 at the hands of the pro-Spanish popular revolt led by Boves; return to New Granada and its civil struggles, which forced him to retire and take refuge in Jamaica, from where he planned new activities to obtain Wellington's support for projects increasingly like pirate raids and that took him twice to Haiti for help. In his well-known *Jamaica Letter*—written to a British resident for public consumption—he dwelled on the social characteristics of the new independent nations. He denied the applicability of the North American federal system or of the "monarchical mixture of aristocracy and democracy which had given such splendor to England" because they were "too perfect." By this he meant that they were too complex, that they required a balance of powers that was very difficult to maintain in the South. He envisaged two alternative prospects to be averted: "demagogic anarchies, or monocratic tyrannies." The solution was to modify the English system, "with the difference that instead of a king there should be an elected executive, eventually for life, but never hereditary if a republic were the aim; a hereditary legislative senate, which in political storms would interpose itself between the popular tide and the government; and a popular, freely elected legislature, with no other restrictions than those applicable to the English lower chamber."[8] Four years later, when Venezuela's independent forces had gained a small local foothold and a national congress was gathered at Angostura (early 1819), Bolívar relinquished the supreme temporary power he had exercised and proposed—without success—a constitutional project. That project emphasized the need for a strong executive to replace the triumvirate established by the previous statute, and a hereditary senate, elected at first by Congress (probably from the military and other leaders of the wars of independence). Elected officials would be granted land and other benefits and would become members of the Order of Liberators, and their children—future senators—would receive special education. A fourth power of a moral and educational type would oversee teaching, the press, and administrative honesty.[9]

One of Bolívar's aims was to form a new aristocracy based on merit acquired during the war with Spain. Economic, political, and cultural privileges would be bestowed on this new aristocracy. At the same time, the state would attempt to form what today we would call consensus. However, Bolívar did not believe it possible to eliminate conflict, and in this his thought must be differentiated from other more conservative utopias. For him, "government" and "people" were "eternal rivals" whose struggles could not be extinguished, but, rather, must be arbitrated by a third force, the Senate. All of this is Aristotle in new dress, or an application of Montesquieu's argument for the existence of separate powers representing different social classes or interests. Bolívar took it for granted that "government" would represent something similar to monarchy.

Most of his ideas were embodied in the constitutional project he wrote for the new republic that was going to bear his name.[10] This same principle he tried to impose on Colombia at the constitutional revision convention in Ocaña in 1828. Some of his partisans were proposing a dictatorship to prevent civil strife and the dissolution of Greater Colombia. In his message to the convention he examined the predicament of the executive in the classical liberal constitution sanctioned eight years earlier at Cúcuta. In that constitution the executive was very limited in its powers but could compensate in times of crisis by appealing to extraordinary faculties, which had to be granted by Congress. Government, then, was either "a miserly source of health, or a devastating torrent,"[11] but the latter only as an exceptional and odious measure. Bolívar proposed to give, by law, greatly enhanced powers to the executive to avoid that oscillation between weakness and near dictatorship. The experience of practically all Latin American countries was to prove the endemic nature of that oscillation between what we would now call weak civilian rule and strong military dictatorship.

Strong Civilian Government

But why should it be so difficult to escape this alternative and establish some form of solid, durable, strong civilian government? After all, there are some countries where this type of government has surfaced in the period under examination or in more recent times. There were two instances of "strong civilian government" during the first political experiments in South America. Though not very democratic under a demanding definition of the term, the governments of Chile and Brazil gave considerable guarantees for peaceful coexistence and basic civilian and political rights. True, both had highly oligarchical features, and in Brazil slavery existed, but both traits also blemished the much extolled examples of the United States, Great Britain, or France.[12] In some measure, the Argentine regime established after the downfall of Rosas in 1852 was also an approximation of this model.

In Brazil it is clear that the monarchy and the sea saved the institutional stability of the country and its unity. The sea allowed the navy to control the separatist attempts both in the North and the South. If Bolívar had had such a weapon at his disposal, the unity of Greater Colombia, and even confederation with Peru might have been more viable. In Brazil, the relative absence of an armed confrontation with Portugal and permanent British support allowed the traditional system of social control and legitimacy, the monarchy, to survive. The massive transfer of the Portuguese court to Rio de Janeiro helped. Several thousand people, many of them of high economic position, suddenly arrived, making Rio de Janeiro one of the most expensive cities in the world.

The political consequences might have been ambivalent. It is true that the number of "*pretendientes*" increased astronomically. But most were individuals with quite a considerable access to economic resources, both those they had in Portugal and were soon to recover, and those that royal favors would create for them in Brazil. They were, therefore, quite different from the insecure middle class (referred to earlier as a Hispanic American trait) that also existed in Brazil. The sector associated with the court was higher in the social pyramid and it enjoyed the benefits of an agrarian frontier adaptable to capitalist cultivation, free from the ravages of war. The clergy was also less important than in the Spanish areas, a fact reflected in the absence of universities during the whole colonial period. Besides, the Portuguese courtiers, as emigrés fleeing from the invading Napoleonic armies, were strongly conservative and counterrevolutionary. The ideas of the "anarchists" were not likely to spread among them. On the contrary, they and their successors provided social and intellectual support for the conservative solutions that were applied to the country after independence.[13]

The Brazilian monarchy was in a certain sense the nearest application of Bolívar's scheme. The emperor was a sort of president for life and was particularly constitutional since the accession of Pedro II in 1840. He wielded the so-called *poder moderador*, inspired by Benjamin Constant, which allowed him to dissolve the Chamber of Deputies and use his influence to have a favorable majority elected. In this fashion, two parties, Conservative and Liberal, rotated in office, following the emperor's sensitivity to social pressure and public opinion. Military coups were avoided for decades. Senators were designated for life, and a very well-endowed nobility performed a stabilizing role, concentrating the more moderate elements of both parties, which were capable of resisting the emperor to some extent because of their life tenure. Provincial dissidence and violent social struggle were not absent from the Brazilian empire,[14] but it is arguable that its centralist but not too rigid organizational structure allowed the maintenance of legality and national unity in a country that was really a conglomerate of different regions. Certainly, other economic and geographic factors contributed to this result. It is also true that social tensions associated with the end of slavery and with the possible transition to a new reign (Pedro II had no male heir) overturned the monarchy in 1889. However, the traditions it created survived for a long time, giving birth to an elastic and adaptive version of authoritarianism associated with the strength of conservative forces based not only on the backward parts of the country but also on more modern areas.[15]

Chile also had a "strong" civilian experience during the regime identified with Diego Portales. The problem was simpler than in Brazil, however, because the country was more homogeneous both socially and geographically and distances were shortened by the sea. In Chile the destruction produced by the war of independence was less than in most other parts of the continent—Brazil excepted— and the adaptation to the new economic system that had England at its center was particularly rapid. In Chile, as in Venezuela, the early republic (1810–1814) created a "tolerant system," which fell victim to internal dissension and eventually Spanish reconquest. When the country was liberated in 1817 with the help of an Argentine army, Bernardo O'Higgins interpreted the lessons of history as requiring a very strong executive, unfettered by elected collegial authorities. Though this might have been justified while the danger of Spanish reconquest was very real, once it disappeared, the lack of institutionalization degenerated into an autocracy isolated from public opinion and subject to the will of favorites. O'Higgins' government (1817–1823) was not, in that sense, an application of Bolívar's ideas, even though O'Higgins, from exile in Peru, later became a partisan of the Liberator. His was not a mixed government but a pure government, based on the executive and its military prestige. That prestige, however well earned, could not operate miracles, particularly once the international war disappeared from the horizon. When O'Higgins attempted an *apertura*, it was too late and he was deposed by a combined military and civilian movement. The political system that eventually emerged after a few years became paradigmatic, during the last century, of what a strong civilian government could be like. It was centered around the figure of a president with great authority, often using the state of siege but with stable methods of succession, based on ample support among the elites and stopping short of unipersonal or despotic rule. The long duration of this system, and its openness in time to popular participation, merit detailed consideration.

The O'Higgins regime, by contrast, had been an attempt to concentrate authority by extrapolating what could have been an adequate answer to the crisis of independence. A seven-year period of what many contemporaries—and certainly O'Higgins' partisans—called "anarchy" followed O'Higgins' downfall in 1823: short-lived weak governments and several changes in constitutions. A new regime was established with a revolution in 1829, which brought Diego Portales to power as main minister. He was never president, and was a minister for only short periods. In September 1831, after a short stint in office, he resigned and returned to his commercial activities in Valparaíso, surprising both friends and enemies. Gandarillas, one of his collaborators, said sarcastically that Portales "despises government, because he prefers to command those who command." But it is not easy to command those who command from outside formal spheres of government.[16]

Chile at independence had a social structure that was peculiar in Hispanic America. Its population was quite homogeneous and racially mixed, with fewer contrasts between extremes of wealth and misery than in other parts of the continent. Agriculture in the central valley, based in viticulture and wheat and with an exportable surplus, had generated some middle strata capable of performing a moderating role. In the cities an artisan and shopkeeping class was present, and there were relatively few slaves and marginals. The dominant class of central valley landholders also engaged in commercial activities, which implied an added factor of homogeneity. Though Valparaíso was more modern and commercial, and Santiago traditional, agrarian, and clerical, the connection of interests between both was intense, so that they were practically a single urban center divided in two. At the time of independence, the intendancy of Santiago included Valparaíso and La Serena in the north, incorporating the majority of the country's population. The other intendancy was Concepción, in the south, near the frontier with the warlike Araucanians, where troops were concentrated. The geographic conflict in Chile separated the Valparaíso-Santiago axis—landed, commercial, and administrative—from Concepción—militaristic and oriented toward expansion in new lands. The clear economic and population predominance of the Santiago area permitted the early consolidation of a centralist regime, which had little difficulty in overcoming its federalist rivals from Concepción and, at a later date, from the mining north. By co-opting a sector of the Concepción army, the Santiago oligarchy was able to sway the odds in its favor. The price was that the first two presidents of the legalistic regime established by the constitution of 1833 were military chiefs from Concepción.

Alberto Edwards, in *La fronda aristocrática* (1928), has given particular attention to the Portalean phenomenon. His analysis is to some extent reminiscent of those of Vallenilla Lanz and García Calderón, because of his insistence on the need for authority after a period of crisis. It differs, though, to the extent that Chilean reality differs from that of Venezuela or Peru. He begins by emphasizing the joint bourgeois and aristocratic traits of the Chilean upper class, the result of a certain social mobility that had allowed people to come up into the higher social circles via commercial activities. A different type of social mobility than the one Vallenilla Lanz saw in his own country's early history, "without selection," as this one was the result of hard work and disciplined effort. Rural entrepreneurs, on the other hand, were mostly agriculturalists, and here we may recall Halperín Donghi's hypothesis about the unlikely occurrence of mobilizational *caudillos* in agricultural areas.

Edwards probably underplays the role of the middle and lower strata, but his description can be taken as a first approximation, remembering that those popular sectors had made an impact during the early years of the republic by forming the so-called *pipiolo*, or liberal populist sector. For Edwards the main potential conflict opposed the "aristocratic hierarchy" against "monarchical power." This is the conflict that erupted in 1810 with the declaration of autonomy from Spain and reemerged on different occasions. Against the authority of government an aristocracy full of the spirit of the "Fronde" raised its head. By giving them this name, Edwards assigns to them sectoral or short-sighted interests, by contrast with the supposedly more responsible and ample vision of the government. This in spite of the fact that he is including as "*frondeurs*" most of the initiators of Chilean—and, by extension, Latin American—independence. What he is trying to characterize is the tendency of groups from the upper classes to grab pieces of state power for themselves, transforming them into private matters and seeking the greatest possible reduction in government functions. With this attitude, unwittingly, the arbitrating power is also reduced and the preconditions created for endemic civil war. This endangers the very same interests the upper classes try to safeguard from state interference.

This point of view differs radically from the one prevalent in early liberal European thinkers like Montesquieu or Burke, for whom sectoral interests represented the basis for a healthy fragmentation of power, not for civil war. Probably the reason for the difference is that in the European experience, when those writers were developing their theories, there was no lack of central power. From the Latin American vantage point, it is more apparent that often anarchy is the result of the short-sightedness with which everyone pulls the rope. Under certain social conditions, though, the same class that breeds "*frondeur*" attitudes, under different leadership may support a more responsible consolidation of authority. The opposition between the "*frondeur*" and the authoritarian attitudes does not reflect, then, a conflict between different social groups, but, rather, between leaders of the same class, that is, between different political sectors of it. They are differentiated only by their adoption of different principles, not by their place in social space. That is why Edwards says that

> *peluconismo*, i.e., the aristocracy, quiescent for twenty years (1830–1850), obedient, giving its disinterested support to any government, was a miracle which immortalized Portales, and the secret of the success of that extraordinary man. Before and after the miracle, the political history of independent Chile is that of an aristocratic Fronde almost always hostile to the authority of governments and occasionally openly rebellious against them. That Fronde deposed the monarchy in 1810 and O'Higgins in 1823, pushed Montt to the verge of ruin some years later,[17] and since then up to 1891, in peaceful or stormy times, slowly demolished whatever remained of the constitutional organization of 1833. Then, completely dominant, it transformed itself into an oligarchy. Liberalism and clerical ultramontanism, those two great spiritual movements of our history, were parallel manifestations of that spirit of Fronde. That is why, despite their apparent antagonism, they were both on the same side at the decisive moments: in 1859 and in 1891. Their common enemy was "Power."[18]

But which is the basis of that power that represents the interests of the nation and is attacked by the same classes whose social and economic hegemony it seeks to consolidate? It is often argued that the linchpin of the Portalean regime, which lasted till the overthrow of Pres. José Balmaceda in 1891, lay in the concentration of authority established by the 1833 constitution. This strong executive would have inaugurated an "authoritarian" but legalistic republic, in which it dominated Congress through the electoral power it wielded via the centralized designation of local authorities and electoral tribunals.[19] But a strong executive and election rigging are not a Chilean specialty. The real conflict was not between the government and a population supposedly interested in exercising its voting rights. It was, rather, about who would be in a position to influence the electors: the central government, or the local oligarchies. Only after mid-century did the central government let go of its control of electoral authorities, first passing it to committees of the "biggest tax payers" and then to autonomous municipalities (free to follow the dictates of local magnates). Progressively, this control over elections was opened up, without revolutions or periods of revolutionary abstention of the type the

Argentine Radical party had to go through to have access to the ballot box. Nothing like that happened in Chile; both the Radical and the Democratic parties gradually obtained representation in Congress, participating in elections that, however distorted and subject to vote buying, provided a channel of expression for new forces covering a very wide gamut of public opinion.

The 1833 constitution, though presidentialist, granted important functions to Congress, including the classical one of sanctioning the budget or otherwise provoking economic paralysis in the government. This possibility was sparingly used if at all for many decades, due to the disciplined official majorities. After Balmaceda's downfall in 1891, though, it became a deadly weapon, inaugurating the so-called parliamentary Republic (1891–1920), which, rather than a constitutional amendment, was a peculiarity of the system of political parties.[20] What characterized the system before 1891 was the unification of opinion around a strong conservative party at first and then an equally hegemonic liberal party. The continuous changes of the 1891–1920 period resulted from the cabinet's agonizing but necessary efforts to conciliate the various factions represented in Congress to approve a budget. The dominant parties of an earlier day were replaced by warring factions and new splinter parties (clerical Conservatives, Nationals, various Liberals, Radicals, Democrats). This situation lasted until 1920, when Arturo Alessandri was elected on a reform platform and strong popular support.

The Parliamentary period has been little studied, and there are many stereotypes attached to it. The general impression is that the ship of state lost its rudder during that time and that Chile forsook the privileged position it had acquired in Latin America. Whether because of this or some other cause, the decline certainly occurred. It was partly caused by the eclipse of nitrate production, but it is difficult not to agree that the permanent oscillation of government alliances was an obstacle to any constructive policy designed to cope with the new challenges, including the incorporation of the working class.

What may be termed the Portalean regime lasted from 1830 to 1891. The first thirty years were under three presidents (Prieto, Bulnes, Montt), each reelected once, of conservative or *pelucón* orientation, and followers of Portales' school of government. A transition presidency helped accommodation with the newly emergent liberal forces, which originated in a division of the ruling party. From 1871 to 1891 four liberal presidents served.

Given the great concentration of power in the executive, how was it possible, without a military coup, to have power transferred from the conservative or *pelucón* party to the liberals? The answer lies partly in the fact that these liberals were only in small measure the successors of the old liberal-populist, or *pipiolo*, party.[21] Besides, the party in power during the first three presidencies was simply the party of those in favor of strong governmental authority. During Montt's presidency (in the 1850s) this party confronted the church with secularizing measures. In the ensuing crisis, it lost an ideologically clerical wing, which adopted the name "Conservative"; the government faction called itself "National," becoming tainted with some liberal elements. The liberal opposition then grasped the opportunity to support the government and influence it. It did not succeed until the government of Montt's successor, José Joaquín Pérez. In the process of supporting the government, liberalism was in turn divided, losing its doctrinaire, ideologically more purist, sector, which remained in opposition. The nondoctrinaire liberals plus the Nationals from the old *pelucón* stem became the basis of the government, occupying so to speak the center. As long as these changes were slow, the political system was not excessively altered by party recomposition.

The scheme is applicable beyond Chile, of course, and serves to explain many government changes during the last century. Divisions in ruling parties created splinter sectors, which entered into alliances with the moderate elements of the opposition, which in turn also divided. Power could then fall into the hands of the new coalition, legitimated by the inclusion of parts of the erstwhile ruling circles. This mechanism of power alternation in societies where opposition is not yet fully legitimated looks very much like the one established by Juan Linz, Guillermo O'Donnell, and others as a way to replace authoritarian regimes: the moderates of the government ally themselves with the moderates of the opposition.[22] It also looks like the rotation of factions in the England of the eighteenth century or during France's Third Republic. This is not so much an effect of the constitution as of party structure.

The Role of Political Parties

Political parties, in Portales' time, were not, of course, what they are today. They were oligarchical with little popular participation, though there were some exceptions, like the Sociedad de la Igualdad, with its artisan sectors.[23] But the idea that power is something that may—or ought to—be obtained through a combination of interests based on a certain organization and a network of communications—"connexions," as Burke called them—is something that today seems obvious but was not so at that time. Not that the use of influences, friendships, personal loyalties, and the like to obtain political ends was unknown. This was always the stuff of politics, because there is no other method to govern, whether in democracies or dictatorships. The peculiarity lies in putting emphasis on the "connexions," on the manipulation of combinations among political actors of similar weight rather than on the leadership. In this sense it may be worthwhile reinterpreting Portales' action.

Portales was the emergent of a social constellation in which *caudillos* had failed. He was a *primus inter pares*, or perhaps not even so *primus* as he seems from a long historical distance. He at least did not consider himself to tower above the others and from his correspondence it is clear that he was not prepared to dedicate himself fully to politics. To recoup his tottering fortune, he was forced to reside in Valparaíso, and only in extreme cases could he afford the luxury of getting involved in public affairs.

Portales was obviously a capable man and may even have been a genius, given the persistence of his convictions. But one of these convictions was to avoid getting permanently trapped in public duties, because he had other more urgent matters to attend to. In 1831, when he felt he had already served his time by occupying a ministerial post for several months and was again living in Valparaíso, his correspondent and commercial associate Antonio Garfias informed him that friends in Santiago considered his return to office indispensable. They caught Portales on a bad day, however: "Tell those b—— who believe that only with me can there be government and order that I am far from believing such a thing, and that if once I moved my a—— and took a club to pacify the country, it would be only so that those f—— and p—— in Santiago would let me work in peace. Tell them that if by mischance I return to govern, it will be to hang from the tallest tree those f—— and p—— and that I shall take the s——off them. And you, my dear don Antonio, don't you write such letters again, because you will get a whipping you won't easily forget."[24]

Pure comedy? It was more a tragedy, because the care of his commercial pursuits, always on the brink of failure, really made it difficult to dedicate himself fully to politics—though he could do it to a certain extent, as, for example, in the organization and training of militia, an important element in civilian participation in the maintenance of order in those days. Not that Portales was averse to using his political connections to obtain some economic favors, but there are limits to this, at least in regimes under some form of collective control. In other words, Portales, perhaps in spite of his intentions, could not afford a full dedication to politics. It would be an exaggeration to say that he limited himself because of some vision about the advantages of partial involvement in politics. But the circumstances of his time and those of his private life led him to have to use an extended structure of "connexions" to realize his aims rather than aiming at absolute personal power.

This created the preconditions for the existence of a political party as a solidary group of people seeking, in Burke's words, "to promote, by their joint endeavours, the national interest, upon some particular principle in which they are all agreed."[25] Not that this happened in Chile because of Portales alone; it was, rather, a collective phenomenon. The seven years during which Portales' star intermittently shone would not have been enough to make an impact on Chilean politics if conditions had not been very favorable. The peculiarities of Portales' life, his combination of strong private and public concerns, converted him into an archetype. But in his time several others—Tocornal, Rengifo, Montt, and Varas—were as important as he in building the system.

The role of the party system in creating the so-called Portalean republic is also congruent with the fact that during most of it the presidents were not the dominant figures. It was, rather, the ministers who led opinion, first Portales, then several others and above all Manuel Montt, who was an influential secretary of state before becoming chief executive. The first two presidents of the period, Prieto and Bulnes, were gray personalities, but for all that no less important in the construction of the polity. The same was true of most of their successors, except Montt and Balmaceda

(Balmaceda, in fact, was overthrown because he overstepped his role). What was dominant was not the president but the clique, or "connexion," or combination of parties or factions in power. The presidency was a constitutional monarchy, still at an early stage in the consolidation of its institutions.

In this sense Portales' Chile is more like monarchical Brazil than like the dictatorships of order so dear to Vallenilla Lanz. The president wielded something like the *poder moderador* of the emperor, changing his cabinet according to the pressures he detected in public opinion. Those changes were eventually reflected in Congress through the recomposition of alliances, if not through free elections, which only in due time became a factor to be taken into account.

The role of the executive in the Portalean regime was very different from that of Portales' contemporary, Juan Manuel de Rosas, autocratic governor of Buenos Aires. Rosas was by definition the indispensable man, chief of a faction or "connexion," but with emphasis on "chief," the connection degenerating into a retinue for all intents and purposes. Though Rosas often expressed his repugnance to continuing in power, he was almost always convinced to remain and continued with the exercise of total power for two decades.

In Brazil both geography and economics created a much more balanced diversity than in most other parts of Latin America. There were four or five regions with a capacity to establish alliances, particularly if there was a political elite prepared to act as a nucleating factor. The attitudes toward concentration of power would then depend on the coalitions among those regional actors. Regions that remained politically isolated might orient themselves toward federalism or even autonomism and separatism if strongly antagonized. This generally was not the case, except at some initial moments. The more common situation was the presence of strong but not overpowering coalitions, creating the bases for a mixture between a centralist and a federal system. Formally, governors were appointed by the emperor, but with great weight given to local opinion. The national executive had enough power to govern, but with some limits set by Congress, which though not genuinely elected was the representative of the regional pressure groups from which the emperor recruited the ministers. The balanced political weight of the regions produced an equilibrium between the national executive and the regional oligarchies represented in the lower house and the life-tenured Senate.

Extended Participation

The fragmentation of authority that results from the existence of checks and balances—legal and social—allowed in most historical experiences a gradual extension of the franchise to ever larger sectors. In the study of popular involvement in the political system it is convenient to distinguish between two concepts: level and mode of participation. The level of participation registers the extension of political rights (especially voting and freedom to organize) to the population. The mode of participation refers to the form taken by popular involvement; it may be mobilizational, based on a charismatic connection between leader and people, or associationist, rooted in an autonomous organizational experience.

A high degree of mobilizationism does not always go hand in hand with an extended level of participation. Many Latin American *caudillista* experiences of the last century were characterized by a mobilizational integration of the masses, but limited to comparatively reduced urban or rural sectors. This is not because under the conditions of the time a high level of participation was unthinkable. The slave rebellion in Haiti in its most intense moments was not only mobilizational but also involved a very high participation by slaves in arms. On the other hand, in industrially advanced countries, it is usual to find a moderately high level of participation, but of the associationalist, not the mobilizational, mode, as in Western European social democracy and—under a different ideological sign—in the North American trade union movement and the Democratic party.

The problem of extended participation was faced by liberal and pluralist thinkers who were reacting to the experience of high participation in Jacobin France and in some early populist movements in the United States. They were concerned with the fact that often a high level was accompanied by a mobilizationist mode of participation, which was not easily compatible with a regime of checks and balances. For the authors of the *Federalist Papers* a complex federal constitution had the advantage of making the sudden access to power of an unorganized popular majority unlikely. In Great Britain, John Stuart Mill argued in *Representative Government* that a system of representation had to fulfill two conditions: (1) that all or almost all of the population have access to vote, and (2) that special representation, via multiple vote, should be given to those with greater capacity, which may be judged not by riches but by education or by the performance of the function of employer.[26] The aim of this special representation is to obtain a balance between opposed interests, because

> a modern community, not divided by strong antipathies of race, language or
> nationality, may be considered as in the main divisible into two sections
> which, in spite of partial variations, correspond on the whole with two
> divergent directions of apparent interest . . . labourers on the one hand,
> employers of labour on the other. . . . If the representative system could be
> made ideally perfect, . . . its organization must be such that these two classes,
> manual labourers and their affinities on one side, employers of labour and
> their affinities on the other, should be . . . equally balanced, influencing about
> an equal number of votes in Parliament.

If votes were given equally to all, "the majority in every locality would consist of manual labourers . . . [and] no other class could succeed in getting elected anywhere."[27]

This latter consideration is central and indicates the perception Mill—and, we may suppose, many others in his time—had about the class structure. The assumption that the manual laborers and their "affinities" would form the majority everywhere probably corresponds to some proletarianizing tendencies of an early capitalist stage. This tendency was later checked by the increase in the middle classes and the consequent social mobility, which influenced many "affinities" of the workers to vote for the conservative or center parties. The result has been that in advanced industrial societies, the parliamentary parity Mill aimed at through qualified voting in fact exists as a result of an electoral balance between the Right and the Left. This equilibrium is potentially unstable because of the different weapons of the contenders. The conservative force depends on a nucleus of upper class and business sectors who form a minority of the population, commanding important economic resources. With the use of these resources, added to the effects of social mobility, the middle and a part of the working classes are co-opted, preventing the permanent electoral majority feared by Mill to materialize, while consensus and institutional stability are generated.

In other historical conditions a balance is not achieved, however, and therefore the principle of one man one vote does not function in the same manner as in the North American and European tradition. This electoral principle, which in one arena produces consensus, in others increases tensions, because it works, so to speak, in an excessively democratic manner. In many Latin American and Third World countries the diffuse conservative influences that operate in the more prosperous parts of the world do not exist. Free elections tend to produce popular majorities without an equivalent force on the other side. That is, results are similar to those feared by Mill; hence the search for new methods of representation, like corporations, or simply the recourse to authoritarian solutions.

Forms of Representation: Parties and Corporations

Pluralist thought originally was concerned with granting representation to different social groups rather than making that representation proportional to their numbers. Thus, John Stuart Mill, in his effort to obtain balanced forces in Parliament, arrived at conceptions that are not too different from what we would call today "corporatism." The aim of corporatist theories is precisely to assure parity of representation for different sectors above the vagaries of elections. The modern liberal system of one man one vote, where it works, produces similar results through the mechanisms of consensus and expansion of the middle classes. Admittedly, one has to interpret institutional proposals in terms of the time when they were formulated. Mill was writing in 1861, when the Disraeli reform extending the vote to urban workers had not yet taken place. On the other hand, corporatist theories, in their fascist garb, go hand in hand with a totalitarian conception of the state. But the theory must not be confused with one of its historical expressions, nor should one attribute to the former all the deformities of the latter. It is not possible either to argue that if Mill were writing today, he would gladly endorse universal suffrage. Most probably, his line of reasoning would lead him to support universal and egalitarian suffrage only in such places as Western Europe, North America, Japan, or Australia. In extreme cases of educational or economic underdevelopment Mill actually justified an authoritarian government "resembling the Saint-Simonian form of Socialism, maintaining a general superintendence over all the operations of society, so as to keep before each the sense of a present force sufficient to compel his obedience."[28] This type of situation is very common today in the Third World, so the eventual need for authoritarian government under those social conditions cannot be rejected on the basis of John Stuart Mill's reasoning.

In Latin America when free representation is established there is a great tendency toward two phenomena that potentially destroy it: Frondisme and mobilizationism. Frondisme creates factions that shun responsibility for the common weal, thus fomenting civil war or decadence by paralyzing governmental functions. Mobilizationism generates popular majorities, often expressed in an authoritarian fashion, with little respect for the rights of minorities and easily regimented, so that, in the last resort not even the rights of the majority are assured. Corporatist theory, revised since the end of the last century by liberal or socialist thinkers,[29] is an attempt to devise a system of representation more attuned to the real distribution of power. To understand its characteristics and the mentality of those who support it, it is necessary not to confuse it with the fascist regimes that tried to apply it brutally, and never more than formally. One of its proponents was Emile Durkheim, who was concerned by what he saw as a society without basic social solidarity, where "anomic" individuals, cut loose from their primary groups and other loyalties, would be easy prey to violence. He did not think the return to traditional forms of life (or what he termed "mechanical solidarity") either possible or desirable. He believed that modern society had within it its own correctives, through the new "organic" solidarity generated by a complex and interdependent division of labor. For him the division of labor, rather than being, as for Marx, the source of classes and class conflict, was the basis of cooperation. But the adjudication of the various tasks and their retributions could be made with greater or lesser comprehension of the mutual rights involved. Writing in 1902 in the preface to the second edition of *The Division of Labor*, he stated that "for anomy to end, there must exist, or be formed, a group which can constitute the system of rules actually needed. Neither political society, in its entirety, nor the State can take over this function. . . . The only one [capable] is that formed by all the agents of the same industry, united and organized into a single body. This is what is called the corporation, or occupational group." Corporations should be largely autonomous from the state, having co-legislative powers, and their effects would be as important in the moral as in the practical fields. The corporations' authorities would be elected, with "representatives of employees and representatives of employers, as is already the case in the tribunals of skilled trades; and that, in proportions corresponding to the respective importance attributed by opinion to these two factors in production." With this latter remark, Durkheim opened up the possibility of a socialist evolution by varying the weight assigned to employers. In the same line, he added that "as we shall say further on, 'as long as there are rich and poor at birth, there cannot be just contract,' nor a just distribution of social goods. But if the corporative reform does not dispense with the other [reforms], it is the first condition for their efficiency. [Corporations] should become . . . the fundamental political unity. Society, instead of remaining what it is today, an aggregate of juxtaposed territorial districts, would become a vast system of national corporations. . . . In this way, political assemblies would more exactly express the diversity of social interests and their relations."[30]

A system of corporative representation has a totally different significance according to whether it is the only accepted one or a complement to other elected bodies. As a complement, it has been incorporated into the program of political parties with a clear popular trajectory, like Peru's Aprismo. The ideology of the latter, as expressed by its founder, Víctor Raúl Haya de la Torre, proposed to add to the traditional executive, legislative, and judiciary powers a fourth one, "where Labor, the State and Capital [would be] *qualitatively* represented."[31] The aim was to provide a legitimate expression to pressures that economic groups exerted anyway. It also gave them some veto power in matters directly affecting them. These powers, of course, are "antidemocratic" in a strict sense. There is little doubt about that. What is open to discussion is whether their operation would produce better or worse results than their absence.

Corporativelike criteria are introduced indirectly into the constitution through the Senate. In all historical experiences, the Senate has had as one of its functions the resistance to a popular majority. The equal representation of small, rural political units tends to favor the conservative sector. Something similar happens in Great Britain with the lower chamber, where constituencies are not all of the same size— rural areas generally have greater weight per person than urban ones. Thus, conservative interests are protected under the more acceptable banners of regionalism and provincial autonomy. This method, though, does not always yield the expected results. In some cases, especially in the Third World, mobilizational phenomena reach the more outlying areas, and then the Senate, far from being a conservative bastion, contributes to the populist majority. This is why conservative or nationalist ideologues often favor the inclusion of an outright corporative component in the composition of the Senate.

John Stuart Mill had already proposed something similar when he argued for the drastic reduction in numbers of born peers; these should be replaced by life designations among individuals who had excelled in some areas, including past cabinet members, governors of important colonies, distinguished professors, and the like.[32] This has been done in practice through the extensive creation of life peers so that the corporative nature of the House of Lords, though not explicit, is none the less real. Its powers are still today not trivial, and they were quite considerable in times when Great Britain had a social condition nearer to that of present-day Latin America. As recently as 1949, the power of the House of Lords to suspend for two years legislation approved by the Commons was applied to the nationalization of steel. Though these powers are exerted sparingly, their very existence forces moderation and compromise on the political forces bent on reform. The Spanish decision, during the process of liberalization of the Franco regime, to include in the Senate forty seats directly appointed by the king was in the same spirit and nearer to the Latin American experience. This was a transitory measure, since repealed, but it helped ease the transition to democracy. The same can be said, from the opposite end of the political spectrum, of the Council of the Revolution, a military body with some veto powers established by the Portuguese revolution of 1975. This council was supposed to guarantee continued respect for revolutionary aims; it lasted several years, until a conservative majority abolished it.

As for political parties, it is difficult to conceive of a free society without their existence by whatever name. In Latin America such a system was established and consolidated in Chile since the latter part of the nineteenth century, and it was both cause and effect of the political stability the country enjoyed for a very long time. However, political parties can be not only an element of control over the state, but a source of constant interference with the government's capacity to govern, as during the parliamentary Republic. Even so, this period in Chile's history permitted an increase in public freedom and the organization of a working-class movement. Despite violent repression—particularly during the first decade of this century—the fact that it was at all possible to use existing liberties to organize resulted in the early formation of a legitimated sector of leftist political parties and trade unions.

In more recent times, during the late sixties and early seventies, Chile experienced an intense polarization of its political party system, to a degree unparalleled in other parts of the continent. There were social tensions—even more acute—in other countries, but in Chile they expressed themselves through a class-based party system. This included a balance between a conservative-liberal force capable of polling a third of the electorate, a strongly organized and socialist-oriented Left, and a Center (first Radical and then Christian Democrat) that occasionally acted as a substitute for the Right. This system, which was quite similar, even in the party names, to the European one, shared with it the characteristic of very explicitly expressing class antagonisms. Some observers argue that this tends to create insoluble antagonisms and violence. The European experience shows that this is not so, however. It is then necessary to explain why in one context the system works rather peacefully while in another it has led to intense conflict and dictatorship. The most current interpretation lays emphasis on the distinction between central and dependent societies. But in Europe the system was also in crisis before the Second World War. Without denying the indisputable constraints created by the peripheral and dependent nature of a society, it is necessary to delve with greater care into the etiology of violence and military intervention.

5. Violence and Revolution

Violence has been studied from two basic positions: one is structural, seeking to analyze society as a whole and pointing to certain relationships, antagonisms, or disequilibria within it; the other, social-psychological, focuses on conditions pushing the individual to violence, which, if repeated in many instances may have social effects. Both must be employed and complemented. It is not possible here to revise completely the numerous theories applicable to this field, but some will be reviewed with the aim of selecting a system of interconnected and formalizable hypotheses.

The Social Psychological Approach

The social psychological approach is mainly associated with the work of Ted R. Gurr and his collaborators.[1] Their basic scheme is an application of theories on the reaction to frustration. It is so simple that it almost becomes common sense, but this is no reason to abandon it. The problem lies in determining the conditions under which different types of individuals accumulate enough frustrations to make them react violently and in how these violent reactions become integrated into social phenomena. It becomes necessary to have a wealth of information about the state of society, type of government, relative force of social actors, and existing channels of political action.

For Gurr, frustration derives from what he calls "relative deprivation," a feeling of having fewer goods, resources, or rights than one feels entitled to. There is an element of individual judgment, certainly not easy to measure, but influenced by social context. It is necessary to consider the actor's previous experience in the possession of those goods, resources, or rights and the situation of others with whom comparison is relevant. This comparison depends on the transparency of social relations, the communication between actors, and the general cultural environment that may stimulate expectations or make privileges seem legitimate. Because of all this, Gurr's approach is not merely psychological, as is sometimes maintained.

To apply Gurr's concepts to society at large, we must differentiate two types of aspiration and attainment: economic, and political or institutional. The economic is measured by the individual's standard of living and possessions and affected by the security or uncertainty in maintaining them. The political or institutional are more difficult to conceptualize and to measure than economic aspirations or attainments. They refer to the degree to which the average individual feels respected, has a sense of belonging, and feels that his opinions are taken into account in the management of the polity. These may become important sources of satisfaction, especially in postrevolutionary situations or after long-sought political changes that compensate for the lack of more tangible economic attainments. How long this compensating mechanism can last is another story; how much relative weight is given to each type of gratification also depends on the psychology and values of each person. Some, whom we might call highly ideologist, care for institutional and political matters; others, more economics oriented, only value bread-and-butter achievements. The ease with which a group or class accepts the setbacks in a political program that it otherwise favors depends on the presence and influence of an ideologist sector within its ranks, attuned to the general long-term goals. The combination of politico-institutional goal achievement and relative economic well-being generates a level of satisfaction whose contrary may be termed "relative deprivation" or dissatisfaction. Ideologism acts as a selector, strengthening or weakening the influence of goal achievement on satisfaction. This group of variables, by producing a certain level of relative deprivation, activates psychological mechanisms in the individual that generate a predisposition to violence. This predisposition is transformed into action according to other facilitating influences, eventually becoming a social phenomenon of revolutionary or civil war proportions. Undue simplifications, however, must be avoided in the passage from the social psychological phenomena centered on the individual to the political or structural level of observation.

James Davies attempted to apply this type of social-psychological mechanism prior to Gurr's studies. His comparative study of several revolutionary processes (the French, Russian, and Egyptian) and other minor rebellions in the United States during the last century was inspired by similar principles.[2] In all these cases he charted for several decades the evolution of what he calls "need satisfaction," principally of an economic type. This concept does not coincide with what we have termed "satisfaction," but, rather, with the economic component of attainments, that is, the objective standard of living and possessions. Davies hypothesizes that the objective, actual need gratification, must be compared with expectations, which in a very rough first approximation result from the extrapolation of historical objective tendencies. He finds that in the cases considered, several decades of prosperity were followed by a sudden fall, which opened a chasm between attainments and expectations, as the latter continued to grow because of the acquired momentum or, at the very least, remained constant.

This discrepancy coincides with what Gurr calls "relative deprivation," and which I have taken as synonymous with dissatisfaction. Quite apart from the different use of names for the variables, the approach is similar, because it is assumed that frustration generates violent attitudes, leading to a revolutionary situation. Davies claims that revolutions occur when a long period of prosperity, which has increased expectations, is followed by a severe and apparently lasting deterioration. The argument is cogent, though the extrapolation from the social-psychological to the political area is somewhat simplistic. To pass from the discrepancy between achievements and aspirations to the generation of violent attitudes in some social groups is a very reasonable first step. What is not present in Davies' studies is the analysis of how the average prosperity in the nation is distributed among different social sectors. Such analysis is necessary to forecast how a certain crisis affects each one of them. The object of study must be disaggregated, taking group actors, not society as a whole, as units of analysis. The scarcity of information requires the accumulation of case studies, but above all reveals the highly hypothetical character of most assertions in this field due to the difficulty of obtaining enough data about the component units of a national society.

The Structural Approach: Violence and Revolution

Structural analyses, in contrast with the social-psychological, emphasize wider aspects of society, its productive apparatus, and its system of social stratification.[3] Marxist analysis is the best known. Its basic hypothesis is centered on the contradiction between what it calls forces of production and relations of production When the relations of production, that is, the system of institutions and privileges, collide with the forces of production (which, to continue to expand, need radical alterations in the social system), a period of revolution starts.

Marx does not take the mere contraposition of class interests as sufficient in the production of a revolutionary confrontation. Class antagonisms, in one way or another, characterize any class-divided society. But their expression depends on the development of class consciousness, which takes a revolutionary form only when productive forces can no longer continue to expand under the existing system of social domination Not that Marx ignored the violent phenomena that happened under conditions not yet ripe in the above point of view. Those violent episodes, or "revolutions," did not represent for him deep and radical alterations, but only coups d'état, or unsuccessful revolts (like those by the German peasants in the sixteenth century or by the slaves in antiquity).

In the Marxist hypothesis a mechanism similar to that of relative deprivation is implicit. Mere misery is not considered sufficient for the generation of violence, much less of revolution because, under traditional poverty, (1) the masses are accustomed to that condition and do not protest against it, and (2) even when they do protest, they are not capable of a successful uprising. Point (1) fits in the social-psychological hypotheses of relative deprivation; point (2) enters the realm of power relations.

Under conditions of high industrialization, technology requires highly trained individuals to adjust to different kinds of work. This, translated into the language of social psychology, is equivalent to an increase in the level of aspirations, which, if associated with a permanent lowering of living standards, must breed a violent mood. Besides, the greater communication between different sectors of the working class, the absence of middle classes, and the elimination of the peasantry facilitate a successful popular uprising. In this scenario, the most solid element is the prediction of a greater organizational capacity and consciousness of their own interests on the part of workers in large-scale industry, in contrast with traditional artisans and peasants. But, as stated in previous chapters, there are two weak elements in the analysis: (1) if middle-class proletarianization were as strong as Marx predicted, the likely result would be the formation of a resistance movement among that class that would appeal to reformist or revolutionary means, but under middle-class leadership; (2) in fact, middle classes in industrially developed areas did not become proletarianized, and the standard of living and prospects of social mobility of the lower strata increased enough to moderate the intensity of conflicts, even in periods when it could be argued that there was a contradiction between forces and relations of production. On the other hand, it is quite likely that in most Third World societies some middle-class sectors, rather than the popular ones, are those that combine enough frustration and organizational capacity to become actively involved in a revolutionary process.

In the Marxist approach, a close association is posited between social classes and political movements; the state is seen as superstructural and rather epiphenomenal, as representing the dominant class. The simplistic manner in which this scheme has often been applied has generated within the Marxist camp itself a reaction that has led to reconsideration of the role of the state (whose autonomy now appears far greater than in the past). The experience of totalitarianism in capitalist countries has been one of the causes of this reanalysis, because when studied in any detail it turns out that the connection between the bourgeoisie and those regimes was not so direct. The other totalitarian experience, Stalinism, also requires explaining the class nature of a state that is very powerful and a creator of privileges.

The assumption that the revolutionary state in such instances continues to represent the working class is scarcely credible. Beginning with the exiled Trotsky's early essays, a "bureaucratic degeneration" was posited as responsible for distortions; no class other than workers and peasants was deemed to exist, given the absence of private property. Later studies, also of Marxist origin, converged toward the perception that not only bureaucratic degenerations, or strata, or social layers, but a dominant class existed, based on the possession or control of the productive apparatus.[4]

There is another line of thought, however, also of Marxist origin but quite innovative, that seeks to approach the problem from another perspective. In this approach, to give a class character to the bureaucracy in Soviet-style regimes seems too risky or unnecessary a step. It opts for a conceptual differentiation between social classes and the state. The latter is considered an independent entity, influenceable by social classes or political elites, but not necessarily representing them. Political struggle, then, whether of a reformist or a revolutionary kind, violent or not, derives from the competition between different groups for control of the state.[5] When the state apparatus enters into a situation of crisis—due to its own dynamic, not necessarily that of the rest of society—the possibility of violence in the struggle for its control is maximized.

For example, in Theda Skocpol's *States and Social Revolutions*, several revolutionary processes (the French, Russian, and Chinese) are compared, not in the light of class relations at the moment of the eruption of violence but in terms of the weaknesses, crises, or maladaptations of the state as a social control mechanism.[6] Skocpol, after reviewing various theories of revolution, rejects the classical Marxist one because of its underestimation of the autonomous role of the state. She denies the validity of Gurr's social psychological approach and of other studies of Parsonian or functionalist orientation that stress contradictions in value systems. She seeks a new synthesis, which must fulfill three conditions: (1) it should not be voluntarist, but structural; (2) it must incorporate the international dimension, that is, imperialism, dependency, or war; and (3) it should reckon the autonomous role of the state vis-à-vis the social structure. This leads Skocpol to emphasize the structural aspects of state formation, which may undergo periods of crisis, especially if under the impact of a lost war (Russia and China) or a serious external threat (France). Though this type of analysis contributes to an understanding of the processes involved, more is lost than gained in rejecting so radically the Marxian hypothesis about the connection between social classes and political phenomena. Admittedly, the state does not depend on the dominant classes in the servile manner assumed by Marx, but their existence seriously limits its freedom of action.

When a political party is studied, it is necessary to explore its anchorage on a set of social actors; the relationship may be far from clear, but generally it will exist. Actors' attitudes create a latent structure, a field of forces within which political leaders and activists operate. The radical revision of Marxist theory adopted by those who, like Skocpol, assign such independence to the state, underestimates the field of forces referred to above and allows political phenomena excessive variability. Though Skocpol does not posit the absolute autonomy or voluntarism of political elites (one of her three theoretical requirements denies it explicitly), she does consider that the logic of state formation and of its adaptation to the performance of national or international tasks are what govern political action. She substitutes a game between groups, defined by their capacity to solve the crises of state formation, for one between actors, based on social classes of a capitalist or postcapitalist nature.[7] Without denying the importance of a given elite's capacity to solve a crisis in state functioning, the approach adopted in this volume sees politics as much more anchored on the structure of social classes or, more generally, on the structure of social actors, which should be split up and separated into their component parts as much as necessary.

Of particular relevance is the situation arising when revolutionary change alters class structure so that it is very different before and after the process. In such cases, some actors exist—as seen already in chapter 3—who may be considered as harbingers of the new postrevolutionary dominant class. Though it would be inappropriate to consider such elites as advanced representatives of a nonexistent class, their presence must be explained in terms of their connections, their origins, and their recruitment patterns in sectors of the class structure. Admittedly, their strategies for the conquest of power will be determined by their capacity to better run the state and control it in competition with others. But the whole class structure that acts as their scenario and their feeding ground cannot be ignored or minimized as a causative and explanatory factor.

Mass Society

Some modern expressions of violence are associated with what has been called "mass society." The phrase was introduced in social science by the attempt to interpret the intense violence and state terror in Nazism and Stalinism. Karl Mannheim, Franz Neumann, William Kornhauser, and others point to the isolation of the individual in a society too anonymous and large for the maintenance of the primary bonds of family, neighborhood, and artisan or peasant work environments. To this interpretation some elements from psychoanalysis were incorporated, leading to the concept of the authoritarian personality.[8] A political authoritarianism capable of activating psychological authoritarianism acquires a certain solidity and destructive force. This type of approach to political processes, developed for the study of industrialized societies in the thirties and forties, can be extended to the Third World or Latin America, where, for different reasons, traditional and small-scale social structures are in crisis. This has been done by Karl Deutsch and Gino Germani, who use the concept of social mobilization to refer to a process of breaking bonds and becoming available for new political experiences.

Charles Tilly, in *From Mobilization to Revolution*, criticizes such interpretations. In his view, mass society theories generally assume that under conditions of breakdown of the traditional order there is a lack of autonomous popular organization, resulting in the prevalence of manipulatory political movements. Violent and revolutionary phenomena are thus undervalued by the "breakdown" theorists of mass society (particularly as applied to Third World conditions) because popular participants in them are deemed to lack clear objectives.[9]

In contrast, Tilly affirms that in many preindustrial or early transition cases, significant popular organizations do exist, some of a traditional variety (Indian panchayats, religious brotherhoods in the Andes), others of a more innovative sort (associations of slum dwellers, spontaneous strike groups, land invasion collectives). When for economic, cultural, or war-induced reasons social tensions are generated, they do not produce an "available mass" à la Deutsch or Germani, but, rather, a host of organized or proto-organized groups. Confrontation leads them to greater radicalization, association with others, access to communication media, and, eventually, violence.

As a consequence of his approach, Tilly uses the word *mobilization* in a different way from Deutsch and Germani. For him, mobilization is not the rupture of traditional loyalties and consequent availability. He calls mobilization the process through which preexisting organizations consolidate, become active, and eventually produce a revolutionary phenomenon.

Leaving aside the question of names, what is important in Tilly's work is the emphasis on the widespread existence of organizations among the destitute, the poor, and the marginal, in both their traditional and their modernizing, migratory settings. A growing body of research is focusing on this subject and often finding more instances of organization than a strict interpretation of the mass society or breakdown theory would predict. It is also true that many revolutionary movements have occurred—and continue to occur—in the peripheral and poorer parts of the world, often with roots in the peasantry and marginal population. More open to discussion, though, is the weight of the autonomous popular associations in those revolutionary movements, or their capacity to act politically at a national level rather than just as locally oriented survival institutions.[10]

In the theoretical construction attempted in this volume, the concept of mobilization is divided into the two components we have already called social and political. Social mobilization denotes the process of breaking the traditional bonds (as argued in chapter 2), whereas political mobilization is better left for organized activity of a violent or peaceful variety. Probably Tilly underestimates the moderating effects political organization has, even when oriented in a confrontational manner, except, of course, in very extreme circumstances.

In practice, in most instances it is difficult to find together, for the popular strata, a situation that includes agitation (what Tilly calls "mobilization"), violence, and autonomous class organization because:

(1) If there is violence and agitation, in general it will be the result of the impact of industrialization, opening to the world market, international war, or religious conflict, all of which break the traditional social structure. This unleashes emotions and frustrations and induces violence, but in general does not facilitate autonomous mass organization. Elite organizations do exist in such cases, superimposed and dominant over the popular component of the alliance, if the latter has taken place.

(2) If an autonomous organization finds roots in the popular classes, it requires a great deal of effort and its leaders will probably be very cautious and will shun an excessively violent policy by seeking legal means of political action.

(3) If a repressive system limits legal activity, the masses may become violent. In that case, the leadership is likely to be transferred to elites, which are better prepared for that kind of action. They will impose their leadership strongly, both before and after the revolution, if it occurs. There is no implication here that the resulting mobilizationist movement is manipulatory. What is asserted is that the leadership usually represents an external actor; whether it is manipulatory or not depends on the circumstances.

In a popular political movement it is important to know not only its ideology and predisposition to violence, but also whether it is based on mobilizational phenomena or on the autonomous organization of its members. In other words, we must distinguish between the two modes of participation, the mobilizational and the associationist. Associationism generally goes hand in hand with a lower predisposition to violence, but it is compatible with many different ideological expressions. Mobilizationism requires the alliance between at least two actors, one a mass component with high mobilization and low (not necessarily nil) organization, the other an elite inclined toward mobilizationism and with affinities toward the popular component.

Affinity, that is, convergence of interests and attitudes, is not enough. The elite must have a mobilizational attitude, which is not the result of spontaneous generation but depends on adequate stimuli from the social context. When the history and development of a mobilizational movement are studied, it is not enough to point to the existence of the elite element with given attitudes or ideologies. That descriptive level is necessary, but a sociological analysis should explore the social tensions responsible for (1) forming that elite out of certain classes or class fragments that are its recruiting ground, and (2) inducing in that elite the required mobilizational attitudes, which are far from natural among middle or upper levels of stratification.

In this area a first hypothesis may be put forth stating that an actor will favor mobilizationism to the extent that its social mobilization exceeds its autonomous organization. A testing of this hypothesis would require that both concepts be measurable on comparable scales. Though the present stage of social research does not allow this precision, it is possible to make approximate and comparative estimates. Favorability to mobilizationism should be found among popular strata, especially in intermediate stages of urbanization or industrialization. In the more traditional situations the low level of social mobilization leads to apathy, to a conservative involvement, or to locally restricted actions. At the other extreme, in solidly industrialized urban contexts, the high level of organization compensates social mobilization, thus diminishing whatever tendencies may exist toward mobilizationism. There may be alliances with middle- or upper-level actors, but they will not be of a mobilizational type. In the Democratic party of the United States, for example, the class character of the social actors involved is very diversified, but the link between them is not mobilizationist but, rather, based on partial convergences of economic interests and political attitudes. In the European social democratic formula there is also an alliance between actors, connected in a nonmobilizational manner, though with a greater element of ideology than in the American case.

Apart from the discrepancy between social mobilization and organization, there are other factors that generate a preference for mobilizationism. These are operative particularly among middle- and upper-level actors, who are usually quite organized and for whom, therefore, the first stated hypothesis would not be applicable. A revision of the literature and of some historical cases suggests the following factors:

(1) Status incongruence. An unbalanced configuration of status dimensions (economic level, prestige, profession, lineage, ethnicity, religion, education, status respect), when very intense or difficult to compensate for, produces acute disconformity and questioning of dominant values.[11] Other things being equal, it may be hypothesized that status incongruence facilitates the adoption of mobilizationist tactics by high-status actors, who otherwise feel threatened by them.

(2) Economic insecurity. This Damocles sword can almost be considered one of the elements of status incongruence, because the actor that feels insecure loses some of its standing in society. However, I am including this variable as a separate factor because of the importance it has in inducing some actors, especially entrepreneurial ones, to accept mobilizational policies as a means of obtaining necessary allies. Among popular strata insecurity is endemic in many countries, particularly during some periods, and produces the above results.

(3) Anomie. This social-psychological factor is important in generating mobilizationist attitudes among intellectual, student, and other middle-level sectors whose cultural malaise leads them to search for security and enthusiasm in a mass movement untrammeled by the petty-mindedness of voluntary association leaders. Admittedly, it might also lead to joining small elitist sects that can provide intellectual certitudes.

(4) Structure of menaces. If an upper- or middle-level actor feels strongly menaced by other (national or foreign) actors of high status, it will tend to perceive itself as being a part of the "people" and favor mobilizationist solutions. If the threat comes from lower stratification levels, the result will be the opposite.

A consideration of these four items leads to the conclusion that mobilizational elites are more likely to appear at intermediate stages of economic development, when the impact of international capitalism destabilizes traditional structures, thus affecting the whole social pyramid. In solidly industrialized countries an acute economic crisis can also have similar effects. What generally will be lacking in these developed cases is an unorganized but socially mobilized mass. However, in some instances, an excess of mobilization over organization may also be found there, among peasant, worker, urban marginal, or middle-class levels. These groups may also be subject to the action of the other four factors outlined above, that is, status incongruence, economic insecurity, anomie, and a feeling of menace. Germany during the Weimar Republic may be taken as a case of this explosive combination of factors leading to widespread mobilizational attitudes throughout the social structure.

Violence, Repression, and Legitimacy

It is necessary to clarify the concept of violence to differentiate it from others with which it is sometimes lumped. Traditionally, violence referred to acts that caused physical damage, destruction, or serious harm to persons or goods, or to the threat of those acts. To this common understanding of the word has been added any type of action that directly or indirectly promotes injustice or seeks benefits from the deprivation of others.

Many apparently innocent acts become part of the "violence from above," more hypocritical but no less destructive in its effects than the necessarily more open "violence from below," which seeks the correction of injustice. Although from an ethical point of view this use of the word may be unobjectionable, sociological analysis needs to differentiate phenomena that have quite different etiologies and effects. I propose to maintain the traditional conception of violence as involving deliberate and explicit acts of physical harm or destruction of people or goods or serious limitations on their freedom of movement. This violence, when exercised by government, takes the form of repression. It then becomes necessary to distinguish between violence and repression. But we shall set aside as pertaining to other conceptual areas all matters referring to the existence of social inequalities, relative privileges, and results of the operation of the economic actions of individuals, businesses, or state corporations. This area is linked to the class structure and the unequal distribution of goods and power. It is as important, if not more, than violence, but it is a different thing. It is a part of the etiology of violence and repression, but it should be separated from them to understand the phenomena involved.

To explore the connections between violence and repression, let us consider an authoritarian regime that had time and opportunity to establish a wide consensus and therefore manifests little repression or violence. As argued above, it is not useful— except as a moral condemnation—to say that the authoritarian use of the mechanisms of consensus is itself an instance of "violence from above." It is, rather, necessary to understand how a system of consensual monopoly works in contrast with one that must rely more heavily on repressive and violent actions. Let us take as an example Salazar's regime in Portugal during its more solid years, around the forties and fifties.[12] In those days oppositional violence was not too great for two reasons: the strong consensus, or passivity, of a large part of the population; and the repression that weakened or intimidated dissidents. Governmental repression was high, but it was exerted along orderly and legal channels and thus did not need to take more open forms of violence: shootings in mass gatherings, kidnapping or assassination of politicians, massacres of strikers. If this did not happen to any great extent, it was because the government was in control of the situation, or the opposition was not strong enough.

By contrast, the Bolivian military regime between 1979 and 1982, during which several presidents and ruling juntas followed each other in rapid succession, resorted to numerous armed confrontations in public meetings in the cities and with striking miners and peasants. Measured in terms of deaths, casualties, imprisonments, and the like, violence was much greater than in Salazar's Portugal. In spite of that, the Bolivian government was much weaker. Even the repression it exerted was not as strong as in the Portuguese case because it did not have the situation under control. This was partly the result of its weakness, in turn due to its lack of legitimacy and to factional infighting within the ruling circles. Often the final episodes of dictatorial governments are weak and violent, though in some cases their weakness does not allow them even to exercise violence.

Stalinism is another paradigmatic case: highly repressive and violent at the same time, because of the way it treated opponents, who were not only repressed in a more or less legal manner but were abducted, deported, or secretly shot. Its successors continue to be repressive, but they are much less violent. Perhaps this is due to the efficacy of the system in distributing some well-being plus its educational and mass media monopoly, which enables it to create a certain consensus. Thus, it approaches the model we have set up for Salazarism.

In Argentina, Gen. Juan Carlos Onganía's government (1966–1970) started as a moderate version of Salazarism: considerable repression, but low-level violence, due to a good measure of consensus or at least a passive opposition. With the eventual deterioration of this supporting or tolerating front, violence was increased from both dissidents and government, as epitomized in the so-called Cordobazo (1969). Onganía's successors within the same military regime, Gens. Norberto Levingston and Agustín Lanusse, increasingly lost control of the situation and were forced to reduce repression and finally to grant free elections. They yielded a considerable quota of power, at least in the specifically political arena.[13] Violence continued to be common, particularly on the part of the numerous groups that had taken to guerrilla tactics.

The takeover in 1976 by a new faction of the military started out with strong repression and violence. It did not have the wide—even if temporary—consensus enjoyed by Onganía, because this time Peronism was more clearly the loser, unlike in 1966.[14] This regime (which left power in 1983) was supported at its inception by a great part of the entrepreneurial and upper middle classes, but not by trade unionists and intellectuals. Society was thus highly polarized. In due time, the economic program and the harm inflicted on some capitalist sectors, which had believed in the new regime, sapped and fragmented that regime's support. This fragmentation, which began outside government circles, soon extended to them, with the resultant clique confrontations and internal coups. This weakness induced a desperate resort to international adventure; when it failed, the ensuing disarray forced elections on a reluctant but hamstrung military regime. In other words, the progressive deterioration of the Argentine military government reflected what was happening at the level of civil society—the coalitions between actors, of whom the military are only one, and not the most powerful.

When violence is confined to small groups, its effects can hardly materialize unless those groups enjoy at least some sympathy or toleration among the population. If that support, however implicit, is lacking, the potential extremists will feel isolated and will not convert their frustration and violent temper into action. To explore this subject further, some other variables must be introduced into the study of violence, beginning with social legitimacy.

In the more democratic societies, both violence and repression are low, except in some isolated cases, like Northern Ireland, which should be considered a separate polity subject to colonial domination. In other European countries violent tendencies also exist among some groups, for example, in Italy, with the Red Brigade and equivalent fascist groups. But their field of recruitment is small and they have not been able to establish alliances with political parties or trade unions. This isolates them and facilitates their control without the state's having to resort to much violence. In other countries, like France, Germany, or Sweden, the incidence of violence among sectors equivalent to those that breed Italian extremism is much lower, or practically nil. This does not mean that frustration or relative deprivation does not exist among them, but the social legitimacy in those countries puts a brake on their actions and makes them feel like deviants without possibility of support from wider circles, so they do not pass from dreams to reality. In Italy and Spain, social legitimacy is somewhat lower, keeping extremist groups relatively active.

Social legitimacy, then, is a moderating factor in the development of violence. It reflects the degree to which social actors judge that society is run in a manner compatible with their values.[15] Though a characteristic of the whole society, it also affects those actors that have contributed nothing to it. Thus, for example, at times Parisian students might have been as frustrated, or felt as deprived, as any students in Latin America. But the fact that they lived in a country with a high degree of social legitimacy also operated on them from the outside, so to speak, inhibiting their tendencies toward violent action.

The Level of Menace: Historical Comparisons

To approach an understanding of violence, it is necessary to appreciate the vicious-circle character it has. A social actor, even if not relatively deprived, may react with violence if it feels threatened by others, especially if the latter are violent or very antagonistic toward the actor we are considering. The concept "level of menace" reflects the degree to which the actor senses the existence of an enemy force capable of inflicting serious harm; the feeling will be diminished if the coalition to which the actor belongs is strong. The hypothesis may be established that a highly menaced actor—in this sense of the term—will react by increasing its predisposition to violence, independently of its relative deprivation.

To see how these variables operate in a historical situation, we can contrast the Río de la Plata area with Brazil during the first half of the nineteenth century. Slavery was a dominant factor in Brazilian society, in sugar and coffee production and in urban commercial and service activities. A good number of the slaves were born in Africa, though the proportion of Africa-born slaves was much lower than in Haiti. In the Río de la Plata region the situation was quite different. Equivalent agrarian labor concentrations did not exist, and a large part of the gaucho rural population was thinly spread over the country and had a high degree of residential instability, like the inhabitants of the Venezuelan llanos.[16] The white and mixed population of Buenos Aires had been very affected by militarization as a result of militias formed during the British invasions (1806 and 1807). In both the urban and some rural areas, social mobilization was much higher than in Brazil. In Brazil the urban and rural masses, especially where they were more concentrated, were to a large degree slave and thus it was dangerous to attempt to mobilize them. Dissatisfied elements of the upper and middle classes had to be careful; appeals to mass agitation were practically forbidden so as not to activate a potentially deadly volcano.

The slave mass in Brazil was a dormant giant, hostile but under control. If activated by external or internal elites, it might irreparably harm the system of social domination. Its nearest equivalent in the Río de la Plata region was the Indian peasants and mining proletarians of Upper Peru (Bolivia), but they were geographically far from the centers of power and, in the period under consideration, they no longer belonged to the same country. Brazilian slaves may be considered as potentially a very strong actor, but in actual fact their autonomous organization was almost nil, though their social mobilization, particularly that of recent arrivals from Africa, was quite high. The slaves, in contrast with the peasants, had fewer motives for respecting the traditional system of authority. Thus, being less integrated into a traditional system of social control, their social mobilization could be considerable. Organizational weight was extremely low, if it existed at all, and mobilizational weight, though potentially high, could not be converted into political power because of the lack of willing leadership elements. This is at the source of the comparatively peaceful transfer of power between conservative or liberal factions characteristic of the imperial period. Admittedly, the celebrated low level of violence of the Brazilian political system covered the daily violence committed against the slaves. It is necessary to distinguish between the violence used to control and administer the slave work force and that employed against open rebellions, which falls more directly in the specifically political arena. Slave rebellions in the Brazilian case were not very extended or intense. Because a high degree of specifically political violence was not necessary to repress these manifestations of nonconformity, the relations between the rest of the political actors were more consensual. The potential popular menace (mostly from the slaves) induced solidarity among the other social actors. Of course, there were regional conflicts, like the war against the separatist Republic of Rio Grande (1835–1845) and the repression of other movements in the North and Northeast. It is significant that the most durable of these confrontations happened in Rio Grande do Sul, a region similar to the Río de la Plata. In the North, elite dissidents, who could not appeal to the masses, quickly failed. By contrast, in the South the incorporation of gaucho hosts was as customary as in Uruguay or Argentina.

The Brazilian and Argentinian situations can be compared with the Mexican one. The presence in Mexico of large labor concentrations in cities and mining areas and of uprooted Indians in some hacienda areas created quite a sizable potential menace. This, which was also the case in Peru, probably explains the much more passive role adopted by capital city elites in both countries at the time of the crisis of 1810.

However, in a peripheral area of New Spain (Guanajuato and Querétaro), the conditions of some of the middle strata were desperate enough to push them to revolt and to adopt a mobilizationist style of leadership, under Miguel Hidalgo and later José M. Morelos.[17] The insurgency remained confined to regional and provincial areas, its extreme violence antagonizing most of the upper and middle classes. However, soon enough many of them were ruined by the destructive effects of the war and thus found themselves torn between opposing forces. The potentially high popular menace and their experience of the early mass insurgency led them to oppose mobilizational strategies and to support stiff repression. Catastrophic oscillations of fortune, though, induced many of them to try new political formulas. The establishment could no longer control political innovators appealing to the masses under the most varied ideological banners.

In Brazil the solidarity of the elites was symbolized by the so-called moderating power of the emperor, which they made possible. In Mexico the masses were menacing and frightening to some sectors of the dominant classes, but not enough to deter their more adventurous elements. The chaotic state of the economy and the destruction of fortunes were powerful mechanisms in the recruitment of mobilizational elites.

Violence-Prone Situations

It is a cliché that violent social revolutions have happened mostly in backward areas of the world, including Latin America. The ideal condition for the creation of violent outcomes seems to lie, however, in countries or areas at a certain intermediate level of development, that is, those that have already been touched by capitalist development, which unhinges and destabilizes traditional systems of social control, like in Northeast Brazil or great parts of Colombia or Peru. In the case of Brazil, the predominant weight of the prosperous Center and South makes the extension of conditions typical of the Northeast unlikely. In Colombia violence has become endemic, with strong rural roots linked to conflicts over land ownership and control. It takes almost clannish forms, often between groups separated by vertical lines, though there is a tendency for it to become more class-based.[18] In Peru the electoral success of a reform-oriented populist party provides an alternative channel for popular demands and aspirations. But the first impact of capitalism on traditional rural areas keeps generating revolutionary elites among intermediate layers of the peasantry or highly marginalized sectors of the small village middle classes.[19] In countries like Brazil and Mexico, although such tensions also exist, and in some places generate violent phenomena in the form of primitive rebels or bandits, migration to the large cities acts as a safety valve, even at the cost of producing other complex phenomena in the new places of concentration.[20] Given this population transfer, the peasant groups that remain in place, having lost the potentially revolutionary ferment that could have been provided by their younger and more ambitious members, tend to conservatism or passivity.

As for the urban working class, its greatest radicalism is usually present at intermediate stages of development. Though the increase in its organizational power may, in the long run, produce moderation, in the short run it may be accompanied by very radical demands that create a revolutionary or quasi-revolutionary situation. This happened during the Second Spanish Republic and in Chile during the Unidad Popular government of Salvador Allende.

In Brazil and Mexico the size of the rural sector gives continued relevance to internal migration and the consequent formation of a mobilized proletariat with little organizational experience.[21] Except in some peak areas like the São Paulo industrial triangle or the Mexican railways or power plants, the dominant pattern for many years is likely to be what Germani called the "availability" of the masses for populist experiences in alliance with assorted elites, generally though not always of a left of center persuasion. The possibility of the radicalization or violent orientation of these movements is always there. In Argentina, by contrast, rural-urban migration is today less relevant, and the trade unions have become more stable, with a permanent and bureaucratized leadership, not always internally democratic but enjoying the confidence of the rank and file. This confidence derives from its record in defending members' rights, confronting military governments with that mixture of strength and softness, hawkish and dovish strategies so infuriating to their critics on the Left but appealing to the common sense of the average union member. This unionism is a hard bargainer, but it is capable of restraining popular demands it deems extreme or impossible to fulfill under the circumstances. In the Brazilian and Mexican cases, the autonomously organized peak sector of the labor movement has some of the traits typical of working class organizations during the first impact of capitalist growth, as in the cases of Chile and Spain. That is, its moderating role is not so marked. As a result, the social tensions produced in the working class are more difficult to manage in Brazil and Mexico than in Argentina, despite the greater weakness of the working classes in those two countries, other things being equal (which is not always the case). Much depends in Mexico on the spell of the revolutionary tradition, which by invoking its million dead extracts loyalty and sacrifice from the masses. It also depends on the type of anti–status quo elites generated in other non–working class strata capable of establishing contact with the masses. This is a sort of Russian roulette by comparison to the more narrowly restricted variability of the Argentine case.

Though in parts of Brazil and Mexico and, to a lesser extent, in Argentina there are conditions that can generate "mutant" revolutionary elements among the middle classes, the more prosperous parts of the country absorb them and offer occupational prospects and mitigate their predisposition to violence. A delicate equilibrium between opposite tendencies takes place in this matter, because the generation of revolutionary elements among the frustrated middle classes may be greater than what can be integrated via economic expansion in the prosperous zone of the economy.

The type of guerrilla that took hold in Argentina and Uruguay was different from the type prevalent in more rural countries. Apparently, this type of guerrilla was generated at a higher level of social stratification, with little or no peasant connections and few working-class roots, although it enjoyed marked sympathy among the intellectualized middle class. It is probably not a coincidence that Argentina and Uruguay during the 1950s and 1960s had, by Latin American standards, a very advanced productive and educational apparatus with a complex division of labor and new professional positions. The severe economic crisis and stagnation that hit these two countries, plus political instability (which had an independent etiology) destroyed many life projects in a group that had enjoyed favorable conditions for a long time. This radical reduction in life chances and the drastic fall in the international status of those two countries produced intense frustration among student and university groups, a sort of Parisian May 1968 without the compensations of the French standard of living. A similar phenomenon may yet affect the equivalent sectors of Brazil and Mexico, which experienced a couple of decades of unprecedented expansion but now see that expansion curtailed by economic crisis. The failure of many insurrectionary experiences, however, will surely affect the behavior of those inclined to follow that road, at least for some time and in countries that consider each other's experiences relevant.

6. Military Interventionism

In developing countries there is often an explosive combination of high capacity to express demands, few resources, and low legitimacy of criteria regarding the allocation of those resources. The result is what Huntington calls "mass praetorianism."[1] This ungovernability with the criteria of liberal pluralism and electoral competition leads to a search for new solutions, of a basically authoritarian character, to facilitate development and capital accumulation. Some regimes, notably in recently independent African and Asian nations, appeal to mass support via symbols of national identification and radical social change. David Apter has called those systems "mobilizational," using the term like we do in this volume.[2] Where that kind of government does not take root, it may be replaced by more direct military rule, without a demanding ideology or mass mobilization. In Apter's view, economic development in the long run facilitates the establishment of democracy, but democracy would be the result, not the means employed.

Taking cues from these approaches, Guillermo O'Donnell has observed the incidence of authoritarian regimes in Latin America, particularly in the relatively more advanced countries. He concludes that under conditions of high modernization but not yet complete industrialization, authoritarian regimes would be the rule.[3] He hypothesizes that the sources for the spread of military "bureaucratic-authoritarian" regimes are of two kinds. First, there is the need, on the part of industrialist and administrative elites, to strengthen labor discipline to make capital accumulation and advanced industrialization possible. In addition, freedom for the popular strata to organize, because of its potentially revolutionary consequences, is threatening to the dominant classes.

Events have forced a drastic revision of this thesis. Bureaucratic-authoritarian regimes in some countries, like Brazil and Mexico (the latter is a marginal case of this type of system), have been successful in "deepening" industrialization, though without much redistribution of income; in other places, notably Argentina and Chile, severe setbacks were suffered by the economy and deindustrialization has taken place.[4]

The gradual or even brusque redemocratization of some of these countries cannot be explained in terms of the theory because, among other reasons, the resultant mood of the masses did not necessarily threaten the existing class system. Under the generic name of "popular political activation" many different phenomena had been bagged together, but these need to be separated and analyzed individually. The most menacing threats to the established order do not always come mainly from the organized working class, but from certain peasant sectors affected by the impact of capitalism, or from "mutant" components of the middle classes. At an intermediate level of threat are to be found the highly mobilized masses of urban marginals and workers, often recent migrants, who are "available" for populist combinations or other mobilizational experiences of a more radical sort. All of these factors can be combined in myriads of forms, a conclusion to which the more recent work by O'Donnell, Schmitter, and Whitehead has also come.[5]

The Military Role: Omnipotence or Illusion?

Let us take the perspective of an extraterrestrial visitor who would notice that some men manage and control weapons while others are forbidden their use. He might conclude that the former would impose their will on the others and that they would accumulate most of the existing privileges, including property. This was close to the situation in feudal societies where the military almost coincided with the nobility and went about armed most of the time. However, even there, force was based not only on the use of weapons but on the capacity to command the obedience of others, which is a trait of society in general, not only of its military segment.

If this aspect were not taken into account, our extraterrestrial observer might be led to believe that real power rested on the privates and noncommissioned officers, who actually man the machine guns, cannons, and rockets, and not on the generals, who have no direct contact with the hardware. In fact, many a nineteenth-century liberal argued that universal military service, by putting weapons in the hands of the people, would guarantee democracy. The experience of the French Revolution seemed to support this conviction, and perhaps it was correct at a time when one man meant one gun. With present military technology, things are different, and universal military service does not seem to safeguard democracy. It must be admitted, however, that a purely professional army might become an even worse menace for a free polity. In a conscripted army the need to handle draftees sets some limits— in extreme cases—to what may be demanded from soldiers. Such an army, though not a guarantee of democracy, facilitates a radical revolution in cases of political, economic, or military disaster, as in the Russian Revolution.

If our observer were to engage in a study of the structures of privilege and consensus, he might come to the opposite conclusion, that the military are just one more of the several ancillary institutions of a dominant order, of which other expressions are the churches and the cultural specialists, and which is dominated by those who own or control the means of production. This is much nearer reality, though a more detailed perception of the internal contradictions and heterogeneities within the dominant circles is still needed.

A further step would lead to a realization that, although the armed forces are not simply an expression of the dominant social order, they may be a reflection of the tensions generated in civil society. These are quite different statements, though both give priority to civil society as an explanatory factor. The first one, which we may call "paleomarxist," holds that the military always, in one way or another, directly or indirectly, represents the interests of the dominant social order. If, as in Peru, the military establishes land reform and other changes, it is only to save the threatened capitalist system.[6] If, as in Portugal, it overthrows a corporatist regime and allows free action to socialist forces, it is only to domesticate them and avoid greater evils. The argument is so closed that it is almost impervious to evidence. It must be admitted that often reality lends it some semblance of validity, however. After all, capitalism is still alive in those two countries, and probably healthier than before the military takeovers. So it is not so easy to dispose of this theory, which, though somewhat antiquated, comes back to life when contrasted to many alternative interpretations that end up by explaining everything as a result of the military's attitudes, evolved as though by spontaneous generation and imposed by sheer force.

The paleomarxist version, however, is weak because of its excessively simplistic perception of the class structure and its conception of how power is distributed in a society. Classical Marxism adheres to the view that power clings almost totally to the economically dominant classes; thus, liberal and democratic institutions are only an illusion. Not only is the democratic dress an illusion, so is the alternative military garb. Even in the *Eighteenth Brumaire*, in spite of its sophisticated analysis of social groups, Louis Napoleon, acceding to power through a combination of military and popular support, was seen as serving, in the last resort, the interests of the only imaginable group in the absence of a social revolution, namely, the bourgeoisie.

In fact, it is necessary to leave things more open-ended, while following the same *Eighteenth Brumaire* and other historical works, in subdividing the class structure into a large number of actors, including some institutional ones. The military is just one of these actors, and its political weight, though considerable, is not overwhelming. If it were, the military could do whatever it wanted, which is not compatible with the preceding analysis. Of course, it can be argued that what the military wants is the result of social forces originating in civil society; thus, it would be capable only of wishing what the social structure put into its head.

Taking this argument in its more extreme form, we would again return to the interpretation according to which the armed forces are only a reflection of what happens in the rest of society. Under certain circumstances, it might be that the military mind reflected not the upper but the middle or even the popular classes. Given its position in the social pyramid, however, it is more likely to be influenced by social actors located from the middle upward. As I have argued, if the middle classes are undergoing a serious crisis, or passing through a process of "mutation," there is a high probability that the military will be quite sympathetic to their point of view. Hence the widespread experience of Third World military reformism.

In the latter case, one may still wonder how these middle-class reformist attitudes are transmitted from civil society to the military corporation. The simplest model would consist in saying that the military itself is a member of some sector of the middle classes; thus it experiences similar economic and social problems and develops the corresponding attitudes. Even if the armed men's position in social space is not exactly the same as that of the middle classes, their social origins, their friends' pressures, would lead to similar results. Admittedly, those mechanisms are in operation, but they do not exhaust the channels of communication between the military and society. It is a fact that the armed forces are to a large extent functional to the maintenance of the existing social order. It is not necessary to subscribe to the paleomarxist hypothesis to accept this fact. The military maintains order and controls the manifestations of violence, thus facilitating the functioning and consolidation of the system. This functionality may be altered under crisis conditions, but while it lasts, it is a central element of the polity. Because of this, reciprocal connections and influences are very numerous, although not always explicitly and open. In the rest of this chapter, the various forms this connection can assume will be examined.

Aristocratic Control: Nineteenth-Century Brazil

One of the simplest forms of relationship between the military and society is found where a strong and solidary aristocracy—preferably under a monarchy—fills the main positions in the army, navy, and militia. Brazil during the last century comes close to this ideal type. The very high potential threat derived from slavery produced the solidarity of the upper classes—as noted earlier—and thwarted any tendency toward mobilizationism or extension of popular participation. Monarchy, or, more specifically, the court, imported from Portugal in 1808, facilitated the fusion of the various components of the dominant classes: Portuguese merchants, native landowners, civilian administrators, and military officers. Though many officers were not of aristocratic origin—at the beginning there were quite a few foreign mercenaries—the circulation of individuals between these positions was considerable. This was particularly so for rural militia, often employed in provincial conflicts and for the the maintenance of order and whose local chiefs, holding the title of colonel, were the primary local landowners. Congruence between the various components and roles of the upper classes was very high. Co-optation was also effected through he occupation of posts in municipal, provincial, and national chambers, the life-tenured Senate, and the Council of State, with titles of nobility granted at important moments of this *cursus honorum*. This was the opposite of what happened in Mexico and Argentina until the century was well advanced. For a system like the Brazilian one to function a very peculiar social and economic context was necessary. There had been practically no war of independence, no sudden economic alteration and breakdown of established economic circuits. By contrast, the presence of all these factors in Argentina and Mexico and the less-restrained agitation of the masses weakened the control the upper classes could exert over the military. This gave the action of the armed forces the appearance of independence. When, toward the last quarter of the century, both Mexico and Argentina consolidated their economies and the traditional sources of agitation among the masses ceased, their political regimes became more stable and military intervention was kept under control. Though this was done under military presidents, what was really happening was a consolidation of social control on the part of the economically renovated upper classes. The solidity of this control, however, was never total in either country. In addition, it was not a reproduction of the aristocratic model, but a local variant of the professionalization of the armies, which was the internationally current development and which remains so in the more advanced countries. This control involved the formation of a professional ethic, which included noninvolvement in party politics. The complexity and increasingly bureaucratic nature of military organization made the emergence of personalist and charismatic leaders more difficult. But it was the solidity of civilian society that imposed respect on potentially rebellious officers, who always exist whether they be a MacMahon in post-Commune France, or a MacArthur in post–Korean War United States.

Professionalization in Mexico was interrupted by the revolution, which was caused by factors other than those considered here. In Argentina professionalization proceeded further, until it almost became a recognized part of political culture in the twenties. In Brazil, meanwhile, the aristocratic system of control had broken down as a result of the social tensions caused by the abolition of slavery. The diversity of regional interests became acute, and the increase in education and in the number of aspirants to middle-class position—in the state, in business, and in the military—facilitated the development of republican ideas. This—which would have been serious enough for the monarchy if expressed in the civilian sector—was deadly when it reached the armed forces. It was the army that overthrew the monarchy, which had abolished slavery the previous year (1888). The abolition of slavery was necessary not only for the general development of the country but also to preserve the real, long-term interests of the existing capitalist system. The monarchy understood this, but many sectors of the bourgeoisie did not share this view, whether because they could not transcend their immediate short-run interests—linked to the previous system—or because they feared the agitation of the liberated slaves. It has even been stated that the Brazilian upper classes took revenge on the monarchy in establishing the republic in 1889. The increased intensity of conflicts among upper sectors, added to the incorporation of middle strata to the arena, created a context facilitating military intervention.[7] The change, however, was not too radical, because the potentially great menace continued to exist, no longer based on the slaves but on the recently liberated black workers and others concentrating in the cities. This was probably behind the consolidation—after a few years of internal military infighting—of the Old Republic's oligarchical but civilian regime (until 1930). The Old Republic supported increasingly greater social tensions, and military agitation was by no means eliminated, although it was kept under control. On the other hand, the previously enslaved population became integrated, reducing the level of menace it implied, though it surely was potentially higher than in Argentina or Chile at the time.

Military Reformism: *Tenentismo* and Ibañismo

The last decade of the Old Republic witnessed the appearance of *tenentismo*, an agitation among low-ranking and young military officers.[8] Their search for reforms adopted the most varied political formulae, ranging from classical liberalism to Iberian authoritarianism and fascism, interpreted as a developmental and nation-building process—something similar to the image many intellectuals had, thirty years later, of Nasserism, that is, an authoritarianism seen as an adequate reply to conditions of underdevelopment, however much it may not be appropriate to the more advanced countries. Samuel Huntington has argued that where the middle classes are of recent formation and are seeking political space within a traditional or semifeudal social order, the military are likely to express the "progressive" program of national construction, economic growth, and industrialization.[9] In developed countries the middle class tends to be more conservative, though if seriously affected by economic crisis or revolutionary working-class agitation it might adopt an "extremism of the center," pitted against both the conservative liberal bourgeoisie and the socialist workers.

In Third World countries middle-class insecurity and downward mobility produce very different reactions from those typical of the European or North American situations. In Brazil a case in point was *tenentismo*, aimed at the oligarchical and foreign control of the Old Republic but also concerned about maintaining order and discipline. The combination was very heterogeneous and differed widely among individuals. The *tenentes* were in the forefront of the basically civilian uprising that took Vargas to power in 1930. It had the support of peripheral sectors of the traditional political structure (Vargas was governor of the state of Rio Grande do Sul), who were unhappy about the prospect of continued São Paulo domination. The rebellion enjoyed the strategic support of provincial militia and had enough sympathy among the regular armed forces to make it impossible for them to perform a repressive role. This situation is often found in other Latin American experiences: the armed forces become paralyzed by internal divisions, or by a lack of adequate connections with hegemonic social classes, thus becoming impotent to stop a basically civilian rebellion.

The Vargas regime, after overcoming Paulista resistance in the 1932 civil war, culminated in the corporatist constitution of 1937, which inaugurated the so-called Estado Novo. The Mussolinian inspiration of this constitution should not lead to confusion between the Brazilian and the Italian regimes. There are many different types of regimes that appeal to authoritarian rule without sharing other elements in their political formulas. Vargas lacked a mass party based on antilabor feelings, so he did not become a South American Mussolini in 1937. He eventually did form a mass party, but this was in 1945, and then with a social support opposite to that enjoyed by Mussolini. Vargas was overthrown by the social classes that had been the basis of fascist rule in Italy. Though Vargas often governed in a dictatorial fashion, repression never reached Italian levels; when he did acquire a large popular following, he lost power, and when he came back in 1950, it was as the result of free elections.[10]

In Chile a military mentality not too far removed from *tenentismo* was expressed in the 1924 coup, which forced Congress to enact the reformist legislation of President Arturo Alessandri, paralyzed by conservative congressional forces and the intricacies of legislative procedure. From 1924 to 1932, Chilean politics were characterized by continuous military interventions, culminating with Gen. Carlos Ibáñez's dictatorship (1927–1931). The armed forces, by intervening, were seeking some reforms and courting popular support so as to undercut the autonomous working-class movement, which had recently joined the Red International. By comparison to Brazil, in Chile the labor movement was much better organized and was perceived as a power contender by the established order. During the first years of the century, it had gone through several violent confrontations with the security forces, as in the 1907 massacre in Iquique, a nitrate-exporting town in the North. If in Brazil the potential menace from the dormant masses was higher, in Chile the popular sectors were more alert and organized, and in a way positing a more concrete and realistic menace to the system. But their strength was legally channeled and counterbalanced by a large middle class. Ibáñez was accused of fascism by his leftist and liberal opponents, and he explicitly adopted in official propaganda the Mussolini example. But in fact his regime was quite different from Mussolini's, primarily because of the lack of a totalitarian mass party. The peculiar traits of Ibañismo (a less successful variety of the Vargas regime of the thirties) must be taken into account to understand the support Ibáñez obtained from the greater part of the Socialist party in 1952, when he returned to power through free elections. Mussolini also had some support from erstwhile socialist and syndicalist groups, but this was a different phenomenon. Such groups were rather few in Italy and not very representative, whereas in Chile the bulk of the trade union and popular political structures (with the exception of the Communist party) joined Ibáñez by cooperating with his government for the first two years. The autonomous nature of this support was revealed when it was withdrawn, leaving the president deprived of most of his popularity, especially from the trade unions. This is important to remember when we contrast this situation with the Peronist experience.[11]

The agitation of the military in favor of social reform, which took place in Brazil and Chile during the twenties, did not occur in Argentina, because of the greater development of the middle classes and the moderation of the trade union movement. During the forties, however, a very peculiar type of civil-military convergence took place in Argentina.

The Military-Industrial Convergence in Argentina

In Argentina the Second World War was marked by a collective psychosis about what would happen after the war ended, especially felt by those who were in closer contact with labor problems and by ideological specialists, like the military, who, due to their circulation through regional barracks and contact with conscripts could better sense the building up of new social tensions. As after the war there was no social explosion, it is today usual to underestimate the voices of Cassandra as purely paranoiac or as coming from those who see the Red menace everywhere.[12] A more careful study of the period in comparative perspective, however, leads to the realization that there were quite solid grounds for forecasting revolutionary upheavals, in Europe, Asia, or elsewhere after the end of the war. At any rate, apprehension was widespread. An important indicator was what businessmen in the Unión Industrial Argentina and some economists and social scientists linked to the *Revista de Economía Argentina* were thinking. The Unión Industrial Argentina organized between 1942 and 1945 a series of conferences to which prominent personalities, including many military, were invited. It was an important instance of military-industrial convergence. The specialized publications of the armed forces contributed to the analysis of the situation.

At that time, many shared a view of the world permanently divided into four great blocs: the United States, Russia, Japan, and Europe under German hegemony. Gen. José M. Sarobe in October 1942 forecast the "material emancipation of Greater Asia," whatever the result of the war, and the incorporation of the Ukraine in the "European New Order," replacing South America as provider of foodstuffs. Argentina might try to hegemonize a fifth area, because "it was necessary to conquer a certain economic autonomy, in order to maintain political independence."[13]

During those years the political and social scene in Argentina was in great upheaval as a result of Pres. Roberto Ortiz's illness and his replacement by Vice-Pres. Ramón Castillo. Castillo was intent on perpetuating ballot box rigging so as to ensure a Conservative victory at the polls. Throughout 1942 the opposition tried to form a local version of the Popular Front, including the Radical, Socialist, and Communist parties and the support of the politicized General Confederation of Labor (CGT). The situation has been analyzed from various angles, but I wish to emphasize here the attitudes of two strategic social actors, the military and the industrialists, concerning two issues: the need to industrialize in order to build up the defense network, and the prevention of potentially revolutionary social agitation, which was predicted to follow the war. For the military, the industrial theme was central, though subordinated to its professional concern with defense.[14] For the industrialists, the protection of industry was a question of life or death; it was needed to consolidate the prosperity brought about by the war.[15]

Col. Manuel Savio, one of the first to be invited to the Unión Industrial conferences, urged his audience to accept state intervention in planning the economy, because "the worst aspect of the postwar is economic chaos."[16] His industrialist convictions are very well known, and of course they implied extensive contacts with the business community. Some, like Unión Industrial president Luis Colombo or Leopoldo Melo, university professor and deputy of the right wing of the Radical party, were concerned with the postwar period due to the foreseeable economic chaos, which "might make more victims than the war itself" and generate vast numbers of unemployed.[17] The economists of the *Revista de Economía Argentina* argued in a series published in the Catholic newspaper *El Pueblo* (1943–1944) that the reopening of imports would mean a "ruinous competition for local industry, provoking unemployment and a paralysis of the present diversification of production." They concluded that "capitalism is an enemy of private property," thus giving a new twist to a long-held conviction of social Catholicism. They warned that the return of peace "would produce a veritable social and economic cataclysm" as unemployment, temporarily held in check by the war, would come back when the war ended. The number of proletarians (most of them foreigners) was increasing, which boded ill for the "social unity of our country." It was necessary to support industrial reconversion and to protect some, if not all, activities, to prevent the formation of "armies of unemployed."[18] The more extreme nationalist ideological group, which after the 1943 army coup was given the governorship of the province of Tucumán, attempted a first installment of its "new order" there. As Alberto Baldrich, the de facto governor, said, they were concerned lest "human desperation lead [workers] to believe those who come with Messianic promises. To prevent Argentina from becoming communist, it must be Christian, not only in religion but also in social organization." Soon afterward he added in a radio talk that those who opposed the government were obstructing "the only possibility of social peace in the somber and menacing days of the coming social convulsions and the turbulence of the postwar period."[19]

What was taking place was a convergence of industrialists, military, and Catholic nationalist intellectuals. For different reasons, they all agreed on a policy of intensive industrialization, protectionism, and production of durable goods and armaments, especially when Brazil began acquiring advantages through its alliance with the United States.[20] This coincidence of economic interests, professional attitudes, ideologies, and fears created the basis for the recruitment of the political elite that brought Perón to power and whose military expression was the Grupo de Oficiales Unidos (GOU). The industrialists, as is often the case, were less in evidence, though some of them, like Rolando Lagomarsino and Miguel Miranda (both members of the Unión Industrial board), became prominent as ministers of Perón's government in 1946.[21] In 1945, however, the Unión Industrial supported the Unión Democrática candidates who opposed Perón. This support has led some observers to deny that the industrial bourgeoisie played any significant role in the formation of the Peronist coalition. Alain Rouquié, for instance, sees no evidence for such a thesis and claims that it was concocted by essayists of the nationalist and Marxist Left. He gives as a counterexample the fact that Robustiano Patrón Costas, the official candidate of the Conservative government, supported by agrarian and foreign interests and against whose candidacy the 1943 military coup was aimed, was one of the largest sugar producers in the country and thus an industrialist in need of tariff protection.[22] If an industrialist in need of protection was in the anti-Peronist band, and if the same was true of the Unión Industrial Argentina, what should one make of the thesis concerning the convergence of industrialist and popular elements under the leadership of Colonel Perón?

Admittedly, in its more simple formulation, the thesis is not defensible. A different situation, however, arises if one is more careful in the identification of the component actors and the elite involved. The latter need not represent anybody but itself. But if it is formed as a result of social pressures acting in certain sectors of the stratification pyramid, it is bound to be affected by its origin. It is not easy to document the specific mechanisms behind the recruitment of that group, but this does not justify falling into some version of the "spontaneous generation" of elites or of their birth as a result of the charismatic capacity of an individual.

What happened to the Argentine industrial bourgeoisie is rather typical of new classes formed within an economic system that allows them some scope but stops short of giving them access to the main levers of command. Classes in the process of formation, "new men," generally have some difficulty in expressing themselves politically because of their recent formation and lack of a long tradition of occupying their positions in a context of legitimacy. Only the more dynamic or adventurous elements of that group or class take the hazardous step of engaging directly in political action.[23] It is highly probable, then, that a great part of that group or class, deeming the existing system of domination next to impossible to overturn, will remain passive and conformist within it, their role being taken up by some functional groups, like the armed forces, the church, or a political and ideological elite. The substitute elite and the group or class whose interests in a sense it represents maintain some connections like those in the military-industrial convergence of 1942–1943.

The study of this type of situation requires that one of the actors be subdivided much more than the others. Thus, it is not enough to inquire whether someone was an industrialist and required protection. It is necessary to specify the kind of industry involved and against whom the trade barrier had to be built. It is one thing to seek protection against Brazilian or Cuban sugar and another to try to stop durable goods from leaving the metropolises. In the latter case, tariff protection means hurting stronger interests and requires a different strategy in the selection of potential allies. Thus, the sugar baron Patrón Costas is not a relevant example, quite apart from the fact that one case is not enough to invalidate any hypothesis.

From Moderating Role to Transformative Intervention

The military had a central role in the formation of the populist coalition that led Colonel Perón to power. But to some extent it also expressed industrialist interests; thus it had a freer hand in dealing with the resistance of the upper classes to its populist policies. This industrial and military role was a result of special circumstances, but these are frequently found in Latin American countries. In less-developed stages, a similar association exists between the armed forces and the middle classes or between the former and the new state bureaucracy.

In the following chapters we shall return to the connection between the military and the trade unionists and to the peculiar political elite formed around Perón. First, however, military interventionism in Brazil should be considered, for comparison.

In Brazil the role of the military has oscillated widely, passing from an organic connection to the Vargas regime from 1930 to almost 1945, to confrontation in 1945, followed by an assumption of what Alfred Stepan has called a "moderating" role between 1945 and 1964. The military's moderating role involved several short-lived interventions immediately followed by devolution of power to a group of civilians. Stability was not achieved, so the system deteriorated until 1964, when the military staged a new type of "transformative" intervention, which went beyond mere "system maintenance."[24]

This transformative intervention, prompted by an increasing level of menace against the military institution (agitation among noncommissioned officers and soldiers, formation of armed groups to support land reform), inaugurated a long period in power, supported by politicians from the business and conservative sectors. It can be argued that a similar situation developed in 1966 in Argentina with the Onganía military coup and, after a short intermission, again in 1976 under General Videla. The Pinochet coup of 1973 could also be viewed as a case of the assumption by the armed forces of a more permanent role in controlling the more developed societies in Latin America. Stepan points out that military interventionism does not spring simply from the military's attitudes, but rather from the constellation of forces in civil society. A solidary civil society would not be vulnerable to armed coups. But it so happens that in Latin American societies the intensity of internal conflict is such that pressures to and from the barracks are uncontrollable. Hence the demand, from civil society, for an occasional moderating role. The accumulation of experiences, and a certain ideological evolution, according to this thesis, lead the armed forces to favor a more permanent assumption of government functions. In this analysis, it is not clear when or how the process can end, though, obviously, if praetorian—that is, multiple and chaotic—demands ceased or diminished, the scenario would be different. In fact, the economic success of the regime in Brazil allowed it to relax controls and start a process of *abertura* not too different from the Spanish one. In both cases, apparently, an authoritarian regime has been capable of liberalization from positions of power.

As to the factors leading the armed forces to establish more permanent authoritarian regimes, most interpretations stress the prevention of a social menace arising from the popular classes. Guillermo O'Donnell took this to be the main function of "bureaucratic-authoritarian" regimes; José Nun has also written about the "middle class military coup," polemically against those who consider the middle classes to be carriers of democratization.[25] According to him, the middle class adopts a democratic mentality only at the early stages of economic development. When the lower strata acquire greater strength and threaten the existing system of social domination, of which the middle classes are beneficiaries, the latter turn to the right, supporting, if need be, military coups. The armed forces should then be considered an organized expression of the middle classes, not because their social origins are, in some instances, similar, but because both are interested in the maintenance of the social order.

In a somewhat different approach, Alfred Stepan allows the armed forces an autonomous role, though subject to controls imposed by civil society. He rejects the idea that the military is the natural representative of the middle classes. In his view, only when the armed forces feel themselves menaced in their own institutional integrity do they intervene to transform those conditions from which the menace arises. Because the menace, though of popular origin, is often a consequence of the upper classes clinging to their privileges, the armed forces, to forestall the menace hanging over *their* heads, may turn against the capitalist privileges perceived as being responsible for the angry mood of the people. Hence, according to Stepan, military interventionism can adopt any ideology, from the Left to the nationalist Center or the Right.

In other words, the association between military values and those of private capitalism need not be permanent. The armed forces' attitude toward the church has often varied in Latin American history, anticlericalism having been quite widespread at some moments, and it is quite possible that a similar rejection might at some point apply to private capitalism. Something of the sort has happened in the Middle East, and to an increasing number of African nations.

In summary, we should consider the armed forces as a separate actor with institutional autonomy; it does not always reflect the opinions or directly represent the interests of other actors. The indirect connections, however, may be much stronger than any direct ties could be.

Actor coalitions are generally balanced (in political weight, that is, not necessarily in votes), because of the tendency toward the formation of "minimum winning" coalitions.[26] Given, then, the approximate equilibrium between political forces in the absence of military intervention, if the military abandons its noninvolvement, it will surely provide the margin of victory to the front it joins. If this is done in violent and repressive conditions, the exercise of dictatorial powers will be aimed at the diminution of opponents' political organization and weight, thus unbalancing the situation even more. However, the political power that must be assigned to the military to understand its relationship with the rest of society need not be excessively high. It is unlikely to be greater than that of the middle classes or the bourgeoisie in a capitalist society or the bureaucracy in a socialist one.

This, plus the fact that under certain conditions the military abstains from political involvement should lead us to affirm that the etiology of military coups does not depend principally on the military's attitudes but on the state of opinion among civilian groups. One of the main components of those relationships is the menace that upper status actors feel as coming from the popular sector. This menace need not always be very high, nor can it be hypothesized that with democracy and freedom to organize it grows. In fact, the contrary may be the case.

7. The Organization of the Popular Classes

According to most early socialist theoreticians, notably Marx and Engels, the formation of an autonomous political organization based on the less-favored classes has very peculiar prerequisites. If something more than a sudden explosion of violence is envisioned, organizational prerequisites are such that only under very special conditions can a popular party thrive. Even violent outbursts, to be successful, require a degree of political practice found among popular strata only where they have undergone the experience of economic, technological, and cultural development. In contrast, theoreticians like Bakunin set more store on spontaneity.

Engels, analyzing the German revolutionary situation in 1848, pointed to the low degree of development that the proletariat had in that country in comparison with Great Britain and France. As a result, the popular political movement had to include other sectors, because "the working class movement itself never is independent, never is of an exclusively proletarian character until all the different factions of the middle class, and particularly its most progressive faction, the large manufacturers, have conquered political power, and remodelled the state according to their wants."[1]

As long as this economic and political development of capitalist society does not take place, some fraction of the bourgeoisie will opt for a popular alliance as a means to power, reducing thereby the likelihood of the formation of a purely working-class political expression. In *Condition of the Working Class in England* Engels observed that Chartism was associated in its beginning with the industrialists' agitation against the Corn Laws. But because of the more developed nature of class relations in that country, a break occurred as early as 1842 between the bourgeois radicals and those with a working-class orientation. From that date on, "chartism became a purely working class movement, and was free from all the trammels of bourgeois influence."[2]

In a report on the Spanish situation in 1873–1874, Engels also argued that "Spain is an industrially very backward country and, therefore, it is not possible to speak yet of an immediate and complete emancipation of the working class. Before that, Spain must pass through several stages of development and put aside a whole series of obstacles."[3] In the Spanish case, as in many others, Engels favored an autonomous organization of the working class, but argued that it had to partake of the political game in alliance with one or the other of the bourgeois factions. It was to be expected that in "underdeveloped" countries, some dissatisfied fraction of the upper or middle classes would form a political party (Pi y Margal's Republicans, English antiprotectionist radicals, Italian Mazzinians) capable of obtaining popular support, because its ideology would be attuned to the mentality of the masses, not yet affected by the urban and industrial milieu.

If the problem existed in the Europe of the last century, it is endemic today in the Third World, including some of more industrially advanced Latin American countries. The historical process is slower and less unidimensional than Marx and Engels thought, however, so the formation of a socialist strategy is less clear. The maintenance of the ideal of autonomous working-class action in the face of the actual populist or radical preferences of that class often leads to political sterility or, worse, wrong alliances.

Leninism was an attempt to solve this problem on the basis of an analysis of the Russian situation, a situation quite typical of countries at intermediate stages of development. Almost all Marxist observers agreed that in such a place the revolution had to be capitalist,[4] because urban workers had no chances of staging a successful rebellion nor could they retain power in case they did. Lenin introduced a new element in this analysis: for him the crisis was so intense and the strength of the working class, though insufficient for the exercise of power, was great enough to frighten the bourgeoisie so that no bourgeois party was capable of leading a revolution. The bourgeoisie, then, would refrain from agitating the waters of popular discontent for fear of facing an uncontrollable storm. Lenin's solution was that the party of the proletariat, which he had already defined as a party of professional revolutionaries recruited from all social strata, should fill in the vacuum and lead the process. The revolution could not establish socialism, but it might inaugurate a special type of regime in which the working class would govern while the capitalists would continue, with some controls, to organize production.[5]

This solution was successful because of a theoretical and practical quid pro quo. The party of professional revolutionaries represented not the working class but only itself, and it became the generating nucleus of a new dominant class, the state bureaucracy. This, paradoxically, demonstrated the validity of the Marxian analysis, though with a twist. It turned out to be true that conditions were unfavorable for a working-class takeover and that only a class trained in the control and administration of the means of production could become socially dominant. But that class happened to be the bureaucracy, which then became a functional alternative to capitalism. As for political power, it is possible to argue—with Lenin, correcting Marx—that government can be exercised by a political elite *different* from the class that is economically and socially dominant. The Communist parties in this type of country have a certain independence vis-à-vis the bureaucracy, in much the same way that the Christian Democrats in Italy enjoy relative autonomy from the bourgeoisie.

Beginning in the 1920s, Víctor Raúl Haya de la Torre attempted to adapt Marxism to local Latin American conditions, as Lenin did for Russia. But in Haya de la Torre's case, the appeal to a class located above the urban workers or peasants was more explicit. Just like Engels for Spain, Haya argued that "in Indoamerica we have not had time to create a powerful and autonomous bourgeoisie, strong enough to displace the *latifundista* classes." He added that the middle classes "are the first to be affected by imperialist expansion, and from them excellent leaders and strong citizens' movements have been formed."[6] It is necessary, therefore, to unite "the three classes oppressed by imperialism: our young industrial proletariat, our vast and ignorant peasantry, and our impoverished middle classes." That is, he proposed not only the alliance of the proletariat with the middle classes (which would have been tactically acceptable to Marx and Engels) but also a veritable amalgam within a single political party of "manual and intellectual workers."

Haya argued that Lenin's Marxist position led him to base revolutionary action on the working class, which in this part of the world was incapable of producing the necessary changes. This criticism was really more applicable to local attempts to copy the practice of Western European communism than to Lenin's own approach to Russia. In Russia the proletariat was also weak, and yet Lenin's tactics were successful, because his party did not act as a representative of that class, nor of the peasantry. It actually did what Haya thought necessary; that is, it integrated sectors of the middle classes, though probably a smaller and more radicalized fraction than the one the Peruvian leader had in mind. On the other hand, in spite of its underdevelopment, Russia had important working-class concentrations, large cities, and enormous masses that were impelled to action through the social mobilization induced by a lost war. All of this applied also to the later Chinese experience. However, in Cuba, which is more like Peru than Russia or China, a "Marxist" revolution was successful. But in this case its initial formulation was more akin to Aprismo than to Leninism. Fidel Castro in his early revolutionary stage was a typical representative of the kind of political movements Haya thought instrumental for the struggle against imperialism; he was capable of recruiting some support even among progressive elements of the dominant country itself.

Leninist ideology is today used to inspire both Castroite movements and other more orthodox ones, namely, the official Communist parties. The Castroite variety is potentially more successful in the less-developed parts of the continent. Orthodox Communists usually are reduced to small minorities, except in Chile, where, until the end of the Unidad Popular experience, they were always the party more closely connected with the trade unions. The Chilean Communist party in practice is evolving along the lines of the Western European ones. Though it is not very advanced on the "Eurocommunist" road, because of its obvious dependence on Moscow while in exile and persecuted, if a political opening takes place in Chile, the party will probably veer toward a genuine acceptance of reformism as a method.

The Problem of Organization: Militants and Bureaucrats

For an organization to be considered representative of the working class, its leadership must be largely manned with members of that class and it should be capable of reflecting the actual wishes and opinions of the membership. But the expression of the wishes and opinions of a great mass of individuals is so complex a matter that it can beat the best-intentioned organizer. This fact was perceived by the early theoreticians of the working-class movement, who proposed, though, conflicting solutions.

Typically, the social democratic tradition has always put great emphasis on the need to fill positions of responsibility with actual workers, on a voluntary basis, except for the higher echelons of the representative structures of trade unions, cooperatives, or party, where permanent officers may be employed. It was taken to be evident that the higher stratum of the working class, due to its educational and factory experience, had a greater chance of filling those positions adequately. At the same time, the danger of forming an aristocracy of labor, or a purely bread-and-butter unionism, was also present. The problem was how to make sure that the upper sector of the workers would have a political conscience beyond their professional interests while involving the lower strata, who often "constitute a sort of social ballast, a mass of people incapable of sustaining generous ideals," to use Kautsky's words.[7] From this perspective, both education and the shortening of the workday should have as one of their main effects the liberation of many individuals for political, cultural, and trade union activism. The running of the diverse expressions of the working-class movement requires an immense amount of associationist activity, one of whose tasks is the maintenance of the values and traditions of the movement, the socialization of new recruits, and the control of mass meetings so as to avoid sudden outbursts of enthusiasm or infiltration by rival groups.

An organization of this type has a great tendency to become integrated in the society it is trying to change. Hence, the many left-wing criticisms of social democracy, beginning with those in the anarchist tradition, who pin their hopes on the spontaneity of the masses. As a political program written by Bakunin said, "What we understand by revolution is unleashing what are known as dangerous passions and destroying what the same jargon refers to as 'public order.' We do not fear anarchy, but invoke it, convinced as we are that anarchy, meaning full affirmation of unfettered popular life, must inaugurate liberty, equality, justice." In his rejection of the Germanic meticulousness of the Social Democrats, Bakunin went so far as to recommend that a Russian friend base political work on "the enormous number of vagabonds, both 'holy' and otherwise, ... 'pilgrims' ... thieves and brigands—the whole of that widespread and numerous underground world which, from time immemorial, has protested against State and sovereignty."[8]

Before the turn of the century, the disciples of the various socialist and anarchist currents were already well established in many South American countries, and trade union activity had also started. Some of the anarchist groups were particularly violent, directing their energies not only against the bourgeoisie, but also against rival political groups, notably, the socialists and the more moderate trade unionists.[9] As an early Argentine socialist militant, Enrique Dickman, said, "It was necessary to organize the defense against these perturbing elements, and trade unions and socialist centers organized it. Against the violence of the aggressors the violence of the attacked was opposed, and soon violence stemmed violence."[10]

This new element of "defensive violence" could only complicate the already-complex problem of organizing a representative structure for the activity of the working class. Defense was necessary not only against intervention from the police or from employers' agents, but also from a type of agitational politics that—in the opinion of the Social Democratic leaders—could only lead the movement to suicide if left unchecked.

Not all the anarchists had the same violent tactics; many, particularly those active in trade unions, were familiar with the dangers of agitation and with the unreliability of the socially marginal elements who occasionally gathered around union locals. The presence of the unemployed—who had nothing to lose—packing union meetings where a strike had to be voted, was, in the same vein, decried as detrimental to an effective strategy.[11]

The problem of possibly contradictory tendencies arising between the elected authorities and the masses was, as would be expected, quite present. Anarchists generally tended to consider mass meetings as more representative of rank-and-file feelings, but actually what they were exalting was spontaneity and immediacy rather than representativeness. Among their own ranks some voices could be heard in opposition to this approach,[12] but the main opposition was expressed by Juan B. Justo in *Teoría y práctica de la historia*. In an important passage he described two instances—one in Great Britain, the other in Germany—where a local branch had declared a strike, although the national leadership was opposed. According to Justo, "the irritated proletarian feeling of a section of the union had overcome the experience and the judgment of the organizers of the whole union."[13] In Justo's perspective, this could be solved by a process of continual adaptation and accumulation of experience via internal conflicts controlled by adequate political ability on the part of the leadership. For the leadership, effective representation involved the capacity to oppose—if necessary, strenuously—important sectors of the represented class.

Militants recruited into the movement can be of many different types, not only ideologically but also emotionally.[14] To the extent that a working-class movement becomes more capable of managing its own affairs and sharing in the administration of society, it inevitably multiplies the causes of internal friction, as the difference in perspectives between leaders, activists, and rank and file creates numerous occasions for protest among discontented militants. The possession of a certain bureaucratic machinery, plus its appeal to the mass of passive members against the militants, is one of the leadership's typical resources. Or course, it also needs a certain number of militants on its side. But the usual situation is for militants—who, after all, are aspirants to positions of leadership—to feel rather frustrated about established officers and, therefore, to become a source of internal opposition. Under normal conditions, they are counterbalanced by other, officially oriented, activists and by the bureaucratic apparatus anchored on the passive rank and file.

The Unidad Popular in Chile provided the main example in Latin America of parties based on the resources of the organized urban working class. It had elements drawn from the middle classes, intellectuals and students, but the specifically grass roots, working-class component, with a rather weak bureaucracy, was very strong, if not dominant.[15] The top leadership, as in practically all working-class parties, came from the middle or upper stratum. These were people not strongly rooted in their class of origin. A very different situation is found in parties that, even if enjoying popular support, have incorporated many elements from the upper stratum, most of whom bring with them a clientele. If the bourgeois elements become too dominant (as is the case in Mexico's ruling Partido Revolucionario Institucional), the party ceases to express the political capacity of the popular sectors.

In this context, let us take a look at a group of parties that can play a reformist role and that are capable of getting a majority at the polls, but that cannot be considered a direct expression of the popular classes because of their excessive dependence on groups higher up in the social scale: the Christian Democrats, the Argentine or Chilean Radicales, the Uruguayan Blancos and Colorados, Peru's Acción Popular, and a few others.[16] Typically, these parties find it very difficult to establish strong links with trade union or peasant organizations on a mass scale. (There are some exceptions, notably, the Christian Democrats, who tie up with Catholic unions or peasant groups.) All of these parties can develop a sizable popular following, including sectors of the marginal population and peasants not previously reached by other popular parties, as was the case in Peru for Acción Popular. The strategic components of these parties, however, are the middle, bourgeois, and professional strata, who control the party apparatus and the ideology. With them the party rises or falls, while a party based on the organizational capacity of the masses depends much more on its trade unions, peasant groups, cooperatives, or grass-roots party cells and cultural associations.

This latter group of parties, representing more directly the lower stratum of the population, can be subdivided into four types:

(a) Socialist labor parties. This type could also be called social democratic, using the phrase in its wider meaning and as coined during the time of the First International. But as "social democratic" has come to stand more particularly for the European experience, the more encompassing "socialist labor" is preferable. These are based on the trade unions, plus sectors of the intellectual and middle classes, with intense associationist practices. Examples include Chile's Unidad Popular, Argentina's Socialist and Communist parties before Peronism, Uruguay's Frente Amplio, Brazil's Partido dos Trabalhadores, and Peru's Izquierda Unida.

(b) "Aprista" or middle-class populist parties. These are based on middle-class associationist activity, plus urban or rural trade unions and peasant groups, often held together in a compact organization by charismatic leadership and strong party discipline. Peru's Aprismo is a primary example, having been the first practical experience of this type. The early Mexican Revolution was based on similar support, though not organized as a party at the beginning. Other cases are Costa Rica's Liberación Nacional, Puerto Rico's Popular party, the Dominican Republic's Revolutionary party, Guatemala's Revolutionary party in Arévalo's time, Venezuela's Acción Democrática, Bolivia's Movimiento Nacionalista Revolucionario, and probably the Partido do Movimento Democrático Brasileiro. Argentina's Unión Cívica Radical and Uruguay's Blancos and Colorados at some stage came close, but their trade union element was never very solid.

(c) Social revolutionary parties. These are based on small elites of revolutionaries drawn from various social origins.They have links with peasants and urban proletarians, and weak connections with existing trade union organizations. Examples range from the Cuban to the Nicaraguan revolutionary movements, and also include Guatemalan and Salvadoran counterparts.

(d) "Peronist" or populist labor parties. These are characterized by strong trade union support under *caudillista* rather than associationist leadership, with a weak following among the middle classes and the participation of a small but strategic element from the upper stratum (industrialists, military). The upper-class component and the charismatic leadership differentiate this type from the socialist labor parties, but there are numerous points of convergence, particularly at the electoral level. The main example is Argentina's Peronism, although Brazil's Partido Trabalhista (today's Partido Democrático Trabalhista) has been evolving in this direction since Goulart's time.[17]

Socialist Labor Parties

Either a simplistic evolutionary or a Marxist perspective would hold that the more urbanized, educated, and industrially developed countries are more likely to have political movements based on the resources of the working class. Though they may have some middle-class participation, the bulk of that class will support other, middle-of-the-road or conservative parties. According to this formulation, one might expect Chile, Argentina, Uruguay, and the São Paulo area of Brazil to be cases in point.

We do find Chile falling in line with expectations. Since the beginning of the century, there has been intense working-class activity on the trade union and cooperative and political fronts, with working-class leaders like Luis Emilio Recabarren. This structure, with some ups and downs, continued until the 1973 coup, and will probably reappear if liberalization sets in.[18]

In Argentina the first ten years or so of this century were a period of agitation, violence, and repression for the labor movement, which was strongly influenced by the anarchists. This began to change by the time of the First World War, although a flare-up occurred during the Semana Trágica. This took place in Buenos Aires in 1919, as a result of a strike in a metallurgical plant. It led to violence that was partly spontaneous and partly fanned by the more radical anarchists. The representatives of the main sector of the organized working class in Argentina, the FORA of the IXth Congress, did not align themselves with the violent aspect of the strike.[19] During the twenties, anarchist influence dwindled and was replaced by revolutionary syndicalism, whose followers called themselves simply syndicalists. Revolution ary syndicalists started out as a splinter group of the Socialist party,[20] although they later recruited from among the anarchists. They followed the traditions of the pre–World War I French working-class movement. They believed more in organization than did the anarchists, but did not wish to have anything to do with the non-working-class allies of the unions. They were the sworn enemies of the political wing of the Socialist party and did not think it necessary to replace it with anything else. The unions should prepare to take over society, via a general strike, followed by worker control of industry. There was a certain anti-intellectual, antirationalist and violent trend in their way of thinking, which had in Georges Sorel a non-working-class friend. In practice, syndicalists tended to be quite pragmatic in their dealings with governments; for them it did not make much difference whether they had to confront a businessman, a Radical minister, a Socialist deputy, or a military intervenor. In a sense, it was easier for a syndicalist to become a labor boss, as he did not have above him the control of an ideologically sensitized party apparatus.[21]

The labor movement in Argentina before Perón was not too dissimilar from its European counterparts in Latin countries at similar stages of industrialization or urban and cultural development. This meant a genuine working-class component in the trade unions, very moderately bureaucratized and based on local branch activity,[22] with some rough handling of opponents, but nothing approaching more recent phenomena. In the political parties (Socialist and Communist), the cooperatives, and cultural and press activities, there was a sizable middle-class element—teachers, intellectuals, and others—present. This latter component was probably stronger than in the European cases because of a lower level of industrialization and the greater difficulty of reaching the lower stratum of workers, as well as because of more insecure political conditions, which made organizing more dangerous. It has been claimed that, because of this, the Socialist party really represented the middle classes and that it made no effort to organize beyond the Buenos Aires area and a few other enclaves. However, socialists, anarchists, and syndicalists tried to go to the "interior," but they found the going hard, because of differences in social structure, limited resources at their disposal, and the constraints of their antiauthoritarian ideology.

In the periodical of the Unión General de Trabajadores, a socialist and syndicalist union federation of the first decade of the century, there are interesting comments on the situation in the sugar areas of Tucumán. Gregorio Pinto, a militant from the Socialist party sent by the federation in 1905 to help organize the Cruz Alta section, observed that, because of ignorance, local people "without a 'man to lead them' believe that they can do nothing. . . . A lot of moral force is required to avoid performing the role of monarch of an authoritarian state." He thought that as long as "there are no people to teach them the contempt for idols and a love for the proletariat as a whole, the class struggle will be an unknown article."[23] The syndicalist newspaper *Acción Socialista*, caring little about offending popular feelings, attacked "idols": "The imbecility of the people creates him, and therefore the caudillo cannot but be the prototype of imbecility."[24] In a more philosophical vein, Gregorio Pinto wrote in the *Revista Socialista Internacional* that

we ourselves have unwittingly contributed to the demise of labor organization in Tucumán. With the trade union practices we have learned, we have been incapable of ordering the peons to "go there" or to "remain here." Instead, we have told them: "the membership meeting will decide" . . . "there are no bosses among us" . . . I believe that in so doing I have fulfilled my duty, but I am sorry to say that sugarcane peons continue to be monotheists. Without an idol there is no struggle.[25]

In Chile the labor movement, led by Luis Recabarren, also developed quite early and with a strong emphasis on grass-roots organization. Contrary to the Argentine case, though, political and trade union activity were widespread throughout the country mostly due to the conditions in the mining North, which provided concentrations of working class too large to ignore. Union activity in the North was potentially very dangerous, and it was strongly repressed by the government (reaching a high point during the famous Iquique strike and shootings of 1907). In the small port towns of the north and the larger cities like Santiago and Valparaíso, socialist activity was not so different from the Argentine pattern, with a combination of syndicalist and social-democratic methods, based on artisans, port workers, and middle-class elements trying to establish mutual aid institutions, cooperatives, and a press to complement union and party activities. In the minefields—mostly nitrates, or *salitreras*—a different model had to operate, with more mobilizational traits. *Salitre* workers, although not exactly like Bakunin's marginals, looked more like them than did Juan B. Justo's disciples in Buenos Aires. Perhaps the greater capacity of the Chilean socialist movement to deal with populism by partially coopting it derived from the character of the birthplace of the organization. The social distance between the miners in the north and the organizers from party or union was not so great, perhaps because cultural and ethnic differences were less evident and trade union practices, having been to a large extent generated in the north, were not so alien to some form of *caudillismo*.

It is suggestive to compare the Argentine situation with the one obtaining in Peru, where, at a somewhat later date, the Aprista party was successful in organizing the workers in the sugar estates of the north and in the mining centers of the sierra as well as the popular and middle-class elements in the cities. Its ideology, though, was not socialist, and it appealed largely to the impoverished provincial middle classes. Paradoxically, it was the more middle-class nature of the Aprista party that allowed it to extend its influence over the country, as it provided locally based intermediaries in positions of prestige and capable of translating the central ideology into more comprehensible terms for the masses by appealing to a commonly held cultural tradition. In a sense, the Argentine situation was not underdeveloped enough to allow for this. Militants and organizers had to conform to the norms emanating from a quite secularized and modernized working class living in the large cities, especially Buenos Aires. This mentality had great difficulty in reaching the "interior" or even the lower sectors of the urban working class.

We must now take Uruguay as another case among the "more developed" regions. Beginning early in the century, there was a trade union movement there with socialist, communist, or anarchist leadership, but electorally not very strong.[26] The Frente Amplio, representing these parties plus splinter groups from the traditional parties, has become an important presence in Montevideo since the 1971 elections, but it has much less strength than similar forces in Chile. The concentration of the Uruguayan economy on primary production, mostly wool and cattle, and the lack of large-scale industry or mining are responsible for the difference. We should add the following caveats to our earlier generalization, then: even if there is a sizable urban sector, high levels of education, and numerous secondary or tertiary activities, if they are small scale, the growth of social-democratic or communist parties may be stemmed. They may exist, as in Denmark or New Zealand, but these countries are more industrialized and technologically advanced than Uruguay.

In Brazil, São Paulo must be singled out for attention. If it were not part of a much larger country, one would be on firmer ground in expecting to find a working-class party. Such did not emerge until rather recently, partly because the existence of so many other actors in the rest of the country affected conditions in São Paulo. Internal migration was constantly renewing the composition of the working class, bringing into it people with a very different cultural and political tradition who had the feeling of climbing the social ladder simply by arriving in São Paulo, however badly housed or fed they might have been at the beginning. The internal migrant to Buenos Aires although he or she may also have a feeling of betterment, soon becomes frustrated because of economic conditions that are much less expansive than in Brazil. Furthermore, the standard of living in the Argentine countryside is not as far from what the migrant experiences in Buenos Aires as the corresponding situation in Brazil. This may be changing, however, particularly for migrants who come to São Paulo from the interior of São Paulo state, or from the better-off regions of Minas Gerais, Paraná, and Rio Grande do Sul. But in general in Brazil the difference between the impoverished interior and the growth poles is much greater than in Argentina, and the reservoirs of cheap labor are more numerous. In Argentina there are certainly regions with as low a standard of living as one can find in the Brazilian northeast, but they involve a smaller percentage of the total population and, therefore, of the migrants. Thus, one can expect internal migrants in Brazil to become the base for a populist variety of political structure, with whatever type of leadership, including sectors of the bourgeoisie or the middle classes.[27]

In recent years, however, industrial growth, educational expansion, and the experience of working in new large-scale factories have created a mutational experience: the growth in the greater São Paulo industrial area of new autonomous metallurgical trade unions, which are the base of the Partido dos Trabalhadores (PT).[28] In this party one can already watch the convergence of a trade unionist mentality and student or intellectual groups carrying the Jacobin legacy under various ideological colors. This combination is similar to the one that gave rise to the working-class parties of Chile or of Argentina before Perón.

In Peru we should consider the case of Izquierda Unida, the conglomerate of small leftist parties that, after a long history of divisiveness and electoral ineffectiveness, have come together and mustered a considerable force with strong trade union connections, particularly in the Lima area. The Communist party is one of the members of this alliance, but a major electoral asset is the somewhat personalistic figure of Alfonso Barrantes, mayor of Lima until 1987. He commands a following that is not channeled into any particular party. Our provisional hypothesis—that the more likely areas for the growth of socialist labor parties are the more advanced industrial and urban conglomerations—would not predict the existence of such a phenomenon as Izquierda Unida. Lima is a large city, but its industrial component is not very strong and the standard of living and educational experience of its popular sectors are also low.[29] Izquierda Unida, unlike a typical socialist labor party, shares the mobilizational character of its rival, the Aprista party, as evidenced by its leadership and by the highly radical and revolutionary ideology of several of its component parties—which verbally are almost as violent as the Sendero Luminoso, though they claim to reject its tactics. One might be tempted to think that it should be placed in the social revolutionary group. The situation is in flux, however, as the whole political system is severely affected by economic crisis and guerrilla activity, so the hypothesis should not be discarded out of hand.

A more serious exception to the hypothesis is the fact that, since the inception of Peronism, there has been no major political party in Argentina classifiable as socialist labor. Peronism, however much based on the working-class vote and organization, does have too many other incompatible traits to be classed in this category; it should be considered a populist labor party. The name "populist" refers to its mobilizational traits and to the existence of very important and dominant non-working-class sectors in its composition. Similarly, in Brazil the main inheritors of the Varguista tradition, the PMDB and the reconstituted PDT, under the *caudillista* leadership of Leonel Brizola, cannot be classed as socialist labor, even if some of their leading elements endorse a social-democratic ideology. The PMDB is excessively multiclass based, which may be an adequate response to Brazilian conditions, but puts it in a different category. In our classification, it was suggested that the PMDB might be marginally included in the "Aprista" category, because of its very dominant middle-class component. As for Brizola's *trabalhismo*, it is in a category similar to that of Peronism (populist labor parties), and it is expanding rapidly under a highly charismatic leadership.

"Aprista" or Middle-Class Populist Parties

Are there other workers' parties in Latin America? We may begin by considering the Bolivian Movimiento Nacionalista Revolucionario (MNR) and the whole process of the 1952 Bolivian revolution.[30] As this revolution was quite radical, coming to power through confrontation with the army, and because of the governmental measures it took (nationalization of foreign-owned tin mines, land reform, and the whittling down of the army), it was not uncommon for observers to consider it as the creation of the combined efforts of workers and peasants. It was often heard that the movement was the expression of those classes, but that it lacked the corresponding (socialist) ideology. This explained its shortcomings and hesitations. It soon became evident, though, that to explain the postrevolutionary situation in terms of class support, it was necessary to add at least some sectors of the middle classes and perhaps also the newly formed "national" bourgeoisie as vital pillars of the regime. The MNR party structure should be described as a combined result of the organizational capacities of sectors of the middle classes plus the somewhat less autonomous efforts of the industrial and mining workers, including the much less autonomous peasantry. As for the miners, they developed a very strong union organization, prepared for a violent defense of their acquired rights. Their leadership, though, was quite *caudillista* and for many years, under Lechín, was of the mobilizational type based on the *caudillo*-follower relationship. It shared little of the associationist character of the socialist labor parties of Chile, Argentina, Uruguay, and Brazil.[31] The party's center of gravity was in the more politically experienced middle classes, while the tin miners performed a shock troop role for their allies.

The peasants, only partially active during the insurrection, supported the revolutionary government that gave them land, but afterward remained as a rather easily manipulated element under the various right-wing and military regimes that followed the MNR's overthrow in 1964. Since then, the accumulation of experiences, violent repression and resistance, and the decomposition of the unity of the MNR are changing the picture. The miners and other working-class groups may become a more vital base of support for a revitalized or radicalized Left inside, or more probably outside, the MNR. They may perform a more autonomous role than in the early experience. But the result is likely to be, in terms of social class composition, not too different from what it was at the beginning: a combination of impoverished or downwardly mobile middle classes, intellectuals, workers, and peasants.[32]

If the MNR had remained uninterruptedly in power for much longer, it might have evolved in the Mexican PRI direction, incorporating most of the newly formed sectors of the middle classes and national bourgeoisie while retaining its ideology and the loyalty of the masses. It would have ceased, however, to be an expression of the political capacity of the lower strata, given the enormous weight of the newly created interests that it would have been forced to accommodate.

Most of what has been said, in general terms, about the Bolivian revolution can also be stated about the origins of the Mexican revolution. This was no feat of workers, peasants, and some intellectuals, as many sympathetic observers and actors would have it, but the result of a peculiar combination of the above forces plus elements of the middle classes and regional bourgeoisie, especially from the north.[33] Given the very modest degree of industrialization characterizing the country by the end of the Porfiriato, the revolutionary power had to sponsor the rise of the new middle classes, the bourgeoisie, and the technocrats, all of whom in large numbers joined the ruling party. In the Mexican case, there was less presence of an organized and rather autonomous unionism than in Bolivia, probably because Mexico did not have, proportionately, a full equivalent of the tin mines to create a dominant concentration of industrial or mining workers.[34] It did have old pockets of rural confrontation between Indian and other types of peasant communities and the landholding haciendas, notably in sugar-producing Morelos, the home of the Emiliano Zapata insurgency. The whole system, though, after a decade or so of chaotic events, consolidated under a strongly centralized leadership, leading to the formation of a party of national integration and mobilization, the Partido Revolucionario Institucional (PRI), which partly represents and partly represses the various worker and peasant groups.

Observers do not agree on the extent of PRI support among the masses. Opponents state that the voting majorities it gets are only illusory or forced, if not actually faked. It would appear, though, that the degree of support the party has is higher than that accepted by its opponents, and that there are elements of genuine representation within its ranks. After all, the party, in its long history, has given land to many peasants, nationalized foreign oil companies, and led a process of rapid, if unevenly distributed, economic development. So it should not be surprising to find large segments of the population loyal to it. But the predominance of manipulative and bureaucratic forms of control of popular organization, plus the influence of capitalist and technocratic elements, rules it out as an autonomous expression of the masses, even of the type we are here considering—alliances between the middle classes and the workers and peasants.

One may wonder whether the conglomeration of interests incorporated within the PRI can last for much longer, or whether some forces are at work that may divide the dominant party in two (Right and Left), or whether, outside its ranks, a new political formation of the socialist labor or middle-class populist variety will be created. In the 1988 elections a splinter group of the PRI, under the personalist leadership of Cuauhtémoc Cárdenas, has obtained a sizable following, but opposition parties on the Left are quite weak. It is sometimes argued that this is due to the repressive atmosphere surrounding any independent organizational effort, once it transcends university or intellectual circles. The argument is not very convincing, though. Social forces work in a very pervasive way and, short of extreme totalitarian suppression, should create oppositional parties when conditions are conducive, these conditions being the result of class conflict, forms of industrial concentration, and the like, and not a function of the police. There are many historical instances of popular parties (beginning with the German Social Democratic one in Marx's own time, and following with the MNR of Bolivia or Peronism in Argentina) that have weathered very extreme bouts of persecution. Certainly, repression against extremist forms of organization exists in Mexico (as everywhere in Latin America). However, one must also consider the many elements in the social structure that are at work to shape the minds of the mass of the population and make them hesitant to join such extremist organizations; thus, it is not only repression that keeps the latter small and isolated. The character of a possible popular opposition force in Mexico need not be thought of as necessarily extremist. It might have—as is the case in many other Latin American countries—a relatively moderate ideology. Such force has been late in developing in Mexico, not because it was seriously repressed when it showed its head, but rather because the existing government satisfied many of the demands and incorporated many of the interests that that force would represent. This is the peculiar characteristic of that strange political animal, the PRI, a party that, because of the double heritage of a successful revolution and a remarkable record of economic growth, has been able so far to deliver the goods to enough groups to isolate those who would wish to organize themselves independently for more radical objectives. This, of course, is changing, as a result of economic stagnation and continual urbanization.

The Alianza Popular Revolucionaria Americana (APRA) in Peru is the most typical example of the parties we are here examining, based on a combination of lower middle class, intellectuals, organized workers, and peasantry. Peru, to a degree even greater than Bolivia, has important concentrations of mining or agroindustrial workers. They provided the base for an early form of trade union organization, which benefited from the collaboration of a political party whose main strength came from middle-class sources and ideology. Aprismo put a great emphasis on grass-roots organization with trade union, cooperative, mutual aid, cultural, and political areas.[35] In this it was somewhat similar to the early socialist movement in Chile and Argentina. But the cultural and work experience of its constituency being quite different, it had to rely more heavily on middle-class, student, and teacher groups. As there was a vast proletariat, both urban and rural, that could not be reached through associationist activities, a mass element was added to the organization. It was based on the charismatic figure of Víctor Raúl Haya de la Torre, surrounded by a solid group of disciplined subordinates and with some attempt at paramilitary formations among the youth of the party. The ideology was a mixture of social-democratic, Marxist, and liberal values.[36]

The Apristas often tried to infiltrate the armed forces, but they were not very successful. Beginning around 1930 with a radical program and a violent predisposition, they had very serious confrontations with the armed forces and tried all sorts of strategies to come to terms with the conservative establishment. These turns and meanders lost the APRA quite a bit of support and cut off its left wing (APRA Rebelde, which also fed other guerrilla groups during the sixties). The APRA, after weathering the very serious crisis of Haya's death, remains a very important expression of the organizational capacities of the less-prosperous sectors of the provincial middle classes and some working-class segments, including rural and mill workers from the sugar areas and peasants from the Indian communities. In Alan García it has found another charismatic figure to unite its component parts.

The Aprista party has been very much criticized by the Left because of its policy of accommodation rather than confrontation with the dominant classes. This policy started with the Second World War and was intensified during the struggle against Gen. Manuel Odría's dictatorship (1948–1956), and the subsequent support for conservative presidential candidate Manuel Prado. The "treason" of the leaders has been adduced as an explanation for the party's lack of a more successful radical record, but the causes are more likely to be found in its constituent groups' limitations, lack of resources, and tendency to operate defensively. In a sense, APRA has fallen between two stools. It has a radical image—earned during the thirties, when it engaged in terrorism and tried to take power by violent means—so that conservatives and the armed forces do not believe it when it promises moderation. Its own rank and file and other potential sympathizers, on the other hand, are disgusted by the lack of militancy and in large numbers join splinter groups or new leftist parties.

By contrast, Acción Democrática, the Venezuelan equivalent of APRA, has been much more successful. It came about somewhat later than APRA, inspired by a similar ideology and with the same type of backing—oil workers replacing miners, and peasants taking the place of sugar workers.[37] Acción Democrática was never as radical as APRA and it did not pass through a terrorist phase. It was attuned to the mentality of the local middle class, which was more prosperous than the Peruvian one, and it was not associated with a tradition of violence and bloodshed. This enabled the party to come to terms with the conservative establishment and the military; that is, it did early what the Peruvian Apristas had attempted and apparently only achieved in the eighties after strenuous efforts.

It accordingly lost some of its more enthusiastic members in the process, its left wing forming the Movimiento de Izquierda Revolucionaria, from which guerrilla groups emerged in the sixties. But the reforms Acción Democrática enacted as a result of being in office, plus the oil-induced economic growth, consolidated its support and now democracy is quite well established in Venezuela. The party enjoys the support of a majority of working-class unions and peasant groups, and it alternates in power with the Christian Democratic COPEI. Though the latter at times appears to have programs of a similar or more reformist hue, the two differ in that Acción Democrática has a greater anchorage among the organized sectors of the popular classes.

To this extent, Acción Democrática is an example of the political organizations we have termed "middle-class populist," to refer to their main traits. The presence of the organized working class and peasant groups as the backbone of these parties is what separates them from those, like COPEI itself, Acción Popular of Peru, or the Chilean Christian Democrats, which lack similar support. Acción Democrática might have developed along the Mexican PRI lines had it monopolized power for long. As this did not happen, the party does not seem to be evolving in that direction. There is an effort on the part of both major parties in Venezuela, though, to recruit adherents wherever possible, and even the support of industrialists and other wealthy groups is not shunned. As the more extreme left wing of Acción Democrática has long been dissociated from it, the ideological pressures against this type of development are less intense than they might have been otherwise. Acción Democrática, though avoiding the PRI syndrome, might evolve in the direction of the American Democratic party, thus including not only the middle classes and the masses within its organization, but also important and influential capitalist groups. As long as it retains its trade union and peasant components, which are quite autonomous and based on grass-roots support renewed in free elections, it can be included as a political expression of the popular classes. It would become a borderline case if the bourgeois component were dominant. If the party lost its trade union and peasant sectors, of course, it would change its nature, becoming more like the Argentine or Chilean Radicales or Christian Democrats, or Peru's Acción Popular: middle-class parties bent on reform, but without much organized support among unionized workers and peasants and therefore a very different sort of political animal.[38]

Whenever there is a weakening, disappearance, or transformation of a middle-class populist party, its place tends to be taken by a more radical, social revolutionary variant on the left. Though conditions may not be ripe (that is, developed, industrialized, urbanized) enough for a social-democratic experience, they might allow for a social-revolutionary outcome, which does not necessarily thrive under conditions of high economic and social development, but rather the opposite.

Social-Revolutionary Parties

During the fifties, Cuba might have been thought to be in a situation not too dissimilar from Venezuela's or Peru's, at a middle stage of development and with a large concentration of unionizable workers in the sugar fields and mills. A party enjoying some form of popular support, the Revolucionario Auténtico of Ramón Grau San Martín and Carlos Prío Socarrás had developed along the lines of middle-class populism, although probably with too much corruption and participation by capitalist sectors.[39] It too did not have the prestigious historical record and economic growth achievements of the PRI. Far from it, the Cuban economy was stagnating.[40] Under these conditions, the party broke down. This allowed the development of a populist experience under Fulgencio Batista, which was a stunted variety of Peronism, or, rather, Rojas Pinillismo or Odriismo, a type to be treated more in depth in the next section. But the Batista experience also failed in arousing the masses, which showed a very high level of political indifference. The Communist party did have some support among them, though conditions did not seem ripe for a consolidation of socialist labor parties after the Chilean pattern. Finally, the general crisis led to the emergence of Fidelismo, as the first successful social-revolutionary movement in the continent to evolve along clearly Marxist-Leninist lines. Fidelismo, by the time Castro came to power, had not built much of an urban base and, even among the peasants, its organization was of the armed, clandestine variety.[41] So it cannot really be compared with mass movements that have had time to develop an extensive organization while in opposition.

The Cuban Revolution and the system of government it inaugurated cannot be understood as being mainly the result of the political struggles of workers or peasants, plus a few intellectuals or Jacobin leaders. Considerations similar to those made for the Bolivian and Mexican cases apply here. However, the middle classes participated to a much smaller degree in this case, and many of their members soon clashed with Fidel Castro.[42] Those middle-class groups represented what may be termed the "Aprista" component in the Cuban Revolution. But the revolutionary struggle was too intense to appeal to most of the middle class, and radicalization within the ranks of its remaining supporters was inevitable.

The people who join radical revolutionary movements can be differentiated from those who support the Aprista middle-class populist parties by the intensity of their alienation and frustration with the dominant system. The more intense traits of the political struggle (generally under conditions of very harsh dictatorship of the Batista or Somoza type) act as a sieve, strongly selecting the kind of activists who can withstand the pressures.[43]

The Nicaraguan situation shows some similarities to the Cuban one, except that a large trade union sector did not exist. The revolutionary formula included the Jacobins of various social extractions plus an unstable peasantry in the throes of adaptation to a capitalist growth that unhinged social relations in the countryside.[44] By contrast, in Argentina the social-revolutionary attempt of the Peronist Left (Juventud Peronista and Montoneros) plus other armed guerrilla groups failed, among other reasons, because there was no sizable peasant sector, and the trade union structure was overwhelmingly against the attempt. Of course, the various Argentine governments (both military and right-wing Peronist) repressed violently the revolutionary attempts, the armed forces having a greater degree of discipline and internal cohesion than was available to Batista or Somoza. But the frontal opposition of the dominant moderate Peronist trade union structure was what made the difference. This factor was wrongly estimated by the revolutionary leaders, who expected to be supported by the mass of the working population, the dominant trade union leaders being considered only bureaucrats who did not represent anybody but themselves and a few henchmen. Though old-style Peronist union leaders did have their henchmen and their own private interests, they were capable of a special type of *caudillista* leadership based on their record of struggles for their unions.

"Peronist" or Populist Labor Parties

Parties in this category are mostly based on the lower strata, that is, urban or rural workers and peasants (where they exist). They will, of course, always incorporate some middle-class elements, but the bulk of the middle classes is not included. This differentiates them from middle-class populist, or Aprista, parties. On the other hand, they enjoy relatively more support among some sectors of the upper strata, notably industrialists and the military.

Peronism has this type of structure, notably in the more developed parts of the country.[45] In the less-industrialized provinces, it looks more like Aprismo, as it includes important sectors of the local middle classes with a rural following. As the next chapter will be dedicated to Peronism, here we will consider to what extent the Brazilian parties heir to Varguismo can be classed in this category of populist labor parties.

The more conservative wing of the Varguista tradition, organized since 1945 in the Partido Social Democrático (PSD), later led by Pres. Juscelino Kubitschek, certainly did not follow the populist labor party pattern. As a matter of fact, the predominance of landowner, capitalist, and middle-class elements does not allow the inclusion of the PSD in the larger group of parties based on the organizational capacities of the popular classes. The PSD was an all-encompassing national integration party, capable of supporting a reformist and occasionally nationalist government as Vargas' was, but not deriving its strength from the political initiative of the masses.

The Partido Trabalhista Brasileiro (PTB), where Vargas incorporated his more popular followers, came nearer to having the structure of a populist labor party. Still, during most of the time before João Goulart's presidency (1961–1964), its trade union base was quite flimsy and the degree of autonomy of its leaders, disparagingly nicknamed "*pelegos*" (straw men) was very low.[46]

When existing political parties were dissolved after the 1964 coup, politicians were forced to coalesce into two new and officially sanctioned parties, the Aliança Renovadora Nacional (ARENA), and the Movimento Democrático Brasileiro (MDB). A great part of the PSD (that is, the right wing of the Varguista tradition), who had been alienated by Goulart's radical policies, joined the ARENA, together with the members of the various anti-Vargas conservative groups. The bulk of the PTB and sectors of the PSD formed the opposition MDB.

At the beginning, the MDB did not have much legitimacy among the intelligentsia and other opponents of the regime, because of the severe limitations under which it worked. But with liberalization since the late seventies, it consolidated itself, incorporating trade union organizations and a lot of middle-class support. It evolved in the direction of the Aprista-type middle-class populist parties, although much adapted to local conditions. The great influence of middle-class elements, and also of those deriving from sectors of the bourgeoisie, placed it in a rather borderline situation, like that earlier attributed to the Democratic party of the United States or like that that Acción Democrática might evolve into if it were more successful in getting support from upper-income groups.

The measures taken by the Brazilian government in 1981 that induced the splitting of the opposition set the whole structure ablaze. Although it is not necessary to follow all of the shifts of political cliques, most of the official structure of the ARENA was converted into the Partido Democrático Social (PDS), which encompassed most elements supporting the military regime. The opposition MDB split up, although the bulk of its members joined the Partido do Movimento Democrático Brasileiro (PMDB). On its left the São Paulo–based Partido dos Trabalhadores (PT) was formed. Out of its populist flank Leonel Brizola's personalist Partido Democrático Trabalhista (PDT) appeared, reduced to a couple of federal units, though with prospects of increasing its influence if economic conditions continue to be critical under the PMDB–controlled government of Pres. José Sarney.

The PDT has continued the development of Goulart's *trabalhismo* in the populist labor party ("Peronist") pattern: not-too-autonomous trade unions, weak middle-class support, and charismatic leadership. The PMDB, after having lost its more leftist and populist wings, could have remained quite weakened, but in practice proved to be very well adapted to fight for electoral support under the new democratic conditions in Brazil. It is based mostly on the urban middle classes, with important additions from the intelligentsia, students, and other Jacobin groups. It does have the vote of most of the lower strata, but it is not strong in autonomous working-class organization. One of the main unknowns for the future is its capacity to maintain areas of organized working-class support. If it does, it will have the characteristics of a middle-class populist party, or of a local version of the U.S. Democratic party. If it lost much popular support either to the PT or to Brizolismo, acquiring at the same time more support among the bourgeoisie, it would fulfill a role similar to that of Acción Popular of Peru, COPEI of Venezuela, or the Radicales and Christian Democrats of various countries, that is, bent on reform but not an expression of the organizational capacities of the popular sectors.

To summarize the classification attempted in this chapter, parties based on the active involvement of the workers, peasants, or lower middle classes have been placed into the following categories:

(a) Socialist labor parties, based to a large extent on urban trade unions, with ancillary support form the middle class and intellectual groups and with intensive associationist practices. Cases in point are Chile's Unidad Popular, Argentina's Socialists and Communists before Peronism, Uruguay's Frente Amplio, Brazil's Partido dos Trabalhadores, and, perhaps, Peru's Izquierda Unida.

(b) "Aprista" or middle-class populist parties, dependent on middle-class associationist activity, plus urban or rural trade unions and peasant groups, often bound into a compact organization by charismatic leadership and strict party discipline. The early stages of the Mexican Revolution, Peru's APRA, Venezuela's Acción Democrática, Bolivia's MNR, and Brazil's PMDB are the main examples.

(c) Social-revolutionary parties, deriving their strength from small elites of revolutionaries drawn from various social origins. They have links with peasants and urban proletarians, although weak connections with existing trade union organization. They are prepared for violent action or for exerting power in a postrevolutionary society via the establishment of a new dominant class structure, as in Cuba and Nicaragua.

(d) "Peronist" or populist labor parties, which combine, under charismatic leadership, small but strategic sectors of the upper classes (military, industrialists) and a mass following with a *caudillista* rather than an associationist mode of participation. The main example is Argentina's Peronism, with Brazil's *trabalhismo* evolving in this direction since Goulart's time. Batista, Rojas Pinilla, Odría, Ibáñez, and Pérez Jiménez attempted, without much success, to organize movements of this type.[47]

This list does not include some well-known specimens that, although reformist and quite capable of obtaining electoral majorities, lack strong ties with the organized workers or peasants or exert excessive dominance over those popular organizations. Parties of this type often perform an important role in the consolidation of democracy, but the social composition of their support turns them into the main antagonists of those based on the popular strata, and thus they are sometimes supported by the Right. They are referred to only tangentially in this volume and include the following:

(a) Parties of national integration, which incorporate many social strata, with a very heavy component drawn from the upper or upper middle classes, as in Mexico's PRI and Brazil's Varguista moderate wing, the Partido Social Democrático (up to 1964).

(b) Military reform parties, led by the military and favoring reform. They are often not oriented toward the formation of a political party but perform such a role indirectly, as Peru's Velasco Alvarado military regime, Bolivia's short-lived presidencies of Busch and Toro during the thirties and Torres in the seventies. If successful in forming a political movement, they might have evolved in the Peronist direction.

(c) Middle-class reform parties, differentiated from the middle-class populist parties in that they do not have strong ties with workers' or peasants' organizations. Primary examples are Venezuela's Christian Democrats (COPEI), Peru's Acción Popular, Chile's Christian Democrats and Radicales, Argentina's Radicales, Uruguay's Colorados or Blancos, and Colombia's Liberal party.

8. Early Socialist Organization: The Argentine Case

In chapter 7 we considered the hypothesis that under conditions of greater economic and social development political parties of the socialist-labor type are more likely to be found. The main exceptions to this hypothesis are the United States and Argentina. In the United States it is usually thought that prosperity and social mobility co-opted and moderated the working-class movement and deflected the socialist trends noticeable at the beginning of the century. In reality, not only in the United States but also in Europe labor evolved in a reformist direction. In Europe it retained its socialist values—however revised—while in America the links with the Socialist party were cut and replaced by a special relationship with the Democratic party. The difference in prosperity may explain the outcome, to which one may add the immigrant characteristics of the United States, which produce heterogeneity in the working class. The large size of the country also generates regional capitalist groups at odds with those dominant at the national level, thus adding a criss-cross effect that blurs class lines.[1]

For a capitalist sector to turn against the dominating order, powerful reasons must intervene. These can be of various sorts, not only regional. In many Latin American countries an antagonism against the agrarian exporting interests can be found among industrialists. If at the same time a sizable sector of the working class is recently socially mobilized, a populist alliance is likely and may replace or prevent the formation of a social-democratic movement. Our hypothesis about the appearance of socialist parties in conditions of high economic development must therefore be revised. That tendency does exist, but it is counterbalanced when one or both of the following factors are present:

(1) a sector of the upper stratum, antagonistic to the establishment or insecure in its position, becomes the source of heterodox political behavior among the elites;

(2) a massive and rapid transformation of the working classes affects the existing political culture, facilitating changes in organization, leadership, and loyalties.

The Argentine Peculiarity: The European Immigrant Impact

Argentina belongs to a group of countries—Australia, New Zealand, the United

States, Canada, and Uruguay—and regions—for example, the south of Brazil—that for a long period were considered almost empty and destined to be filled by European immigration. But how does one fill an empty country? And how empty were these countries?

At the time of mass migration, by the mid-nineteenth century, the United States was certainly not empty, but, rather, formed an organized society with solid political traditions and an industrial and military force capable of imposing itself on the international scene. It had, true enough, empty territory, but the newcomers would find there strong political structures to which they would have to adapt as junior partners.

The opposite prevailed in Australasia and the Río de la Plata, but with some differences between the two. Australia and New Zealand were, for all practical purposes, empty, while Uruguay and Argentina were already occupied by a population that had fought for its independence and formed a state. Thus, toward 1820, when settled Australia was little more than a penal colony with some thirty thousand inhabitants,[2] Argentina (excluding Paraguay, the Alto Perú, or the Banda Oriental, which only nominally formed part of the new nation) already had more than five hundred thousand.[3] Canada was in an intermediate situation between the United States and Australasia.[4] But both in Australasia and Canada, the human transfer took place under British institutional control, and the great majority of immigrants were British nationals. Thus, during their formative period these nations had a sizable quantity of immigrants, but few foreigners.

In the three cases, almost all immigrants came from the British Isles, which means that they retained their nationality; the voyage to Australia, New Zealand, or Canada was like an internal migration, a transfer to a far-off, somewhat autonomous province of one's own country. Political and civil rights, habits, and way of life were retained, with only the logical adaptations due to labor scarcity and other cultural traits. No doubt, the cost of the return trip made a difference. A new nationality was in the making, but very gradually, within the limits marked by the colonial power, which, rather than dominating a foreign country, was extending the boundaries of its own nation and preparing for a slow and not too conflictive future separation. The social, political, and national development of countries such as Australia, New Zealand, and Canada took place, thus, as a part of the expansion of the mother country in new lands. The result was not the amalgam of two societies, of two cultures, of two forms of life; it was, rather, a mutation, under favorable conditions, of a part of the British population under the institutional control of the metropolis, one of the more advanced societies of its time.[5]

The situation was very different in the Río de la Plata and the south of Brazil. There the *criollos*, practically independent since about 1810, were already developing their nationalities. After an authoritarian period, represented in Argentina by Rosas, a modernizing, liberal, and often anticlerical elite was formed, which tried to "Europeanize" the country by bringing massive numbers of immigrants from overseas. The mixing of the new with the old populations and its dominant social

Table 3.
Percentage of Population by Birthplace

	Australia[a]			New Zealand[a]			Canada		
	1871	1901	1921	1891	1901	1921	1871	1891	1901
Native born	61.2	77.2	85.2	58.6	66.8	74.4	83.0	86.6	87.0
Other Australasian		0.7		2.6	3.5	3.9			
British Isles & possessions	38.8	18.0	12.5	35.6	27.1	20.1	14.0	9.9	7.3
Other (foreigners)		4.1	3.3	3.2	2.6	1.6	3.1	3.5	5.7
Total immigrants	38.8	22.8	16.5b	41.4	33.2	21.7	17.1	13.4	13.0

Sources: Census of the Commonwealth of Australia, 1921, vol. 2: 62, 92; *Official Yearbook of the Commonwealth of Australia*, 1901–1911, p. 121; Ministry of Supply and Services, Immigration Division: *Immigration Statistics* (Ottawa, 1978); *Interamerican Statistical Yearbook*, 1942, p. 116; *Census of the Dominion of New Zealand*, 1921, part 2: 13; *Official Yearbook of New Zealand*, 1914, p. 118; *Reports of the Immigration Commission: The Immigration in Other Countries* (U.S. Senate, 61st Congress, Document 761, 1911).
[a]Aboriginal population not included.
bSupposing a percentage of "other Australasians" equal to that in 1901.

system, however, proved to be more difficult than expected. The arrival of an enormous mass that was not only immigrant but also foreign created special political and social problems. For the traditional elites to maintain control of the process would have demanded a capacity that they did not have. The result was a Babel, a prosperous and commercial Carthage that did not know how to govern itself, to adopt the metaphors of the day. At some moments it seemed that immigration, far from creating a cultivated population adapted to the formation of a modern country where work and property would be respected, would be the source of violent solutions of various signs. The nationalist reaction against the danger of being flooded by the tide from overseas was not late in coming.

The size of the tide can be seen by contrasting the situation of the Río de la Plata countries with that of Brazil, Chile, and the United States. The special situation of Argentina can be seen in table 4. The proportion of foreigners was the highest, practically double that for the United States during the formative period around the turn of the century. In Uruguay the number of foreigners was very high (higher than in Argentina) around 1880, as a result of the particularly empty character of that country and the fact that much immigration had concentrated in Uruguay when conditions were not very favorable in Argentina under Rosas' government. But proportions for Uruguay fell for the new century to levels similar to those of the United States.

A comparison with table 3 shows that the total percentage of immigrants for Australia and New Zealand was similar, or even higher, than for Argentina. But, as already seen, they were not foreigners, the number of whom, by contrast, was minimal. Canada had proportions close to those of the United States for immigrants, but mostly from the British Isles, and therefore not foreigners. The United States,

Table 4.
Percentage of the Population by Birth Place, Selected Countries

	Argentina			Uruguay		Brazil	Chile	United States		
	1869	1895	1914	1879	1908	1910	1907	1870	1890	1910
Native born	87.9	74.6	70.1	69.0	82.6	94.6	95.9	85.8	85.5	85.5
Foreigners	12.1	25.4	29.9	31.0	17.4	5.4	4.1	14.2	14.5	14.5
(Italians)	4.1	12.5	11.9	—	—	—	—	0.0	0.3	1.4

Sources: National Censuses, 1869, 1895, 1914 (Argentina); *Anuario estadístico de la República Oriental del Uruguay*, Dirección General de Estadística, 1890, book 7, p. 12; *Síntesis de estadísticas de la República Oriental del Uruguay*, 1927, p. 5; *Annuaire Statistique du Brésil*, 1916, p. I:xvi; *Interamerican Statistical Yearbook*, 1942, p. 118; *Censo general de la Población de Chile*, 1895; p. IV:463; *Censo de la República de Chile*, 1907, p. xix; U.S. Bureau of the Census, *Immigrants and Their Children* (Washington, D.C., 1927), pp. 5–7.

like Argentina, did have many foreigners, not only immigrants, but their proportions were much lower and their position in the social stratification pyramid was different.

In summary, it can be said that (1) Argentina had one of the highest percentages of immigrants, double that of the United States and Canada, and similar to that of Australia and New Zealand, but (2) in Australia and New Zealand, the great majority of immigrants were British and therefore not foreigners; the same was true for Canada; therefore, (3) the numerical impact of foreigners was, for Argentina (and at times in Uruguay) the greatest, creating a situation totally different from that of Australia and New Zealand and, for other reasons, also different from that of Chile and Brazil. More similar to Argentina and Uruguay was the United States, but with only half the percentage of foreigners; (4) the qualitative influence of foreigners in Argentina and Uruguay was more destabilizing to the local social system than in the United States, because the institutional and political force of the latter was far greater and therefore could absorb the impact better.

The Problems of the Amalgam

The majority of those who were to be amalgamated into Argentine society were Italians, especially from northern Italy. For various reasons, the trans-Atlantic Italian current favored South America at first. In North America, even if the expansion of the economy promised future prosperity, it was necessary to compete with many others who were already established, like the Irish, Germans, Nordics, and Jews. Among foreign communities in the United States the status of Italians was not high, due as much to their low educational levels as to ethnic prejudice.[6] The Italians, because of the difference in language and other cultural traits, remained at the lower end of the pyramid, especially in contrast with the native born, already experienced in business, education, political, and trade union fields. The Italians in North America were considered bad unionists and were often used as strike breakers. It was not easy for them, particularly in the East, to have access to land. They remained concentrated in the Little Italies, where the Mafia rather than the trade union dominated.[7]

In contrast, in South America the relative lack of North European immigration left more space for the Italians and other South Europeans. The comparison with the Argentine natives of the lower and lower-middle strata favored them, because of the locally low level of education and due to ethnic prejudice. Immigrants, even if poor and without technical training, formed part of the aristocracy of the skin, more obviously in Brazil, but also in the Río de la Plata.

Foreigners were flooding the prosperous parts of Argentina. Although throughout the country they formed somewhat less than a third, in the cities like Buenos Aires and Rosario they were more than half; if only young adult males are considered, the percentage is even greater.[8] Among the ruling circles who watched this phenomenon, the perception was that "half our population" was foreign, which exaggerated the statistical facts but reflected accurately the situation in the more important centers of the country. It was thought that this tendency would continue indefinitely and create special problems if these foreigners did not become citizens or were not educated in national values.

Foreigners, with few exceptions, did not adopt Argentine citizenship, in contrast with what happened in the United States. There are several reasons: in the *criollo* ruling class not everybody was enthusiastic about facilitating citizenship; in the foreign communities, there were also those who did not favor it and considered it an abandonment of the homeland.[9] Beneath these attitudes there was a structural fact, that is, the relative lack of force and prestige of the Argentine state in comparison with the ethnic community of origin. In the United States the country's government and institutions, despite their occasional corruption, were seen clearly as having more force, prestige, and capacity to protect than the European consulates. The opposite happened in the Río de la Plata and Latin America in general, because of the scant development of the rule of law in these latitudes. For the foreigner it was better to retain his or her nationality and thus the protection of the consulate, rather than to try to share the benefits and guarantees Argentine institutions were supposed, but did not, confer on the citizens.

In short, immigrants felt superior in the scale of ethnic prestige to the nation in which they lived, particularly in comparison with the majority of the local popular classes and also with the few participants in the *política criolla*, with its *caudillos* and electoral violence. A local consolidated and respected middle class was either lacking or too weak, due to the country's embryonic industrial, technological, and educational development. Also lacking was the associationist activity that had so impressed Tocqueville in his North American tour. According to the modernization project of the elite, all this was going to be provided by the immigrants themselves, under the guidance of the patricians.

To complicate matters, a wave of violence shook the European working-class movement, mostly in southern Europe, in the last decade of the nineteenth century. The philo-Europeans of yesteryear began to be afraid of a dying Europe that, in crisis, threatened to send to America its worst elements. Many came, with bomb in hand, or so it seemed. Well-known intellectual anarchist leaders crossed the ocean, as did more obscure militants.

For the young Joaquín V. González, who wrote a university thesis entitled "Revolution" in 1885, it was necessary to educate the people to avoid a fate similar to that of the Roman Empire, a victim of praetorianism. Reforms and the development of the spirit of association were the remedy for revolutions.[10] In his maturity, a minister during Roca's second presidency, he tried to establish an important electoral reform, with secret voting and single-member constituencies, to facilitate the representation of minorities and occupational groups that might be concentrated in a given locale.[11] Toward the end of his life, writing in 1920, he regretted that Argentina did not have, like so many other societies, "the degree of culture which would allow it never to lose the solidary, ethnic and national bonds."[12]

Education was a very important aspect of the formation of the "solidary, ethnic and national bond." The support given to education by Argentina's conservative liberal regimes must be seen as aiming not only at instruction, but at the nationalization of students, in particular, to counterbalance the effects of the education administered by the immigrant groups themselves. Foreign-language schools were very common and became the motive of important debates. Italian mutualities often maintained their own schools. In 1881 an Italian Pedagogic Congress was held and produced a polemic with Sarmiento, who attacked the divisionism introduced by foreign-language schools. The following year President Roca's government organized another official Pedagogic Congress, to prepare public opinion for the adoption of free, secular, and compulsory education.

As has been mentioned, foreigners, particularly southern and eastern Europeans, found themselves in the Río de la Plata in a social position quite higher, in comparison with natives, than in the United States. This facilitated their mixing with the nationals. From the point of view of social assimilation, it can be said that the amalgam was more successful in South America than in North America. The lack of ethnic ghettoes—by comparison with the United States and Canada—is an indicator of the greater ease of assimilation, which quickly dissolved the first congregations of overseas communities. The latter had good opportunities of social mobility via commerce, artisan work, and industry, and—though to a somewhat lesser degree—through farming. Ownership of land was very restricted in Argentina, and several attempts at establishing an equivalent of the Homestead Laws never succeeded. But a great number of immigrants became tenants of small and medium farms, and others benefited from colonization schemes in the provinces of Santa Fe, Entre Ríos, and part of Córdoba. The situation in the United States was not much better for South and East Europeans, because, even if land was more subdivided, in most cases it was already occupied by the time they arrived. As a consequence, the most capable agriculturists among the Italian emigrants (from the north of the peninsula) came to the Río de la Plata because there they could better apply their skills. This is one of the reasons for the greater percentage of northern Italians in Argentina than in the United States and also helps explain the higher status of the Italian community in the Río de la Plata.[13]

The social amalgam, therefore, was for most immigrants a success. In the case of the political amalgam, however, things were different. Not that in the southern European countries participation was very high, but there were minorities that got involved in political action. It was for their equivalents among the immigrants that intervention in Argentine affairs was more difficult. Even so, numerous groups of foreigners, of various nationalities, sought a role in local political life or were forced to get involved in defense of their interests. Thus, for example, settlers in the province of Santa Fe, mostly Swiss and German, participated in the Radical revolution of 1893.[14] Among Italians, Mazzini's and Garibaldi's influence, very strong among the firstcomers, also led them to political and even armed involvement, part adventurous and part mercenary.[15]

The Early Intellectuals of the Labor Movement

The trade union movement was largely formed in Argentina by foreigners, as could not fail to be the case, given the demographic composition of the country. In this there is a vivid contrast with the situation in the United States, where trade unionism was based principally on the native born, though also integrating the immigrants. In Argentina—and in Uruguay—immigrants from the European South were the main source of labor in the urban and prosperous rural areas, and they engaged in trade unionism as an expression of their own interests. The native labor force, of *criollo* origin, in the places where it dominated, like the sugar industry of Tucumán, did not participate in the trade union experience until much later, with only few exceptions.

For the immigrants, unionism was a way to defend their standard of living without being citizens. For many there were also ideological motivations of an anarchist or socialist type. An important minority existed with intellectual or journalistic training; from the beginning it was active in Argentina. It enjoyed a sort of captive audience among compatriots who in the Old Country probably would not have paid attention to its message because of ignorance, lack of opportunity, or a "know nothing" attitude. In Argentina this mass, however unwillingly, had experienced something new: social mobilization, anomie, the break with traditional figures of authority (the priest, the *padrone*, the chief of the extended family) and with the certitudes of life in a small village. This situation made them more prepared to listen to new messages. But there was still some difficulty in accepting ideas so opposed to those they held before migrating. These same ideas, expressed by an Argentinian activist, surely would not have had much impact on their minds or their hearts. But when they heard them from someone coming from the Old Country, there was a world of difference. And, given the type of immigration, the majority of popular intellectuals or ideologues belonged to the Left; they were at the very least republicans, very seldom Catholics. The influence that the new ideologies might have had in the Río de la Plata socioeconomic milieu was reinforced a hundred times through the fact that they became almost national traits for immigrants. To support those doctrines became a form of consolidating one's self-image, so dramatically deteriorated during the voyage to America.

To this was added for the Italians their peculiar kind of nationalism, which had certain revolutionary, and no doubt anticlerical, traits. The role of the Mazzinians is very important in this sense, and their campaign for a certain type of "petty bourgeois" socialism, or radical socialism, antedates by at least fifteen years the formation of the Socialist party, which, though more leftist in theory, in practice occupied a not too different position in the political spectrum.[16] Other foreign groups were also spreading socialist principles, like the Germans of the Club Vorwaerts, and beginning in 1890 Avé Lallemant, also of German origin, expounded Marxist social democracy from the weekly *El Obrero*.[17]

Anarchists were dominant in the working-class movement until about 1910; their influence declined afterward, especially after the First World War, even though they were active in the Semana Trágica of January 1919 and the strikes in Patagonia in 1922. Among the anarchists were leaders from Europe who functioned as organic intellectuals of the working class. Anarchists did not have too much success in conquering the native Argentine intelligentsia, even if there were exceptions, like Leopoldo Lugones, who published *La montaña* with José Ingenieros, and the more permanent support of Alberto Ghiraldo, director of the artistic, literary, and political fortnightly *Ideas y Figuras*. This organic link between the working class and an intellectual group that often maintained a standard of living like that of the lower classes, that is, as typographers, artisans, or petty employees, was consolidated by the common ethnic identity, in the restricted national sense or in the wider one of European origin. This organic link, however, did not extend to the rest of the native working class, which, admittedly, did not possess many of the economic, cultural, and environmental conditions for the development of class consciousness. The abyss that separated them from the organized foreign workers made their evolution in a socialist or anarchist sense difficult; those were *"cosas de gringos."*

The Socialist party, in contrast with the anarchists, had more solid links with those sectors of the citizenship that participated in elections, probably because its ideology was more easily understood by certain petty bourgeois elements—teachers, artisans, and the like. Electorally, socialism was very successful right after the Sáenz Peña law guaranteed access to the ballot boxes in 1912. Obviously, the anarchists could not, following their doctrine, compete in this area. The majority of the urban working class, being foreign, did not participate in the elections. The anarchist propaganda of ignoring elections coincided with the immigrants' natural diffidence toward the institutional and political system of the country. The few foreigners who took up citizenship, and a great part of the potentially leftist public of the city of Buenos Aires, however, voted for the Socialist party. This electoral orientation became more credible after the Sáenz Peña law, that is, after 1912, coinciding with the decline of the anarchists.

The Early Argentine Political Party System

Even if the identities of parties were not clear during the formative era of modern Argentina, and even if their characteristics often were too personalistic, some traits can be discerned. Beginning in the 1870s, an establishment government coalition was progressively formed, which in 1880 became the Partido Autonomista Nacional (PAN), afterward simply Nacional. It was sometimes divided by personalities but generally it represented the stronger elements of government available in the country.

For a long time, PAN's main opposition was Mitrismo, first as the Liberal party and then as Unión Cívica.[18] This party, based in the province and, above all, the city of Buenos Aires, had wielded power during Mitre's presidency (1862–1868), but had lost it at the hands of a coalition of provincial interests that became progressively more conservative, even if anticlerical and modernizing. Mitre, with quite a strong local base among the petty bourgeoisie, both native and foreign, and among commerce in general, could have returned to power as the leader of a strong liberal movement.[19] Equilibrium between the rather conservative party of Julio A. Roca (the PAN) and the more liberal and popular party of Bartolomé Mitre would have resulted in a classical European scheme.[20] In Chile something like this existed, facilitating the process of alternation in power and extension of popular participation and democracy. Why not in Argentina?

In Argentina parties did not have adequate organic connections with the possessing classes. The PAN, even if conservative and favorable to the interests of the oligarchy, was too much in the hands of *caudillos* and their electoral *comités*, which mobilized marginal sectors of the population during elections in order to intimidate their adversaries. As Tulio Halperín Donghi has remarked, Sarmiento complained about the "property owners'" lack of control over the ruling party.[21] If one were to read Sarmiento literally, it would seem that the PAN was a sort of populism *avant la lettre*. This would be a mistake, because Roca's followers' manipulation of elements from the underworld was only a peripheral part of his strategy. It was not a mobilizational politics appealing to the masses as, under the conditions of a previous era, was the political formula of Juan Manuel de Rosas and other provincial *caudillos*.

But the use of the elements from the *comités*, even if not properly speaking mobilizational, was necessary because of the propertied classes' lack of direct involvement. One could say that the government performed the role of a *condottiere*, to whom the dominant classes delegated the defense of the political aspects of their interests, without asking about the details.

The weak organic connections between political leaders and their constituencies were also present in Mitrismo, even if its leaders were more capable of putting a crowd in the street, as was shown in 1890. The greater part of the bourgeoisie and petty bourgeoisie, being foreign born and without citizenship, was poor support for any party that might have represented them. In the more prosperous region of the country, the proletariat and a large part of the private white-collar employees were also foreign and therefore not very closely and organically related to political parties.

Not that the bourgeoisie and the proletariat, that is, the foreigners, were totally outside the political system. Some links existed, as could not fail to be the case, because such a large and resourceful group could not remain totally outside the political arena, to which they had to accede to defend their interests. It is, however, necessary to distinguish among different forms of political participation:

(1) violent protest in extreme cases, which includes taking part in armed movements and civil strife, as in 1880, 1890, and 1893, or in general strikes like those at the beginning of the century, or the Semana Trágica, or the events in Patagonia in 1922. In all of these cases, there was a lot of foreign participation;

(2) organization in defense of economic interests, which ranged from the forma-

tion of labor unions to industrial or commercial chambers, where foreigners were also quite active. Curiously, foreign businesspeople were less successful than trade unionists in this area. Given their resources, one might have expected a more developed and united commercial and industrial representation structure. It would seem that the higher one went on the social scale, the less motivation existed for reactive participation, surely the dominant type in movements of violent protest, and the more possible it became to concentrate on the administration of one's own affairs, leaving class affairs in professional hands;

(3) support and participation in a political or ideological movement, a much more complex level than the other two. There are several forms of participation and various possible motivations, conscious and otherwise. In general, one can say that between a certain class and a political movement there is a circulation of elites, a mutual interchange of experiences, ideas, and resources, economic or cultural. This circulation—symbolized by the link between class and organic intellectual in the Gramscian conception—was obstructed in a society where such a large part of the more strategic social classes were foreigners. National politics, particularly electoral politics, was "*cosa de criollos.*" The main economic forces, the social classes characteristic of the modern country, remained outside and did not become involved. As a result, the native sector—landowners, military, public employees, popular marginals—operated to some extent in a social vacuum; it did not receive enough inputs and controls from the rest of society.

If this analysis is correct, several consequences can be deduced:

(1) conservative parties had apparently "populist" traits, because their *criollo* character made it difficult for them to recruit support among social classes with a more bourgeois mentality, particularly outside the landowners;

(2) liberal parties (Unión Cívica, Mitristas), whose support should have been the bourgeoisie or the middle class, were weak because of the foreign character of their potential constituency, with which they could not build organic connections;

(3) for similar reasons the moderate socialist and radical-socialist currents were never very strong; even if the Socialist party tried to represent this ideological sector, it did not do it with conviction and could not consolidate its human bases, which to a large extent were also foreign;

(4) rather than a liberal party (for the bourgeoisie and a sector of the middle classes) or a radical-socialist one (for the lower middle class and labor), a populist movement became dominant, based on the *criollo* sectors of the population (the Unión Cívica Radical). This party, lacking organic connections to the majority of the bourgeoisie, remained populist and personalist. It was not leftist enough to obtain trade union support, but it was too mobilizational to consolidate its bases among the more prosperous bourgeoisie, which, being foreign, could not control it. From its beginning, the Radical party had more moderate sectors, in tune with the mentality of the established bourgeoisie, but they were systematically pushed aside by the leadership during the period under consideration.

The System under Threat and the Nationalist Reaction

Between 1890 and 1920, not only the political but also the social system of Argentina was quite threatened by possible internal revolutionary commotions. The human mass that filled the city of Buenos Aires and a large part of the Pampa region was of a very peculiar type because of its lack of roots, personal and family instability, and therefore potential violence. Emigration was a trauma of a magnitude difficult to conceive, particularly during the first years of each individual's experience. This concentrated mass, socially mobilized, in a state of availability, is the classical component for agitation, violence, and combinations of all sorts, of a populist or revolutionary type. It may not have had the conditions that an orthodox Marxist interpretation requires for a triumphant revolution. But rebellions in periods of low industrialization are much more dangerous than those hypothesized by Marx for advanced industrial societies. The fears of the dominant Argentine classes, continuously expressed by their more varied intellectual and political representatives, were not pure paranoia.

The revolutionary menace at the beginning of the century had two components, namely, (1) sectors of the native middle or upper middle classes not adequately incorporated into the system of domination, which was too oligarchical and exclusive. These groups expressed themselves through the Radical party; and (2) the popular mass, mostly immigrants, subject to anarchist influence and ready for violence. These components are not too different from those that started the Mexican Revolution in 1910. *Mutatis mutandis*, Francisco Madero is the equivalent of the native middle and upper middle classes, that is, the Radicales; Emiliano Zapata and the other agrarian leaders might be equivalents of Argentina's immigrant mass. If the political system did not open up, the continuation of the rebellions and conspiracies of the Radical party, which erupted or were attempted every two or three years, would end up by igniting the fuse. The working-class movement and the anarchists did not sympathize very much with the Radicales, but it was impossible to foretell what would happen if by chance one of those Radical revolutions were to last a bit longer, starting a civil war and a frantic search for allies. The ideological convictions of the anarchists, which led them to refuse collaboration with the Radicales, were, ironically, a defense against the above possibility.

But could one rely on this guarantee? According to the example of the Mexican Revolution, no, because of the strong collaboration of several anarchist groups with the revolutionary process.[22] More than the purity of anarchist or socialist convictions, the revolutionary combination was made more difficult by the massively foreign condition of one of its elements.

The social distance between the two possible components does not mean that there were no cases of participation of foreigners in the activities of the Radical party. The "farmers in the revolt" of Santa Fe in 1893 have been mentioned, and there was another very important instance, in 1912, when an agrarian strike was organized throughout Santa Fe and Buenos Aires by tenant farmers, mostly

Italians.[23] This strike was strongly supported by the Radical party, which had just won the government of the province.

Antiforeign components in the Radical party, however, were very pointedly represented by Senator José Camilo Crotto, who tried to block the election of the Socialist Enrique del Valle Iberlucea in 1913 by arguing in Congress that it was the result of a foreign plot. Del Valle Iberlucea counterattacked by regretting that the initial orientation of the Radical party in Leandro Alem's time (when Lisandro de la Torre also belonged to the party), which favored foreigners, had changed under Hipólito Yrigoyen into a xenophobia.[24]

The nationalist reaction affected large sectors of the Argentine political spectrum, especially the armed forces, landowners, and intellectuals connected to the native upper classes, like Leopoldo Lugones, Ricardo Rojas, and Manuel Gálvez.[25] A great part of the modernizing elite progressively abandoned its liberal convictions and supported various forms of authoritarianism. Lugones himself is an example, as are Gen. José F. Uriburu, Carlos Ibarguren, and others who ended up as supporters of fascism.

An important expression of this nationalist reaction was the formation of civilian armed groups during the Semana Trágica in January 1919. The Asociación del Trabajo was created to watch over trade unionism, and the Liga Patriótica was constituted as a paramilitary mass movement. A few years later, the revolution of 1930 represented the arrival to power of those elements, but still mixed with many liberal-conservative components, who only wanted a temporary corrective to the excesses of the second Yrigoyen presidency.

During the military government of José F. Uriburu (1930–1932) and the early part of Gen. Agustín P. Justo's presidency (1932–1938), the repression of the working-class movement forced the Confederación General del Trabajo (CGT) leaders to follow "apolitical" lines, as did the syndicalists and some socialist trade unionists.[26] The latter had a difficult relationship with their party, which insisted on controlling union leaders, increasingly in command of important resources. The Italian experience was there to show that a certain number of union leaders, both socialist and syndicalist, under stressful conditions, had gone over to fascism.[27] The case of socialists from various social origins joining fascism was not uncommon in those days. Oswald Moseley, in Great Britain, was a well-known example.

In 1935 a reorganization of the CGT was undertaken, as a result of a sort of internal coup engineered by the socialists and their loyal railway unions. The syndicalists were set aside and slowly withered away as an organization, although their philosophy did not disappear. In their resentment against the Socialist party or the growing Communists, they were fertile ground for new political alliances or unorthodox combinations.[28]

In Chile during the Ibáñez dictatorship (1927–1931), particularly at the beginning, some sectors of the labor movement also tried to get something from the new order, which had promised to break the deadlock created by parliamentarianism. That first wave of Ibañismo having passed, the labor movement reemerged under socialist and Communist leadership and perpetuated in the Frente Popular, which came to office in 1938. A similar strategy was under way in Argentina during the early forties, with great possibilities of success. An Unidad Democrática was being organized with all main parties from the Radicales to the Left, excluding, therefore, mainly the ruling Conservatives, who maintained themselves in power by rigging the elections. With the wave of democratization that would surely follow the end of the war, a peaceful change toward democracy and social reform might get under way. This was not to happen as expected, though, as the political and social map of the country was changing too fast.

9. Mass Organization and the Rise of Peronism

During the Second World War Mexico, Brazil, and Argentina, because of a qualitative change in industrialization, were ripe for a transition to large-scale trade unionism. Of these, Argentina had the highest level of urbanization and education and the largest industrial base relative to its population, so the process there could be expected to be particularly intense. This type of change, which has happened at different speeds in different countries, is often accompanied by alterations in ideology. When the evolution is slow, the results are less radical, as was the case in Great Britain. Even there, however, in the 1890s there was a certain discontinuity. This led to the so-called new unionism, which reached to the lower strata of the laboring population. The new unions were oriented more toward socialism than were the older unions of more skilled workers, in part because the lower educational experience of their members left more space for ideologically motivated militants of a middle-class origin to perform a role in organizational tasks. These politically oriented organizers had less competition from economically motivated worker activists than in the case of the craft unions.[1] On the other hand, in time craft unions also generated ideologically oriented leaders, with the result that a gradual evolution of the whole movement in the direction of social democracy took place, with minor waves of radicalization. But at no moment was the political formula of the Labour party, once established at the beginning of the century, seriously challenged.

In France conditions were quite different. Unionization had to contend with a greater degree of persecution, so when a friendly government was established by the Popular Front in 1936, there was a sharp increase in membership. Something similar, but on a smaller scale, had happened during the First World War and immediately after. These sudden increases involved a consolidation of the Communist party's influence. This party, in the twenties and thirties, had an advantage over its rivals, as it could rely on international support from the Soviet Union, important not only materially but as a provider of an emotional appeal of high visibility for the new entrants into the ranks of the unions.[2]

In the United States there was also a great expansion of union coverage during the New Deal. This expansion was accompanied by a change from the craft unions of the old American Federation of Labor to the factory-based ones of the Congress of Industrial Organization, more closely associated with the New Deal politicians. At any rate, in the United States the labor movement never had a very definite political expression like the British one, so the change, although not trivial, was not fundamental. Unionism remained a junior ally of progressive leaders in nonsocialist parties.

In Argentina the Second World War, and the advent of Peronism (since the army coup of 1943) saw an increase in union membership from some five hundred thousand to about three million in a period of four or five years.[3] The majority of the working class passed from a social-democratic and Communist orientation to a populist one, involving an alliance with a sector of the dominant classes. This alliance was quite different from the one obtaining in the Democratic party in the United States. It was not mainly the result of conscious bargaining but was accompanied by a very intense political mystique and identification with common symbols of a high emotional content. Trade unionism changed from socialism to a commitment to nationalism and redistributive social welfare, accompanied by corporatist sympathies. How did all this happen?

Early Attempts to Co-opt the Labor Movement

One must begin with the various attempts on the part of Argentine governments to take control of the labor movement. These attempts, before Perón, were unsuccessful and therefore not too well known or studied, but they did occur. Hipólito Yrigoyen, after coming to power through free elections in 1916, tried to cope with the rather violent working-class temper of his time. He used strong repression occasionally (the Semana Trágica of 1919 and the Patagonia killings of 1922), but he also looked for alliances among union factions. As the election results show, nationwide the majority of the voting native lower classes favored the Radical party, the main exception being the city of Buenos Aires, which often had a socialist plurality. Union members, though some may have voted for the Radicales, supported the socialists, the anarchists, or the syndicalists in their unions. Ideologically motivated activists of the Left were numerous enough to control the labor movement, getting the acquiescence of the rank-and-filers, even if not necessarily their vote in the national elections. President Yrigoyen tried to make inroads into this structure by using the more amenable syndicalists, who were less linked to a party structure of their own than the socialists and were less violent or extreme than the anarchists. But nothing came of his attempts.[4]

After the 1930 military coup, some members of the government tried a fascist-inspired new deal with labor. A mixture of harsh repression against the more violent anarchists and compromise with the moderate socialists or syndicalists was tried. The government planned to have a couple of well-known unionists, from the Unión Ferroviaria and the CGT, stand as candidates for the Cámara de Diputados for the conservative party (Demócrata Nacional), which was to be the heir to the 1930 revolution. Again, this attempt came to nothing.[5]

Roberto Ortiz, who had been a lawyer to the British railways and knew the unionists quite well, also tried his hand at controlling parts of the movement while he was a minister with Pres. Agustín P. Justo and during his own presidency (1938–1941). He supported a group of disgruntled syndicalists who had been displaced from the Unión Ferroviaria and the CGT by socialists and others, but he did not succeed in establishing a friendly union sector.[6]

At about the same time, the Socialist party suffered a left-wing division with the formation of the Partido Socialista Obrero. Several Trotskyites were involved, as well as others who afterward joined the Communists. It has been argued that the Radicales, via the newspaper *Crítica*, were active in supporting this dissension so as to reduce the very great electoral weight the Socialist party had in the city of Buenos Aires. Again, nothing much remained of this effort.

In spite of the tensions and divisions within the ranks of the unions, and the amenability of many leaders to compromises with the government in exchange for some immediate benefits—usually for the union, not for themselves—the labor movement had not been destroyed by the unrelenting pressure from a series of governments, democratic, semidemocratic, or dictatorial. When in 1943 a new military coup took place, one might have expected the same thing to happen. And in fact, one of the first things the new government did was to intervene some of the main unions (Unión Ferroviaria and Fraternidad), dissolve one of the two CGT's existing at the time, and persecute political militants of the democratic and leftist parties.

Things started to change with the policy of the new secretary of labor, Juan Domingo Perón. The very peculiar situation created contained the following elements:

(1) The war had produced a deep division among the dominant classes by automatically protecting industry and thus creating many newly enriched entrepreneurs who faced disaster if after the war a thoroughgoing protectionist policy were not adopted, a policy not to be expected from the ruling conservatives;

(2) The process of industrialization, and the cessation of European immigration, was attracting great masses of internal migrants from places with little or no union or leftist political traditions. These people were not easily absorbed into the existing union structure, with its complex array of institutions, local meetings, balloting, committees, and so forth;

(3) The government decided to support a program of social welfare and industrialization, which meant the maintenance and expansion of employment. The division and confusion among the capitalist sectors of Argentine society facilitated the adoption of innovative attitudes among its individual members, leading some of them to support the risky plans proposed by Perón, which involved the mobilization of the masses.

The Changed Cultural Milieu of the Working Class

What was the impact of all this on the existing organization, not only the unions but also the closely connected leftist parties, the cooperatives, and the cultural and recreational institutions closely connected with this system? Given the historical experience of the country, a combination of repression plus attempts at co-optation was to be expected. Quite likely also was that some people in the labor movement would favor open resistance while others would prefer compromise. A unified policy could not be applied because of rivalries between the various groups and the notable independence of many organizations, especially some unions. But the movement as a whole had enough experience to defend itself. There would be victims, there would be "traitors," there would be changes of position, all of them probably forgotten after a few years, as had been the case before. But this did not happen. The onslaught was successful. Why?

The new military government (1943–1946), with Perón first as secretary of labor, afterward as vice-president, made concessions to the workers. After a short spell of persecution, a better deal was offered to unions and persons who had problems pending in the Departamento del Trabajo, a predecessor to the Secretariat of Labor. Later more concrete and massive measures were taken in the areas of remuneration, social services, and relations with management in the workplace. This has led some students of the process, notably Miguel Murmis and Juan C. Portantiero, to argue that, given the new perspectives opened up by the labor secretary and taking into account the previous practice of reformist pragmatism on the part of the workers, it was only natural that the latter should decide to support a government that was helping them so liberally.[7] According to this view, decades of economic growth without redistribution had produced so many pent-up demands that it was easy for the new authorities, particularly under conditions of prosperity and full employment, to deliver the goods.

This interpretation has been developed polemically against the earlier studies of Gino Germani, which point to the great influx of internal migrants coming into the larger cities, bringing with them traditional attitudes and therefore not easily involved in the more modern or Europe-oriented culture of the labor movement.[8] Among these traditionalist attitudes one must include the tendency to participate in paternalistic political systems. According to this approach, the new migrants would be the main support of Peronism, and one should expect to find most of the old leaders and activists among the resisters to it. It so happens, though, that quite a number of old labor leaders went over to Perón. It is not easy to know how many, but the revisionists base their thesis on the impression that the number of active supporters of Perón is much larger than earlier believed. Further research, which distinguishes among national, regional, and local leadership, is necessary to clarify this subject. It is also necessary to consider the fate of the political allies of labor, that is, the Socialist and Communist parties. Their weakness after the advent of Peronism does not justify ignoring the very central role they played before.

The crux of the revisionist interpretation is that the process of "Peronization" was a natural adaptation to new alliances on the part of a labor movement basically intact in its cadres and internal structure. The formation fo the Partido Laborista—one of the main supports of Perón's electoral victory in February 1946—by several old-time union leaders in October 1945 is cited as an example of the autonomy of the decision. This party's forced dissolution a few months after the electoral victory is glossed over as being the result of other factors. Equally ignored is the fact that most Laborista union leaders had to accept the verdict without discussion; those who opposed the decision were quickly set aside or more seriously persecuted.[9]

The revisionist approach, dissatisfied with an interpretation based on demographic changes due to internal migration, attempts to shift the emphasis onto the evolving attitudes of labor leaders and union activists, who are supposed to have decided, in their greater numbers and quite autonomously, to join a new class coalition. This concern with attiitudes is correct, but the view is quite seriously distorted, ignoring as it does some of the more important prerequisites of an autonomous labor movement.

What is necessary, if research and theoretical thinking on this subject are to make further strides, is to analyze in greater detail the internal dynamics of a system of representation of working-class interests and the many ways in which it can be distorted. The system of working-class representation, as it was constituted before Peronism, was not able to defend itself adequately against what was obviously an attack, because it was suffering from a crisis in its connections with its own environment. This crisis was partly due to the effects of mass migration, the proportions of which are difficult to challenge.[10] This does not mean, though, that one should expect to find most of the old established workers as anti-Peronists, or that Perón's electoral support was confined to the migrants. What the massive influx produced was a radical change in the social environment of workplace and neighborhood and, therefore, in what constitutes the source of union and political party activity. Unions were accustomed to having a few militants, a larger, though not too great, number of members coming to meetings, and a still larger number—but still a minority of the working class—taking up membership. When Perón, as secretary of labor, undertook his policy of redistribution and social welfare, suddenly masses of previously passive workers started demanding results. Not only new migrants, but also old apathetic members suddenly came to the meetings or participated in shop steward elections.

Had it been merely a question of increased activity, or new entrants into the industrial labor force, the situation would have been much easier to handle. The new entrants might have produced an increase of not necessarily wise militancy, but the change would not have been so great. The strategic fact was that, at the same time, the government was making a concerted effort to control the labor movement with a combination of force, persuasion, and corruption. This combination had been used before, and has been used often since, with little success. Yrigoyen, Uriburu, Ortiz had failed, as Frondizi and Onganía would later fail. Why did Perón succeed?

Partly, of course, because his policy was more clearly prolabor. The deep division within the dominant classes created among those in power many supporters for his risky prolabor policy. Otherwise, it would have been smothered, or kept within more moderate and therefore ineffectual limits by the pressure of the establishment. In addition, economic conditions were better than ever before, so there was a bigger cake to share.

These cannot be the only reasons, however, as they fail to explain the repression and persecution of so many components of the old labor movement and its political allies. All attempts to control the labor movement have generally been partially successful: they influence some unionists who genuinely believe in the program, they buy out others, they intimidate quite a few. But the working-class organism usually reacts, it resists the attempt, because under normal conditions it is adequately connected with its social environment. During the war years, when Perón's onslaught came, the environment was changing so fast that the movement lost its capacity to fight back. The balance of forces that kept the movement alive and made for circulation and mutual understanding between union and party officers, activists, and rank-and-file, was radically altered. The more ideologically motivated activists, one surmises, received the brunt of official persecution and lost their sources of influence and patronage. Those more preoccupied with economic results, who had traditionally been held at bay by the former, could now have the upper hand. To topple the equilibrium in a more definitive manner, a very large number of previously passive workers—old or new entrants into the labor force— were demanding an emotional stimulus that could be easily understood and felt.

Not that the old system was constitutionally incapable of providing an emotional commitment. But it was of a different sort, and the images of identification it provided were very obviously tarnished by decades of political bargaining and compromise. By contrast, the new "idols" were better suited to the crystallization of collective sentiments the farther removed they were from everyday working-class life, like Perón and his wife, Evita. The combination of government pressure, cooperation by quite a few leaders and militants, and the demands created by the new entrants effectively liquidated the old system. The old active minority was partly co-opted and partly replaced by another minority, more closely connected with the newly awakened mass feelings. The result was a transition from what can be called a system of representation to one of *caudillismo* with mobilizational links between leadership and followers. And if any system of representation involves some manipulation and distortion of rank-and-file attitudes, the *caudillista* variety increases the element of manipulation while maximizing the feeling of spontaneity.

In Chile the socialist working-class movement resisted several populist attempts emanating from government circles, first by Arturo Alessandri and then by the two Ibáñez experiences (1927–1931 and 1952–1958). In Argentina the different result of the process has a lot to do with the duality between the older, more established and organized sector of the working class, which had some traits of a labor aristocracy, and the new migrants, socially mobilized but with little organizational experience and therefore prepared for a mobilizational leadership. The pre-existent labor movement simply did not have the capacity, even if it had possessed the will, to provide the *caudillista* structures necessary to channel the process. In general, for an autonomous working-class movement, it is very difficult to set up a *caudillista* type of leadership, due to the nature of the social distances within its ranks. It can, given certain economic prerequisites, erect a bureaucratic organization, but that was still premature on both sides of the Andes. In Chile, however, the socialist movement, especially its political sector, did have some *caudillista* traits, although largely restricted to a local level. It had enough of the virus to be immune to it, so it was capable of resisting the challenge, which came with quite a lot of force, above all with Ibáñez in 1952. He could have become a Vargas or a Perón; he did not for a number of reasons. Probably among the Chilean upper strata there were not as many cleavages generating anti–status quo elites as in Brazil or Argentina. But a comparable increment in the numbers of the working class did not occur, either, and the cultural differences between the pre-existent associationist system and the newly mobilized internal migrants were not so great. As a result, the pattern of loyalties, traditions, and prestige structures within the working class was not so radically altered.

In Argentina, by contrast, the mass influx meant a radical demographic transformation for the larger industrial centers, almost of the proportions of the one that happened around the turn of the century. The major cities underwent a phase of fermentation during two historical periods. The first one corresponds to the international European migration, around the turn of the century. It produced the agitation of the great strikes and anarchist attempts on the life of prominent political figures. After this, during the twenties, confrontation diminished: prosperity, social mobility, family reconstitution among foreigners transformed them into either a peaceful petty bourgeoisie or a solid working class, oriented toward bread-and-butter trade unionism and reformist socialism operating within the existing system. But near the end of the thirties and especially during the Second World War, another fermentation began, supported now by the internal migrants. Again a condition of social mobilization, dissatisfaction, and potential violence emerged.

If the situation is contrasted with that prevailing at the beginning of the century, one can see that now the two components—the dissatisfied elite and the mobilized mass—had more of a chance of becoming fused into a political movement. For the new *criollo* immigrants, culture, tradition, and ethnic identification operated in the sense of making them more easily influenceable by a nationalist and military elite than by the leaders of the working-class movement who, after the lull of the twenties and thirties, had a somewhat "bourgeoisified" mentality. The first-generation Argentines were also beginning to have a more local than European mentality—partly due to the very success of the social amalgam that continued its operation under the aegis of Argentine prosperity.

Argentine Industrialists and the Peronist Elite

To complete the analysis of the formation of Peronism, we must return to the subject of the Argentine industrialist class, touched on in chapter 6. Any class that begins to consolidate in the womb of a pre-existing social formation stumbles along for quite some time before it finds an adequate political expression. In the Argentine case, the proportion of foreigners—far more than in the other cases considered, with the exception of Uruguay at the end of the nineteenth century—created a political void, an incongruence between the social base and the legal structure representing it. The industrial and commercial bourgeoisie and the proletariat were formed, from an economic point of view, very solidly, under conditions of great prosperity, with a successful social amalgam. But in the field of politics the representation of these classes was inadequate. Of particular consequence, because of the very great incongruence created, was the lack of adequate representation of the bourgeoisie. In contrast with almost any other country in similar economic and social conditions, in Argentina there existed an urban capitalist bourgeois class almost totally foreign and therefore with little political participation during the formative years.

The industrial bourgeoisie's lack of political experience was felt particularly when it had to confront the situation created by the Second World War. The 1943 revolution was clearly inspired by nationalist sectors of an antiliberal hue and concerned with the deterioration of the regime established in 1930. As those groups were rather unpopular among practically all class levels, in a short time the revolution was left without support. Perón reversed this predicament, building the alliance between army and people. Under this mantle he also included right-wing intellectuals who, because of their nationalism, joined the process and accepted its populist orientation. Besides, Perón's policies were attractive to the numerous sectors of the industrial bourgeoisie who were concerned with the coming crisis of the postwar period. Those groups naturally needed tariff protection radical enough to allow their production ventures, started chaotically in the hothouse atmosphere created by the war, to survive. They did not get enough of a response from the political parties, which, because of decades of prosperity from the export-oriented, low-protectionism formula, were not prepared to try new recipes. Their traditional constituencies, from the upper and middle classes and from the better-off sectors of workers, had benefited from the Argentine position in the international division of labor and thus could not be expected to change their preferences too quickly.[11]

Industrialists, as suggested above, lacked organic connections with political parties and thus remained isolated and endangered. Their convergence with the sectors in the military government influenced by Perón was a natural result of their predicament. Perón performed an invaluable role as the center or pinnacle of a political group or elite that brought together apparently irreconcilable elements, giving to each one an indispensable role. But Perón would have been helpless without the concurrence of very special conditions that facilitated the recruitment of a wide group—at elite levels, though—prepared to thrust itself along political paths. In turn, this elite would not have had success without the changes occurring at the level of the popular mass.[12]

The social actor we refer to as the Peronist elite was the result of the operation of social tensions that, during the war years, affected some strategic sectors of Argentine society, mainly the armed forces and the industrialists. Not that Peronism was a creation of the military, much less of the industrialists, but its existence was made possible by the frustrations, anxieties, and internal schisms affecting those actors. The peculiar conditions under which this elite was formed facilitated its expression through a mobilizational movement, with charismatic leadership capable of building a popular following. Some intellectual and professional groups, marginal to the existing prestige and power structures, became connected with the new actor in the process of formation. These were the nationalist, often profascist, intellectuals and others with more of a Social Christian outlook. These two groups of ideological specialists had no connections with the labor movement except the few afforded by the Catholic church. But having close communications with the Peronist elite—which in part they also helped to form—they gained access to the working class, whose mentality they had a chance to influence, especially at trade union leader levels. The situation may be diagrammed as follows.

Figure 3. Communication Structure at the Inception of the Peronist Movement

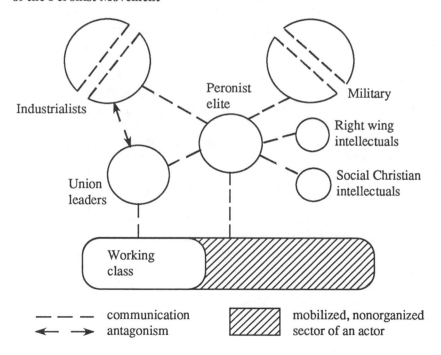

— — —	communication
← →	antagonism
▨	mobilized, nonorganized sector of an actor

The diagram shows the Peronist elite as a very centrally located actor. It had, from the start, easy communications with a sector of the industrialists, with the military, and with the two previously mentioned ideological nuclei. As a result of the strategy developed from the Secretaría de Trabajo y Previsión, it acquired solid connections with the union leadership (a part of the old one, and the new elements created under war-induced industrialization). Besides, given the mobilizational attitude adopted that elite acquired a wider sphere of influence over the masses recently integrated into the urban patterns of life, or sensitized to political stimuli via the radio and mass demonstrations. In a broad interpretation of the term, the "Peronist elite" would include not only the social actor we have termed as such, but also the fragments of the military and the industrialists and the nationalist and Social-Christian ideologues. Trade union leaders were partly co-opted, acting under the pressure of the new circumstances brought about by the massive influx. When, soon after the 1946 electoral victory, a serious confrontation pitted Perón against some of the old trade unionists who had supported him, the latter's lack of independence became evident. The opposite of what was to occur to Ibáñez happened in Argentina. Thanks to the operation of the mobilizational mode of participation, to which old union leaders were not very accustomed, they were expelled or subordinated.

One may ask whether, if Peronism had been successful in its economic policy, it would have integrated within its ranks most of the entrepreneurial and middle classes, as happened in Mexico to the Partido Revolucionario Institucional. To the extent that it is possible to answer these questions, it seems that this outcome was not very likely. The Argentine entrepreneurial and middle classes were more consolidated by the time the experience under consideration started than in the Mexican case. At the same time, the presence of the working class loomed much larger in national politics, and there was no peasantry comparable to the Mexican one. Under those circumstances, it was much more difficult for a government to gratify a majority of the industrialists, the middle classes, and the workers. It would have been too large a coalition, incorporating too many interests. It was possible—as did happen—to include a minority of the business community and a working-class majority, but not representative majorities of both sectors.

After the downfall of Peronism in 1955, preceded by a short period of radicalization and confrontation with the church, conditions for the permanence of the Peronist elite in its traditional format no longer existed. For one thing, the military became, almost entirely, an opponent of the regime. The industrialists were under greater cross-pressures. If Argentina had undergone a period of intense economic development, the minority of industrialists who had created the conditions for the emergence of the Peronist elite would probably have become reintegrated into the majority of their class and adopted conservative attitudes. This development would also have been prodded by the bad experience most conservative classes—including businesspeople and the military—had had during the last couple of years of the Peronist regime (1954–1955). The reality, though, was that industrialists continued to face very bad times, so the forces generating politically unconventional attitudes among that social sector remained in operation.

The memory of the extreme radicalization that Peronism again underwent in the early seventies, however, is a factor making it more difficult for political innovators among the upper strata to get involved in a Peronist coalition. It is necessary for them to be very intensely affected by insecurity or by a feeling of being menaced by other high-status social actors (including foreign interests) to take the step of adopting populist or left-of-center attitudes. Some of them can, of course, always be motivated by more purely personal or ideological factors to abandon the attitudes dominant in their class, but this is a different phenomenon from the one that generates populist elites.

10. Reform and the Politics of Social Democracy

For a long time, much of the Latin American intelligentsia has been attracted by the promise of social revolution, or by the hope of radical change brought about by a progressive faction of the military. The routinization of charisma within authoritarian institutions in Cuba and the failure of the Velasco Alvarado regime in Peru have stimulated a search for alternative experiences. This search for new experiences has been made more realistic by the demise of several right-wing dictatorships, which has created space for individuals who had grown accustomed to being permanently barred from nonrevolutionary access to power.

This has led to a reevaluation of democracy, and to a spate of books, articles, and seminars on how it works. Obviously, for its consolidation, it is necessary to secure civilian control over the military; it is also essential to create conditions of welfare for the majority of the population, which in turn requires adequate rates of economic growth. What is less obvious, but nevertheless I would suggest true, is that:

(1) economic growth does not necessarily depend on setting up a "progressive" coalition including the popular strata. It is as likely to be promoted by a conservative government, in which the strategic role is played by private entrepreneurs;

(2) civilian control over the military depends not so much on pruning out the authoritarian elements of that corporation as on achieving a minimum level of solidarity between political parties and interest groups, so that their conflicts do not spill over into violent or disruptive social agitation;

(3) the consolidation of democracy requires the existence of a powerful reformist political party based on the lower strata of the population, capable of expressing their demands and at the same time controlling them, so as to maintain the level of conflict within safe limits.

These propositions are not very palatable to the Left, and are not always easily acceptable by social scientists. The Left tends to be somewhat voluntaristic in its treatment of the military, thinking that assertiveness on the part of a civilian government is what is needed, together with punishment of officers involved in the violation of human rights, or not fully readapted to democratic life. The Left also, at least in its more activist fringes, believes that intensification of social conflict is necessary in order to curtail established privileges and extend economic and social rights to the mass of the population. Therefore, anything approaching a social pact, an incomes policy, or a consensus-building *"concertación"* smacks of immobilism. The Left, finally, is remiss to admit the role that a right-wing, industrializing coalition can perform, because of its conviction that the hour of capitalism has passed, at least in the underdeveloped parts of the world. These traditional tenets of leftist thinking are increasingly being subjected to revision and self-criticism, but the process is slow and painful.

On the other hand, the hallowed convictions and practices of the Right do not help it to achieve a better understanding of the situation, though its blind spots are complementary to those of the Left. It is only slowly leaving aside its dreams of "law and order" dictatorships, and its distrust of popular and leftist parties and of what it considers trade-union abusive vested interests. Often the Right, in its attempt at building an ideological package totally opposed to statist progressivism, lapses into extreme versions of laissez-faire individualism. These fly in the face of the concrete experiences of modern economic development in the Third World, as in Korea or Taiwan, which though capitalist have been anything but laissez-faire oriented, and have involved a very active role of the state. The Right also is not aware of the extreme danger for democratic stabilization involved in the existence of a mass of unemployed or professionally displaced people, created by uncontrolled market mechanisms. In present-day advanced nations, the standard of living and existing social security make these negative effects, when they are at all present, bearable. But a similar situation, in the thirties, bred fascism in Europe, and today is likely to imperil democratic transitions in Latin America and other parts of the Third World.

It so happens that both Right and Left are necessary for democratic consolidation—a fact that is quickly becoming a commonplace in sociological analyses. I would add that both Right and Left are also necessary for a policy of social reform, if this is to be kept within moderate channels. Without a Right, social reform tends to become too radical, and to create a reactive set of mind among conservative groups, capable of influencing the military. Of course, in some cases radicalization may lead to revolution, but this is unlikely in most of Latin America. Therefore, quite apart from the desirability of revolution, it is better to keep within the bounds of the rules of the game. Not only the rules of the democratic game, but also the less-known rules of the reformist game. Let us then explore in this final chapter some of these rules.

A Caveat on the Transference of Ideology

In Western Europe, the creation of the socialist ideology almost coincided with the formation of the first organized nuclei of the working class, which quickly adopted the new values. European social democracy, however, is not simply socialism plus democracy. It involved an adaptation to the peculiar national conditions of the countries where it took root, coming to terms with the interests of the local bourgeoisie. It required participation in a political system that, particularly at the beginning, was grossly slanted in favor of the dominant classes. To obtain the support of trade-union leaders it was also necessary to make concessions to their pragmatism and economism and to tolerate their attachment to bourgeois parties, like the British liberals or the French radicals, or to the political expressions of the churches. But these were obviously remnants from another era, previous to the time when the working class acquired the capacity to organize itself. In contrast, in the Third World it is typical for a populist movement to compete successfully with socialism for the allegiance of the masses and to appear as their main representative against the middle and upper classes.

In mid–nineteenth century Latin America, at the time of the creation and first expansion of socialist ideology, conditions were not favorable for autonomous working-class action on any scale. In fact, they were hardly ripe for the consolidation of the bourgeoisie as a ruling class. Strangely enough, however, a tradition of popular revolt did exist, ranging from Túpac Amaru, the Haitian slaves, or the Mexican insurgents to radical *caudillista* movements like *Artiguismo* in Uruguay. In the European experience, equivalent phenomena had converged with the tradition of popular struggles that socialism recognized as being its forerunners. In particular this was so for the French Revolution, which despite its complex class support, has always been considered, in its most radical facets, a formative element of socialist ideology. In other words, socialism is, to a large extent, a commentary and an extrapolation of events during the great French Revolution and other revolutionary processes in 1830, 1840, and 1871.

Latin American popular rebellions and mobilizational experiences are more bereft of ideological interpreters; they have not been as incorporated into the main body of a theoretical construction aspiring to universal validity. It is not that they absolutely lack intellectual heirs and interpreters, but, in general, what exists is a more directly political and strongly nationalist hagiography. Thus, for example, the Mexican insurgents of 1810 are included in the Mexican pantheon but they are not sufficiently well known or taken seriously in the rest of the continent. The same happens to the other episodes referred to above, which at most are the object of a patriotic cult, but have not become part of a universalist narrative with ideological value.

All of these Latin American experiences were either ignored or seriously distorted and misinterpreted by Karl Marx and his early followers. They were not studied as an essential part of the theoretical system needed to better orient the struggle for socialism, as were the French or British revolutions. This same attitude was, to a large extent, adopted by the first socialist thinkers in Latin America, especially in the Southern Cone, intensely affected by European migration and considered "empty," not only of population but also of relevant political traditions. The situation was somewhat different in other parts of the continent (Chile, Peru, Mexico, and Cuba), which, although less developed, did have important working-class concentrations in agroindustrial and mining areas. There, intense class conflict emerged somewhat earlier than the theory would have predicted. This led social thinkers and political theorists on the Left in those countries to look more for national traditions whose relevance was more obvious because of the lack of such a radical change in the basis of population as characterized Argentina, Uruguay, and southern Brazil.

Between 1910 and 1917 several revolutionary processes took place in countries of the periphery. Although anticapitalist traits became dominant only in the case of Russia, the Mexican and the nationalist Chinese revolutions should not be forgotten. As an earlier generation believed the Zeitgeist had swept through France at the moment of the fall of the Bastille, ignoring the fall of the Alhóndiga of Guanajuato to Hidalgo's hosts in 1810, so a new intellectual group perceived a basic difference between the Russian Revolution—a part of the world historical process—and the Mexican Revolution—a local episode without a valid theoretical reading beyond Mexico's frontiers. Haya de la Torre's attempt to build his political system on the Mexican example is a significant exception, although not strong enough to counteract the tide.

I do not pretend to adopt a closed nationalist perspective, much less to deny the importance of the French or Russian revolutions. But the degree of intellectual elaboration and concern they—in contrast to the Mexican Revolution—have occasioned among Latin Americans is simply an expression of the cultural dependency that so seriously affects intellectuals in this part of the world.

In Argentina the Second World War created a particular combination of social forces that facilitated the emergence of a new political experience, Peronism, as we saw in chapter 9. The socialist movement, in practically all its shades and component parties and sects, stood in opposition to the new challenger, interpreting it as a local version of Fascism. Only a small proportion of the ideological and party activists, and a somewhat larger sector of the more pragmatically oriented trade unionists joined Perón's movement. The intellectual frame of reference most of them had was based on an extrapolation of the European experience and made a different reaction difficult to imagine. Although Perón was offering important advances toward social welfare, his moorings in the authoritarian military regime of 1943–1946 were obvious, and outspokenly Fascist individuals held positions in his entourage. The cards were distributed in such a way that it was extremely difficult to play the hand held by the Left and the intelligentsia. There was a circular causation mechanism at work, because the maldistribution of the cards was itself in part the responsibility of that same Left and intelligentsia, who, because of their rigidity, had antagonized too many individuals and groups and thus made them available as partners of a new political experience.

The crisis of the Perón years resulted in a very deep chasm that has separated most of the intelligentsia from the bulk of the working class, a typical phenomenon in Latin American history, but by no means universal or irreversible. It was not typical of Argentina before the advent of Peronism and need not remain so. The problem of the connection between an intellectual elite of predominantly socialist ideas and a working-class movement of a more pragmatic orientation is basic to the analysis of the prospects for reform in Latin America. By extension, it is also very relevant to the consolidation of democratic regimes in that part of the world.

The Role of the Middle Classes and the Intellectuals

As is well known, middle- and high-level administrative, professional, and scientific strata increase in numbers in both capitalist and bureaucratic collectivist societies, so much so that they may even be more numerous than manual workers. We must distinguish, however, between the role of this new middle class in consolidated capitalist and in revolutionary circumstances. The choice, given the present level of development of the forces of production, is not between capitalism and socialism, but between the capitalist and the bureaucratic collectivist modes of production. Both are based on the existence of dominant classes, in the former the bourgeoisie, in the latter the bureaucracy. Socialism as a distinct mode of production based on highly egalitarian autonomous units, independent of the state, with little or no hierarchical division of labor, is a Utopian goal, given the present or foreseeable technological system. If socialism, here and now, cannot become an established order, then it must be a movement, predominantly based on the less-privileged classes, toward changes that are never final. The reality of the bureaucratic collectivist mode of production complicates matters, because to a large extent it has run away with the theoretical clothes of socialism, distorted unrecognizably by Lenin, Stalin, and Mao.

Technicians, administrators, and professionals, as a social group, experience serious difficulties in their life chances in Third World countries, where revolutionary conditions often exist. These conditions usually express themselves through occupational groups that undergo a process of mutation. What has been called in earlier chapters a "nucleus" of a class becomes a strategic political actor. Its access to power depends on its capacity to establish effective alliances with popular sectors. But even if the masses—peasants, marginals, proletarians—are the battering ram with which the enemy fortress is destroyed, only the new bureaucratic class can occupy the positions of command. This, being inevitable in the present state of technology, cannot become the basis for a criticism of the bureaucratic collectivist regimes. The form in which power is exercised in them is, of course, another matter.

Where capitalism is more consolidated—despite occasional crises—the technicians and other administrators do not differ too much in their attitudes from the property-holding middle and upper classes, and they become the main numerical support for the Right. Under conditions of lesser economic development the greater incidence of frustration reduces the electoral support for the Right, encouraging the growth of a Center party to take its place, like Christian Democracy in Chile or Radicalism in Argentina. In decidedly Third World countries dissatisfaction among the middle classes is so great that it may even affect such groups as the military or the clergy, leading them to violent anticonservative political involvements, as in Iran and most of the Arab world.

Practically in any social system a certain sector of the middle classes adopts a leftist ideology. Factors leading to that attitude range from the personal and psychological to the structural. Where there is a wide social pyramid, with relatively good or at least passable occupational chances, most middle-class individuals, as stated above, orient themselves to the Right (as in Europe, the United States, Japan, or Australia) or to basically moderate Center parties (as in Chile or Argentina). Very specific ideological or cultural factors must be in operation on a minority of the middle classes to generate among them anti–status quo ideologies. A rather small "enlightened middle class" sector is thus formed, not excessively oriented to the conquest of power, because it lives rather comfortably within the existing structures. Where the social pyramid is narrower in the middle, frustrations push to militancy different types of persons who more impatiently seek political power and are more capable of using ideology for that purpose. Their success as leaders is partly based on the weakness of labor organizations and the prevalence of a more easily manageable peasantry. By contrast, in developed areas, union leaders can successfully compete for leadership positions with the middle-class intellectuals, for whom they feel less status respect.

The revolutionary sector generated within the middle classes in Third World conditions is much more dangerous to the established order than its equivalent in developed areas. Under high industrialization the prospects for radical and violent changes in the system of domination are out of sight; not so where the first impact of capitalism is being felt. In the industrially advanced countries (with the partial exception of the United States) the main component of the popular coalition is generally the unionized working class. It may have allies among the intellectual and middle strata, which because of their training can provide a lot of the leaders. But these allies, though necessary for the working-class movement, are not likely to overpower it. Neither are they menacing, strictly, to the dominant classes. The bases are thus created for a moderate type of politics, which, though far from conservatism, produces only gradual reforms.

Intellectuals constitute a special group within the middle classes who, due to their skill in the manipulation of symbols, appear to be somewhat independent from their immediate class determinations. Their connections with the new bureaucratic class of professionals, administrators, and technicians, however, are numerous and varied, so much so that often they act as organic intellectuals of that class and not of the proletariat or the peasantry. Something similar happens to students. In their majority they study in order to accede to technological, administrative, or professional positions, which generate a social perspective and a mode of life quite different from those of intellectuals in the restricted sense of the term.[1] Students, however, given their youth and marginal incorporation into the labor market, retain greater freedom from class determinations, which makes them more similar to intellectuals and differentiates them from professionals and administrators. But for reasons analogous to those stated above, they often express the power strategy and politics of the new middle class, even if not consciously so.

The Relevance of the Party System

The party system, particularly in countries in the process of consolidation of democracy, must be viewed as a channel for containment of potentially disruptive forces, such as the military and the economic Right, as well as the more activist Left. If the economic Right does not have access to the electoral field—that is, if it cannot hope to win an election—it will try to redress things in its favor via the armed forces. There is a circular causation mechanism in operation here, because the armed forces themselves will feel threatened if they do not have enough friends among the political parties. A powerful party of the Right is the best solution from their point of view, at least in most cases.[2] It must also be stated that, regardless of the number of friends the armed forces may have among the political leadership, they will feel hamstrung to intervene if political and associationist leaders are sufficiently solidary among themselves as to refrain from knocking at the barracks. This is why at the beginning of this chapter (and more in detail in chapter 6) it was hypothesized that in order to make the polity secure from military intervention a certain level of solidarity between political parties or pressure groups is necessary, rather than a high degree of democratic conviction among military officers. Of course the latter would help, but it is more difficult to get, and it takes longer to materialize. Though extreme nondemocratic and authoritarian individuals should be, if possible, eliminated from the armed forces, there is a perverse tendency for them to be reproduced at lower or junior echelons of the hierarchy, if social conditions are bad enough. It would be unwise, then, to spend the modicum of power a civilian government in the process of democratic transition generally has, in pruning the military of its more menacing heads, because the operation, like an inexpert cutting of a cancer, may generate more malignant cells than it eradicates.

By contrast, comparative experience shows that when there is lack of sizable civilian support for a barracks takeover, this does not occur, or is much less likely to occur, and much less permanent in its effects. The Argentine experience between 1983 and 1989 (at the time of writing), in this sense, has one radical difference from what went on in that country since 1930, or even earlier, up to 1983. These last six years have been the only period within that larger time span when practically all parties and corporations have been solidly in favor of the maintenance of the democratic regime, when it was threatened by barracks revolts (the Aldo Rico and Mohammed Seineldin attempts of Easter 1987 and early and late 1988). During these events a few civilians were known to side with the rebels, but they were heavily outnumbered in practically all political parties and pressure groups by those loyal— for whatever reasons—to the regime. Some of these parties and pressure groups, while rejecting a military coup, do however feel empathy for the predicament of the soldiers and would concede some of their demands. Though this propinquity between military and civilian factions incenses the moral feelings of a section of the population (and of the social science community) it is good for the consolidation of the democratic system, as it increases the number of social actors with a stake in it.

If we now consider the Left, its more activist fringes are often on the verge of turning to violence and revolution. The existence of a reform party open to them, and capable of controlling them, is essential for channeling their energies into constructive tasks, also giving them a stake in the system. The coexistence of these activist elements in the same party with a working-class majority is no easy matter. The material conditions under which the working class is formed in highly urban and industrial areas make it pragmatic and diffident toward millenarian ideals about total social change. Labor pragmatism, however, is compatible with ideological commitment, but only if the latter does not get in the way of practical politics. In most countries where socialism is strong as a party, that is, where it takes a social-democratic form, a fusion has been worked out between the ideological mentality of the intellectuals and the pragmatism of the trade unionists, particularly their chiefs and bureaucrats. If this fusion is lost, intellectuals fall prey to ideological sectarianism, and trade unionists adopt versions of corporatism or economism.

In the relatively developed countries—including several in Latin America—the two most sensitive issues for the formation of a strong reform movement are the role of trade union leaders in it and its relationship with populism. The function of intellectuals, which is also central, depends very much on their understanding these two problems adequately. Every political movement, however class-based, is in fact a coalition of social actors. In this coalition it is necessary to identify the mutual affinities or antagonisms as well as the relative status and communications between its member actors. In some cases there may be some actors who, being antagonistic toward each other, remain in the coalition only as a result of their common attraction to a third one, which acts as a nucleus. Ideological influences of some actors over others will depend partly on the existence of a communications network, because otherwise there will be no circulation of ideas. Generally, in a large coalition, there will be one or more actors preoccupied with ideological mattters. Though all actors have some ideology, only some are ideological specialists. Often, especially in populist movements, ideological specialists are opposed to each other, and their ideologies may be different from those of the rest of the members of the coalition. Thus, in the grand alliance put together by Peronism to return to power in 1973, at least four ideology-generating groups were included: a classical *justicialista* Center with Social-Christian overtones; a noninsurrectionary "national" Left; an insurrectionary extreme Left; and a semifascist extreme Right. The group around Perón himself formed another actor, with quite a considerable weight, but more pragmatic. A social-democratic ideological sector was conspicuously absent.

In the European working-class movements, neither the extreme Right, the insurrectionary Left, or the Social-Christian elements are present. The ideological field is thus reduced to the moderate social democrats (or Eurocommunists) and the socialist Left, mostly nonviolent. In Peronism, with the passing of time, the violent Left has been practically eliminated, and the profascist Right very weakened as a result of the Renovación movement. Peronism thus is progressively being reduced to having two main sources of ideology within its ranks: the classical *justicialista*, and the "national" Left. Under these conditions, the incorporation of moderate socialist components is less difficult.

In the European historical experience, the social-democrat (or Eurocommunist) intellectuals have established a close communication with trade union bureaucrats. In this way, socialist ideology influences the working class through the intermediation of national, regional, and local union leaders, who serve as the transmission belt.* Direct communication between most intellectuals and workers is not great because of class differences and professional specialization. If it were not for the intermediation of the trade union leaders, the intelligentsia would have much less access to the masses. As for the socialist Left, it is usually recruited among stratification levels somewhat lower than the professionalized social-democratic intellectuals, and includes numerous rank-and-file activists near, in social space, to the working class. There is, as a result, considerable communication between the socialist Left (strongly ideological) and the working class, but the values and attitudes of both groups are quite different. Though the socialist Left has the true interests of the workers very much at heart, it does not equally respect their actual current opinions. A barrier is thus erected between the socialist Left and the majority of the working class, the latter being provided with moderate or economistic values by the chain of communication formed by the social-democratic intellectuals and the union bureaucrats.

This is not the only connection between those intellectuals and the rank and file, however. There is another intermediary group, well connected with both, namely, the party organizers and volunteers of low middle or working-class extraction who share the dominant party ideology. Their stratification level is similar to that of the socialist Left, but in general they are not so ideologically intense, although they can operate as transmission belts. They perform a similar role to that of the union leaders in providing social-democratic intellectuals access to the working class. This channel, however, is not totally independent, because party organizers and ward activists are well connected with union leaders also. Therefore, if social-democratic intellectuals attempted to use the party structure against the union bureaucrats, they would soon find the going rough.

Within the type widely defined as social-democratic, there are two varieties in the European version. One is represented by Labour parties (in Great Britain, Holland, Belgium, and Scandinavia); the other may be called Social Democratic in the restricted sense (of German and Austrian origin and also applicable in France, Spain and Italy, and, by extension, to Eurocommunism). Historically, the older parties belong to the social-democratic variety, influenced by Marxism and with a centralist approach and great concern for ideology. In them the role of intellectuals and middle-class activists has been quite significant. This has something to do with the more recent industrialization of those countries. It is also the model that more directly influenced socialism in Argentina, through Juan B. Justo and the Vorwaerts group.

In contrast, the British case, which is the classical Labour model, reflects a situation in which the working class was organized at a quite early date, mostly by its own efforts.[4] The result was an economically oriented and professional trade unionism, slowly expanding to incorporate the rest of the working class. The strength of the union movement, and the large number of leaders it generated, created a resistance to the penetration of the intellectuals and their ideologies during a great part of the nineteenth century. Almost until the First World War, Germany was considered the classical land of socialism; England and the United States were the great exceptions, where, in spite of industrial development, the working class remained attached to liberal or bourgeois democratic conceptions. The evolutionist perspective shared by many socialist theoreticians led them to forecast a shift of the ideological spectrum to the left in those two countries, which were the main centers of international capitalism. This shift did not occur in the United States; to the contrary, the weak but non-negligible connections between some American Federation of Labor unions and the socialist movement were severed, and more pragmatic links forged with the Democratic party, which under Franklin D. Roosevelt had rekindled its reformist traditions, although in alliance with quite conservative elements in the South and in the city machines.

In Great Britain the road to a working-class party was finally taken around the turn of the century, but socialist ideological elements were incorporated only sparingly, to the dismay of continental observers. The party adopted a highly federal structure, reserving a privileged—and not very democratic—role for the trade unions, which were massively incorporated into the party. The British Labour version is of interest because of its highly federal structure, opposed both to the Leninist model and to Karl Marx's projects since the days of the First International. It is also interesting, from a North or South American perspective, because it represents a successful fusion of socialist intellectuals with a pre-existing labor movement, which had developed its own political traditions and habits. In the United States, several attempts at repeating the British experience failed, perhaps because the appeal of short-run economism and the advantages gained from alliances with nonsocialist popular parties were so tangible that they overcame any other consideration.[5] In Latin America the equivalent problem is the connection with the populist movement, an even more intractable potential ally than the British liberal trade unionists of the beginning of the century or the pragmatic North American ones.

The Social-Democratic Party Model in Latin America

In Latin America, Aprismo is the more typical local adaptation of the German organizational model of social democracy. Even though in Haya de la Torre's thought the Fabian and Labour party influence was very marked, the movement he formed in Peru had from the beginning a very disciplined and *"verticalista"* structure highly concerned with ideology. Intellectuals, among them Haya himself, and other erstwhile student leaders played an important role. The party exercised constant supervision over trade union, professional, and peasant groups. The main difference with the European social-democratic model is that instead of a strongly organized working class there are comparatively weak trade unions with somewhat *caudillista* leadership. The role of the labor movement as backbone of the organization is substituted by that of a middle class, organized and disciplined in tightly knit cells. Popular and working-class support, and especially the peasant following, are to a considerable extent mobilizational, demanding a charismatic leadership role. This role was performed with great skill by Haya de la Torre.[^] His successors may have to adapt to different conditions, although Peruvian social structure still demands—to a lesser extent than fifty years ago—that type of organizational cement, as is shown by the role performed by Alan García.

Within the concept of Aprista parties several others of a similar kind are included, notably Venezuela's Acción Democrática and Costa Rica's Liberación Nacional. Apart from these, the other major example of application of the German social-democratic model was the Socialist party of Argentina; the Communist party of Chile approached this pattern, with Leninist elements added. Leninism, however, is not a well-adapted organizational form for industrial and urbanized milieux, like Western Europe and, to a lesser extent, Argentina, Uruguay, and Chile. It either degenerates into sectarianism or it adopts near–social democratic forms, as in Italy.[7]

In Argentina, socialism, until its eclipse when Peronism appeared, was more in line with German or French social-democratic patterns than with British ones. It had a clearly democratic doctrine and rejected the dictatorship of the proletariat, but it was rigidly centralized and concerned with purity of doctrine. It exercised too close control over the behavior of its trade-unionist members, without being capable of imposing a charismatic leadership on them, as the Apristas did. The massive transfer of loyalties to the new Peronist movement between 1943 and 1946 was to a certain extent a rebellion of the trade unionists against the excessively rigid supervision of their strategies by party leaders.[8] Actually, however, a degree of tension between a mature trade unionism and a party structure with important intellectual and middle-class participation is quite normal in any popular movement.

An important aspect of the organization of a reformist party is the kind of connection it creates between the bulk of the party structure and the intellectuals, professionals, and technocrats who are close to it. These groups require a good deal of independence to attend to their professional careers. Because of their higher standard of living, they have always been suspect in working-class parties, but they are an essential ingredient, especially once the reformist nature of the movement is acknowledged. In the European experience many of those professionalized intellectuals and the political leaders representing them have collaborated from an early date with middle-class parties or held important civil service posts. From a Sidney Webb to an Alexandre Millerand, the examples are numerous. In Latin America, to draw some inferences from a European comparison, two facts must be considered: (1) a professionalized civil service does not exist, high posts in public administration being obtained only through political influence, and (2) many of the bourgeois reform governments have not been led, like the European ones, by Liberals,

Radicals, or Christian Democrats, but by the military (like the 1943 regime in Argentina and that of Velasco Alvarado in Peru), or by authoritarian civilians (like Vargas in Brazil), or they derive from unfair elections (as in the case of Frondizi and Illia in Argentina). Given this situation, the predicament of an intellectual or a technician who wishes to contribute his skills to public service is particularly complicated. It is not realistic for most of them—acting with that combination of selfish and altruistic motivations found in any social group—to wait until there is an honorable, legally elected civilian government, preferably socialist, in the meantime isolating themselves in private professional activity. The problem transcends the purely individual, as well-trained professionals, with experience in public life, are necessary, not only in government, which is obvious, but also in building a party. It is not enough to have intellectuals, medical doctors, teachers, or human rights lawyers, whose professions enable them to be independent and to become the moral conscience of the community. It is also necessary to have economists, technicians, administrators, and experts in the social services, health, and city planning. A reformist party must create a place for these types of people, must accept and tolerate their tendency to become involved, while pursuing their careers or attempting political action, in governments that are beyond the pale if seen from the perspective of the more ethically oriented group of rank-and-file activists.

In the British Labour experience the Fabian Society created an environment in which those professionals and technicians had an opportunity to act, given the parameters of time and place. It included many public officials, and—anathema to the activists—many of its members belonged to the Liberal party or cooperated with governments of that color. The work of its members and their accumulation of experience were facilitated by the highly federal nature of the party structure. The environment of the Fabian Society was tolerant of the predicament faced by technicians and intellectuals when undergoing their experiences in government (or in private business), thus permitting the maintenance of solidarity and socialist self-perception.[9]

In the other European countries, socialist parties also created formal or informal mechanisms of this type to incorporate intellectual elements without submitting them to an excessive party discipline. In Chile the tradition of participating in electoral fronts, already strong and accepted in the thirties, performed a similar role. Beginning with the Popular Front of 1938, heterogeneous and contradictory allies, ranging from the Communists to Radicals and Christian Democrats, were incorporated. The profusion of small parties, some of them almost rubber stamps, in the political fronts continually formed and re-formed by the Chilean Left gave it a highly federal structure, which allowed intellectual and professional groups to seek to establish their own strategies.[10] The Socialist party was never very rigid in its internal organization and has incorporated some *caudillista* elements. From the start it adopted organizational forms reminiscent of French syndicalism, with a wide array of local trade unions, cooperatives, and cultural associations. The weaker nature of Chilean trade unionism and the greater status respect in that country facilitated intellectual leadership over the working class, by comparison with Argentina. There was an important rebellion in the ranks of the Left, however, when Gen. Carlos Ibáñez returned to power in free elections in 1952, heading a movement similar to Peronism. At that moment a majority of the working class took the populist road. It was accompanied by a sector of the Socialist party, which split and took most of the membership, although it was resisted by the Salvador Allende group and the Communist party. The antipopulist Left rump was reduced to a small percentage of the electorate in 1952. But when after a couple of years economic troubles forced President Ibáñez to adopt a more conservative policy, the labor and socialist component of his support abandoned him, and the populist formula dissolved. The *caudillista* traits of the socialist leadership in Chile, plus its long tradition of participation in political fronts—which requires tolerance of the characteristics of allies—facilitated the process.

In many countries in the area, the continuing economic crisis in the late eighties has stimulated the growth of an electoral Left, often at the expense of populist parties. Thus, in Peru Izquierda Unida is becoming a serious challenge to the APRA; in Ecuador Izquierda Democrática has acceded to the presidency, even if with a minority vote; in Brazil both the left populist Partido Democrático Trabalhista of Leonel Brizola, and the Partido dos Trabalhadores (based on the São Paulo new unionism, but with important extensions in the rest of the country) have registered local victories in the municipal elections of 1988, at the expense of the moderate Partido do Movimento Democrático Brasileiro (PMDB); in Uruguay the Frente Amplio, a coalition of leftist parties, may become the main opposition; and even in traditionally PRI-dominated, "one-and-a-half-party" Mexico, a dissident PRI group led by Cuauhtemoc Cárdenas in alliance with the Left is likely to bring a permanent alteration to politics as usual. Last but not least, redemocratization in Chile is also likely to bring again to the fore an important Left vote.

In Argentina, the multifaceted nature of Peronism has been referred to often enough in this volume. The current *"renovación"* is producing a greater homogeneity in the party, but the process is only beginning and inevitably it has its setbacks. Compared to the Brazilian PMDB, Peronism has always been much more trade union based, and is thus less prone to challenge from a Left new unionism. Most of the intellectual Left, after its ideological frenzy of the seventies, when it believed it could incorporate itself within the Peronist movement, turning it into a revolutionary force, has agonizingly reappraised its traditional convictions to such an extent that it may have inadvertently thrown out the baby with the bathwater. When redemocratization occurred in 1983, Peronism appeared to be too tainted with authoritarian traits, and its working-class component was underrated by the currently fashionable revisionism of Marxist stereotypes. As a result, most members of the "modernized " Left joined the new political coalition that was being formed under the leadership of Raúl Alfonsín on the basis of the traditional middle-of-the-road Radical party (Unión Cívica Radical), which had been polling about a quarter of the electorate for decades. This left-leaning anti-Peronist nucleus, paradoxically, then became a magnet for the various disparate elements of the Right, allowing Alfonsín to win the presidency against a Peronist movement unsettled by the death of its leader. The pack of cards was again wrongly dealt: the moderate Left was allied with the Center and the Right, in its vote for Alfonsín, and found itself pitted against the Peronist working class and labor unions, which enjoyed support from rather unsavory characters on the extreme right. In contrast with what happened in 1946, when Perón was constitutionally elected over a wide coalition of opponents, this time the moderate Left won, but with the wrong allies—wrong, that is, if a socialist project was its aim; correct, probably, if only a consolidation of democracy was intended.

The situation in Argentina resembles somewhat the predicament of the democratic Left in Italy, mostly represented by the Socialist party and other minor groups that have been forced to cooperate with the right-of-center Christian Democrats rather than with the labor-based Communists, because of the still-uncertain democratic convictions of the latter. Ideological renewal has been proceeding very fast in the Italian Communist party, but not fast enough to impress large sectors of public opinion. It is necessary to allow more time for the process to unfold. Looking back to the Argentine situation, a similarly philosophical stance should be taken in the analysis of the potential for change within Peronism.

This comparison between the Italian and the Argentine party structures assumes a certain equivalence between the Radical party and the Christian Democratic cum Socialist alliance. On the other side of the main conflict line, the Peronists would occupy a position akin to that of the Communists. I believe the comparison is basically appropriate, though many caveats must be appended, as the social and political structures of the two countries are quite different, and the class composition of Peronism is much more encompassing than the one backing the Italian Communist party. Ideologically, most Peronists would rend their clothing before accepting that they occupy a position similar to that of the Communists, whose ideology they strongly condemn (as do many Apristas and Social Democrats). As much importance, however, should be given to the class nature of a party's support as to its ideology in judging its long-run prospects for change.

Conclusion

The rules of the reformist game, under a democratic regime, are basically the rules of the formation and functioning of a party system. It is important to include the proviso "under a democratic regime," because not all reformist programs take place under such conditions. As a matter of fact, in most Third World and Communist countries reform is either blocked, giving way to revolution, or else it is in the hands of one-party civilian or military regimes. In those instances the ruling party is a different sort of political animal from the competitive parties that vie for power in more open regimes. Latin America is today the main area of the world where a party system is in the process of being formed and is acquiring enough strength to reflect local social forces adequately. Probably we are entering a period of major party recomposition, in several other Latin American countries. The pressure toward the consolidation of clearly conservative parties on one side of the spectrum, and of social-democratic ones at the other end, will be mounting. If this process does take place, eroding the effectiveness of well-known and time-tested political expressions, it will be accompanied by an increase in social tensions and unpredictability of outcomes. Both social scientists and political actors might as well brace themselves for a stretch of increased occupational hazards.

Appendix: A Theoretical Model of Political Processes

One way to advance sociological theory is to integrate hypotheses into a systematic model. Each hypothesis describes relationships between variables, eventually in the shape of a mathematical or other type of formula. These formulas require well-defined and measurable concepts. The combination of the various hypotheses—some of which may be derivable from others—forms the model. A special type of model can be used to describe and explain a political process over a stretch of time by dividing the time span into smaller units, or periods. In each period the state of the system is described by the total set of variables used. Some of these variables are exogenous, some endogenous. The exogenous variables' values must be given by the observer in each period; the endogenous ones are calculated by the formulas incorporated into the model, that is, by its sociological hypotheses. In the first period, though, many normally endogenous variables may also be given, forming together with the rest of the exogenous variables the initial conditions.

The endogenous or exogenous character of a variable depends on the hypotheses adopted in the model under consideration. An exogenous variable is not more causal than the others; it is simply a variable whose values and changes cannot be calculated on the basis of the set of hypotheses considered; thus, they must be given by the observer. Endogenous variables have a dependent status in the hypotheses used to determine their values, but they can perform an independent role in other hypotheses. The model is called a simulation model because it copies, or simulates, the actual political process as it unfolds over time.[1]

It must be said, before proceeding, that any attempt to describe such a complex and multifaceted thing as a political process using a limited set of variables and hypotheses must inevitably simplify reality, with the risk of oversimplifying it. If formalized or mathematized hypotheses are considered, the difficulties in measurement are so great that the whole enterprise must be clearly seen as experimental and heuristic. If properly used, though, this system of hypotheses can help in thinking about the relationships between the various dimensions or components of society. Given the peculiar nature of this effort, it has been committed to an appendix, so as not to mar the text of the book for those who do not appreciate formalizations or who consider the whole process incapable of successful completion.

I must also say from the start that I am not a hard-core practitioner of the art of modeling, as I admit the partial validity of many of the criticisms leveled against it. But I believe that cautious approximations, which I approach from the angle of a sociologist with historical interests and some training in mathematics, are useful in this field. The model developed in this appendix will only be outlined in its barest bones, with minimum mathematical references, so as not to scare away many potentially interested readers. In thinking about and writing the book the model has performed an orienting role, and I have done some runs with various versions of it. The excessively preliminary type of elaboration of the formulas and the unreliability of most necessary data make it inadvisable to publish the results, at least at this stage. As will be seen after examining the variables incorporated into the model, the scope is very wide: so many aspects of a social system are included that it is unrealistic to expect to have solid information about all of them.

This is one of two possible scientific strategies, the other being a decision to cover just a few variables, preferably those about which some reliable data exist. This would greatly impoverish the theoretical scope of the model; it might even be the approach recommended by hard-core modelers, but I do not belong to that group.

Historical Generalizations and Sociological Hypotheses

General propositions about society can be expressed at different levels of abstraction, using different types of variables. The lowest level—keeping close to recorded facts—gives what are called empirical generalizations. These are records of observed regularities linking certain phenomena. If these records are based on historical processes, we can speak about them as *historical generalizations*. They express in summary form a series of processes that bear some similarity to one another. No attempt is made at this level to derive those patterns from some more general laws or regularities. In some cases, the relationship may be stated as holding only in certain historical periods or areas.

A further step in scientific generalization attempts to formulate laws, or relationships between variables, that should hold universally or under conditions specified by using general variables, not particularistic determinants of time and place. A concrete historical process, then, should be the result of taking some particular initial conditions and applying to them the effects hypothesized by the general laws. As these laws are usually very tentative, having a low degree of confirmation due to lack of precise measurement and experimentation or of enough comparative situations, they are better called *sociological hypotheses*.

The distinction here established is somewhat similar to the one posited by Karl Popper between *historical* and *sociological laws*.[2] A historical law, in his conception, attempts to predict a historical sequence, given some initial conditions, without specifying further contingencies or combinations of variables that might alter the course of events. This "prophecy" or long-term forecast is condemned by Popper as unscientific and is contrasted with what he calls sociological laws, which specify relationships between variables and do not refer to whole historical processes or sequences.

A sociological law cannot predict the future because its purported effects are contingent on the values of the independent variables and must be combined with the operation of a multitude of other laws, all of them establishing equally contingent relationships. To this must be added the fact that most sociological laws—or hypotheses—should be interpreted probabilistically, not in a determinist fashion.

In this Appendix the theoretical propositions explicitly or implicitly put forth in the text of this volume will be rehashed in two rounds. On a first round, the main historical generalizations will be reviewed. On a second round, more abstract or general hypotheses will be established, building with them a theoretical model, so that, in principle, each historical generalization could be deduced from the application of the model's hypotheses to diverse initial conditions.

To begin with the historical generalizations, they have been numbered from G1 to G20, and grouped under the following headings:

(1) political cleavages in advanced industrial societies

(2) political cleavages in relatively industrialized developing societies

(3) political cleavages in underdeveloped societies feeling the first impact of capitalist growth

(4) political cleavages in societies settled in "empty" areas

(5) militarism and civilian control in nineteenth-century Latin America

(6) authoritarianism and democracy under dependent capitalism

(7) the organization of the popular classes

Political Cleavages in Advanced Industrial Societies

G1: In a modern industrial society, there is a bipolarity of interests between employers and workers that tends to produce a class-based two-party or two-coalition political system in which the middle classes are mostly co-opted by the dominant ones and the working class has a socialist ideology (Western Europe and Japan), unless

(a) there are strong ethnic, national, religious, or language differences (J. S. Mill, Lipset-Rokkan) or regional conflicts, which weaken working-class solidarity and generate antagonisms and divisions among the upper and middle classes (United States, Northern Ireland), or

(b) deep economic crises generate unsettled sectors of the upper and middle classes, which adopt anti–status quo and mobilizational tactics, thereby taking advantage of social-psychological tensions in mass society (Mannheim, Nazism in Germany).

G2: The working class has radical and violent attitudes during the early stages of industrialization and it tends to moderation as a result of economic development, reform, and increased social mobility; thus, economic growth facilitates the consolidation of democracy (Lipset).

Political Cleavages in Relatively Industrialized Developing Societies

G3: In a relatively industrialized and urbanized developing country (or area), a tendency to class-based political bipolarity does exist but is very often counteracted by

(a) the presence of unsatisfied sectors of the bourgeoisie and the middle classes seeking position in a more fully developed capitalist system (Marx, Engels),

(b) the existence of strong ethnic, national, religious, language, or regional conflicts,

(c) the fact that often the relatively industrialized and urban part of the country forms a small percentage of the nation (Brazil, Mexico), and

(d) the fact that the working class has high social mobilization but low autonomous organization, as a result of its recent rural migratory origin (Gino Germani; Argentina after World War II).

G4: As a result of the above, mobilizational multiclass-based parties with popular support rather than social democratic ones are typical, whereas conservative parties are weak, having been unable to co-opt much of the middle classes.

Political Cleavages in Underdeveloped Societies Feeling the First Impact of Capitalist Growth

G5: Underdeveloped societies undergoing the first impact of capitalist growth through connection to world markets or foreign investments are likely to have

(a) dissatisfied status incongruent and insecure elites among the upper and middle strata, the military, the clergy, and the intelligentsia, some of them affected by the revolution of rising expectations, others suffering downward mobility or the threat of it (Iran),

(b) masses of socially mobilized but not yet autonomously organized working class, often with high concentrations in mining and agroindustry (Deutsch, Germani),

(c) proletarianized peasants due to the demographic explosion and the impact of capitalist businesses on the existing land tenure structure.

G6: As a result of the above, there is a tendency for the formation of a potentially revolutionary coalition between dissatisfied elites and mobilized masses. The resulting menace prompts the dominant sectors to a repressive policy, or, alternatively, to the creation of a modernizing autocracy. If the revolutionary coalition comes to power, it can form a mobilizational regime (Apter), which will be the more radical the fewer elements of the upper strata it has within its ranks.

G7: After the revolutionary elimination of capitalism, a new bureaucratic class must be formed to organize production. This class becomes socially dominant, although it does not necessarily exert political power directly (USSR, China, Cuba).

Political Cleavages in Societies Settled in "Empty" Areas

G8: In societies settled in "empty" areas, under conditions of high labor scarcity, there is early strength of trade unions and a tendency for the formation of labor parties (Australia, New Zealand, to a lesser extent in Canada) with the exceptions stated in G1 (a) (United States).

G9: In settler societies where

(a) the country is less "empty," with a nonnegligible native population, and

(b) immigrants are also foreigners and do not take up citizenship because of the weakness of the political system of the receiving country,

there will be a tendency at some moment for the internationalist, foreign-oriented culture of the labor movement to be superseded by a national-popular reaction, based on internal migrants and nationalized descendants of foreign immigrants (Argentina).

Militarism and Civilian Control in Nineteenth-Century Latin America

G10: If there is a potentially menacing class, even if not yet mobilized, and economic conditions are not excessively unsettled, the dominant classes will be unified, will avoid mobilizational tactics, and will be able to control the armed forces through an aristocratic civilian regime (monarchical Brazil).

G11: If there are intense antagonisms between sectors of the dominant classes and unsettled economic conditions, there will be a lack of control over the military, leading to what may be called "military anarchy" (early nineteenth-century Mexico, Argentina before Rosas).

G12: If liberalization or the adoption of democratic institutions proceeds too much in advance of the actual distribution of power among social classes, the result will not be a solid liberal or democratic regime, but rather

(a) Frondisme, that is, the fragmentation of power among sectors of the elites, which makes effective government impossible, and/or

(b) mobilizationism, that is, the appeal by dissatisfied elites to mass participation under *caudillista* leadership.

In both instances, a situation of "civilian anarchy" is created, leading to military intervention (Alamán, Alberdi, Edwards).

G13: Military or civilian anarchy is controllable if

(a) one military group overpowers the others, using as a base a growing social class or helping to create one, and establishes a stable autocracy (Díaz in Mexico, Rosas in Argentina);

(b) one dominant "connection" or coalition is formed between economic groups and politicians, establishing a strong civilian government (Portales in Chile).

Authoritarianism and Democracy under Dependent Capitalism

G14: Democratization under dependent capitalism creates conditions such that

(a) popular activism thrives, generating a menace to the existing system (Huntington, O'Donnell), which is unable to deflect it through social mobility, reform, or extended prosperity, due to the limits set by dependency;

(b) the degree of work discipline expected by managers when attempting intensive industrialization is impossible to establish except by repression of trade union and other rights (O'Donnell).

G15: Under conditions of limited popular participation, a democratic regime of sorts can exist, although with malfunctions due to lack of consensus or episodes of increased popular participation. These episodes generate military interventions of a provisional, corrective, or "moderating" type. As popular participation increases, generating a serious menace to the established order, the military is stimulated to a more permanent type of intervention, of a "transformative" type. This can be

(a) a combination of repression and eventually radical reform to deflect the menace even at the cost of sacrificing the interests of part of the civilian dominant classes (Stepan; Peru's military regime), or

(b) a "bureaucratic-authoritarian" regime oriented to economic growth and permanent repression of working-class activity (O'Donnell; Argentinian, Brazilian, and Chilean military regimes).

G16: Autocracy oriented to economic growth and stability may produce two different types of effects (differently emphasized by contrasting theoretical systems, probably operative under different contexts):

(a) it may succeed in establishing order and economic growth, forcing the dominant classes and the military into more technocratic and professional roles, and the popular opposition into less mobilizational or violent tactics, thus creating the conditions for eventual gradual liberalization (Vallenilla Lanz; Spain, Brazil), or else

(b) repression may lead to blockages of information and communication and to an accumulation of frustrations among not only the popular but also the middle or upper sectors of society (Apter), thus endangering order and growth and forcing ever-greater degrees of repression in a vicious circle leading eventually to a social revolution (Cuba and Nicaragua) or to widespread guerrilla activity (Argentina).

G17: Under modern conditions control of the armed forces can exist if

(a) a full representative system is established, so that all classes feel adequately represented and give up expectations of total domination of society, coming to agreements and pacts and keeping control over their own extremists (Linz, O'Donnell-Schmitter), or

(b) a revolution is successful in establishing a new order initially based on violence but able to create a hegemonic system of civilian domination, which keeps the military under control (Mexico, Cuba).

The Organization of the Popular Classes

G18: In the more rural countries of the periphery, the main sector of the popular classes is the peasantry, which may become politically activated through the leadership of middle-class elements, either of a social revolutionary type or of a more moderate populist ("*aprista*") variety (Central America and the Caribbean, Peru, Venezuela).

G19: In the more urban countries of the periphery, the main sector of the popular classes are the trade unions, which may become politically activated through the leadership of external elites in a populist formula ("Peronist" type) or in alliance with sectors of the middle classes or the intelligentsia (socialist labor parties) (Argentina, Chile).

G20: In countries of the periphery, the political role of the intelligentsia is marked by its tendency to adopt ideologies created in the more developed industrial countries or to follow the model of successful Third World revolutions. As a result, its role is particularly difficult in the relatively more developed areas, where it resists association with working-class populism and tends either to the purist ideological Left or to collaboration with middle-class reform parties or governments (Argentina, Brazil, Mexico).

These historical generalizations classify situations or processes and establish associations between them either by predicting series of events (as in G2, G9, or G12) or, more commonly, the permanence of some traits as long as some other conditions, which define the situation, remain in operation (as in G1, G3, and most others). Still, they do not detail the processes involved in maintaining each situation, and to that extent they are less useful in planning action for interested social actors, or in studying closely the evolution of a political situation. By remaining quite close to historical facts, however, these propositions are easily understood, and in the cases where two or three of them must be applied in conjunction, it is possible intuitively to follow the operation of their combined effects.

For a more detailed analysis of the interaction processes involved in the maintenance—or change—of each situation, we must now turn to a system of *sociological hypotheses*, linking variables to one another, not to whole historical sequences.

The Structure of the Model

In contrast with the historical generalizations, each of which deals with different situations, the theoretical model here developed establishes relationships between variables that should be valid under the most diverse conditions. Given the approximate nature of the discipline, however, the more those conditions diverge from those characteristic of Latin America in the last century and a half or so, the less accurate the model will be. The variety of Latin American situations, country by country and time period by time period, is great enough, however, to accommodate cases drawn from other areas, short of extremes like those of postindustrial or feudal and archaic societies.

In the following description of the structure of the model, I shall make no attempt to justify or explain the hypotheses I incorporate, as they have been in most cases already dealt with in the text.

To begin, society is seen as divided into a number of social actors, mostly stratificationally defined or based on ethnicity and religion, but including also institutional ones like church or armed forces, the government, political and ideological elites, and foreign interests. Actors form coalitions with the purpose of coming to power and bringing about changes or preventing them from occurring. For this purpose, society is also seen as consisting of a number of social controls, which are ways of running things, based on legal, institutionalized, or customary practices. Actors have attitudes toward those social controls and attempt to change them when forming part of the government. Social controls can be classified into economic and political, taking the latter in its wider sense. Economic controls can be, for example, prevalence of private property, protectionism, support for agricul ture, and deficit financing. Political controls are, among others, centralism, repression, level and mode of participation, support for education, and immigration policy. Each actor has a certain attitude, favorable or unfavorable, toward each of these controls.

Actors have a set of characteristics: nationality; ethnicity; religion; language; region of origin; status; status incongruence; standard of living; level of expecta- tions regarding standard of living; economic insecurity; organization; social mobi- lization; organizational or political weight; mobilizational weight; communications with other actors (which form a matrix). All of these variables are exogenous and are mostly self-explanatory. The political weight of an actor is its strength or power, which depends on several factors not enumerated in this model (resources, central- ity of position, prestige, and the like) and on its degree of autonomous organization. So the political weight of an actor can also be considered its organizational weight. The actor also has a certain amount of social mobilization, on the basis of which a mobilizational weight can be defined. Although both organizational and mobiliza- tional weights are exogenous, they are proportional to the values of organization and of social mobilization of the actor considered.

Next, a group of actors' attitudinal variables must be considered: anomie; psychological authoritarianism; ideologism; ideology (which has six dimensions, namely, nationalism, conservatism, pluralism, populism, egalitarianism, and statism); satisfaction; predisposition to violence; attitudes toward economic con- trols (economic interests); attitudes toward political controls.

Anomie and psychological authoritarianism are well-known concepts. Ideolo- gism refers to an actor's tendency to give high priority to ideological questions of any orientation. The various ideologies, or ideological dimensions, appear in the above list. Some well-known ideologies are absent from this list of dimensions, but not from the theoretical concerns of this model. Thus, "liberalism" has a different meaning in Latin America and the United States, so it is better to reduce it to its components, probably a combination of pluralism, populism, egalitarianism, and statism, in the North American use. The Latin American definition of the term would wipe out all but pluralism from the above list and add important components of conservatism. For similar reasons socialism is absent from the list of ideological dimensions, its nearest surrogate being egalitarianism, with statism a good runner- up. Specific Latin American ideologies like Aprismo are also absent, being reducible to a combination of populism and egalitarianism, with fluctuating elements of pluralism and statism. Favorability to dictatorship is not explicitly included, although it is present implicitly in a very low or nil value of pluralism. Favorability to dictatorship (or, more generally, to repression) is taken to be an attitude toward a social control (repression) that may vary somewhat independently from an actor's ideology. Thus, an actor may be relatively high in pluralism and at the same time (maybe for conjunctural reasons) favorable to repression, as in some liberal developmental dictatorships, or "strong governments" of Latin America's past.

Satisfaction and predisposition to violence are both endogenous and will be dealt with later on.[3] Attitudes toward social controls have been referred to before. It must be added here that attitudes toward economic controls are the same thing as economic interests, or, rather, subjective economic interests. That is, we abandon the quest to know the "real interests" of each actor. Not that the subject is unimportant, but it is better for the moment to keep to what the actors actually think they want (both in economic and in political matters).

With this list most of the basic variables of the model have been introduced and described. A few others (mostly constructed variables) will be seen later, but are not considered here for simplicity in the exposition of the model. What we have, then, is a list of variables characterizing each actor and some social controls applicable to society as a whole.

Once we know the values of the variables for a given period, the next step involves calculating, on the basis of each actor's attitudes, their attraction to or rejection of others, so that political coalitions can be formed. Of these coalitions, the strongest one will come to power, and from there it can inroduce some changes in the dominant social controls. With this, the period under consideration is finished. The next period (after six months, or a year, or whatever is chosen) must be treated in the same fashion, namely,

(1) specification of the new values of exogenous variables,

(2) calculation of the values of endogenous variables for each actor, using the model's formulas,

(3) calculation of the new coalitions on the basis of the changed attitudes and other actor characteristics, if such changes have taken place,

(4) determination of which is the winning coalition and the setting it up in power, and

(5) calculation of the changes in social controls brought about by the winning coalition.

Coalition Formation and Political Cleavages

Between any two actors the similarity or difference between their attitudes toward the existing social controls (i.e., their economic interests and political attitudes) creates an affinity or an antagonism.[4] If we take only one social control or issue at a time, we get between any two actors a partial affinity, calculable according to several alternative formulas not given here. The total affinity or antagonism should be the result of averaging out the partial affinities, but not all issues have the same relevance or weighting. One way of calculating relevance is by making it proportional to the total amount of conflict existing around the corresponding issues. The amount of conflict depends on the political weight of the actors and their partial antagonisms over a given issue (pp. 41–45, 138–141).

Actors are attracted to (or repelled by) others according to the affinities or antagonisms existing between them. It can be supposed that a certain force of attraction (or repulsion) is exerted proportional to the affinity and to the political weight of the attracting (or repelling) actor. Thus, a matrix is created which allows a calculus of coalition formation. There are several possible mathematical formulas for this process, which are not given here. The result, however, will generally be a number of coalitions, among which antagonisms will exist. At this stage the principle of the "lesser evil" may make the coalitions feel a certain solidarity with those against whom there is less antagonism. In this manner a structure of tactical affinities will exist on the basis of which the same calculations as before will lead two or more coalitions to form a front. To distinguish these types of coalition, the earlier, more solid ones will be called "fusions," to emphasize their greater unification of purpose, and the tactical ones will be called "fronts." The stronger front, as will be seen later on, accedes to government.

It is necessary to differentiate among actors some of whom, because of the guardian nature of their functions, are expected, under relatively modernized social environments, not to interfere in the political process by forming coalitions. Even when abstaining from direct intervention, however, they have interests and attitudes, but they express them differently. These actors are considered as potentially noninvolved, even if often they do take part in politics, shunning their noninvolvement (as a result of feeling menaced, usually).

Before starting the calculation of coalitions, then, we should separate the noninvolved actors, if there are any. After the fronts have been determined without their participation, it is important to know which front the noninvolved actors feel closer to. When front formation has been completed, abstaining or noninvolved actors are allowed to join the process of coalition formation. The resulting coalitions, which do not actually form during the period considered, will be called "potential fronts." They will materialize, though, if at some future time the noninvolved actors become involved as a reaction to feelings of menace.

Fusions (or fronts) should look very much like political parties. As has been seen, political parties are not normally taken as individual actors (an ideological party elite may, though). A party should result from the coalition of several actors. The model can also work, however, if it becomes necessary to take in one or more intractable political parties as actors in their own right.

In judging the similarity of a coalition to a political party or movement, it should be borne in mind that the coalition is only a latent structure, not an exact description of society. The fact that an actor appears in a coalition does not mean that all of the individuals who, according to the definition of the actor, belong to it must also support or vote for the party symbolized by the coalition. It is enough if the greater, the more important, or more organized part of the actor is so incorporated. If necessary, subdivision of actors may be necessary better to reflect reality.

The main cleavages in a society are those between fronts. The political cleavages hypothesized by the various historical generalizations listed earlier cannot be predicted using only the theoretical formulas of this model, because the results of their application are contingent on "initial conditions." Initial conditions, from a model point of view, are not only the values of all the variables in the initial period, but also the values of the exogenous variables in the following periods. The model does not presuppose any particular values for those initial conditions; it simply calculates the results for any set of them.

A special type of coalition, which can be called mobilizational, comes into existence when it includes at least one mobilizational leader and one actor with more social mobilization than organization. A mobilizational leader is an actor that has high status and an attitude favoring mobilization as a mode of participation.

The political weight of a coalition is normally equal to the sum of the political (i.e., organizational) weights of its member actors. But in the case of a mobilizational coalition, its total political weight results from adding up the mobilizational instead of the organizational weights of its members. Within a mobilizational coalition the distribution of power and influence, however, depends on the organizational weights of its members. Thus, a highly mobilized massive actor with low organization can contribute a lot of strength to a coalition but have little say in deciding its policies (pp. 33–48, 134–137).

The ideology of an actor is calculated in two steps. Actors that are high on ideologism are considered ideological specialists who generate ideology on their own. For them, ideology is exogenous, because the model does not attempt to enter into the arcane factors that determine ideological preferences for such groups.[5] Once ideology is thus generated, it spreads through influence, which runs through channels provided by the communications matrix referred to in the previous section. But this network operates in a special way: influence is unidirectional, from the ideological specialist to the other actors, provided there is a minimum of affinity between them. On the other hand, members of a solidary coalition (i.e., a fusion) pass on to each other the "contacts" they have, that is, their structure of communications. This mechanism defines the concept of accessibility of an actor from another actor, based on the communications existing between them, or provided by an ally of the ideological specialist. The ideology of a nonideological specialist, then, will result from the ideological influences it receives. These influences originate only from ideological specialists, are proportional to the accessibility of the receiving actor from the various ideological specialists and to the affinity uniting them, and are cumulative from period to period (pp. 38–41, 143–146).

In table 5 the main variables seen so far have been displayed for easy reference.

Table 5. Basic Set of Variables

Actor characteristics

Nationality, ethnicity, religion, language, region of origin

Status, status incongruence

Standard of living, level of expectations, economic insecurity

Anomie, psychological authoritarianism, ideologism

Organization

Social mobilization

Organizational (or political) weight

Mobilizational weight

Relationships between actors

Matrix of communications

Matrix of accessibility (based on communications, affinities, and structure of coalitions)

Matrix of affinities (based on economic interests, political attitudes, satisfaction, and predisposition to violence. If negative: antagonisms)

Interests, attitudes, and ideology

Economic interests (attitudes toward economic controls)

Political attitudes (attitudes toward political controls)

Ideology (nationalism, conservatism, pluralism, egalitarianism, populism, statism)

Structure of coalitions

Fusions (based on affinities and political weights)

Fronts (based on tactical affinities and fusions' political weights)

Potential fronts (fronts that would form if noninvolved actors were included)

Structure of menaces (based on structure of coalitions, antagonisms, and violence)

Main cleavages (determined by structure of coalitions)

Cycle of violence

Satisfaction (if negative: relative deprivation)

Predisposition to violence

Types of actors

Potentially noninvolved (e.g., church, military)

Actually noninvolved

Ideological specialist (high in ideologism)

Mobilizational leader (high in mobilizationism and with high status or organization)

The Cycle of Violence

To this point, the model has mapped the political scene by calculating the main coalitions and thus the prevailing cleavages. It has also determined the ideology of each actor (and therefore the average ideology of each coalition) and has taken into account the existence of some special, "guardian" actors, which may be noninvolved in the process of coalition formation, although they do have attitudes and interests and are ready to join one of the fronts if stimulated to do so. Now we must examine a set of variables associated with violence.

As an introduction, the variables satisfaction and legitimacy will be considered. The satisfaction (or its opposite, relative deprivation) of an actor may have two sources. One is linked to its economic well-being, the other to its institutional goal fulfillment, that is, the degree to which society is run according to principles (social controls) attuned to the actor's beliefs (attitudes). In both cases, satisfaction is a relative phenomenon, depending on the interplay of gratification and expectations. Thus, in the economic field, gratifications are measured by the standard of living, affected by economic insecurity; expectations refer to the standard of living the actor feels entitled to, that is, to its realistic aspirations. The relationship between the two (gratification and expectation) gives the economic satisfaction. In this sense, the economic satisfaction or feeling of well-being of an individual or group may vary independently of its actual standard of living, depending on the psychologically and socially induced level of aspirations. As for institutional goal fulfillment, it depends on the contrast between the state of the existing social controls and the actor's attitudes toward them. The smaller the gap, the greater the feeling of satisfaction or of institutional goal fulfillment. Some of these goals may be economic, but they must be distinguished from the "consumerist" feeling of economic well-being. Thus, agrarian reform may be one of the economic controls desired by a certain actor, which will feel goal fulfillment if it is enacted. But the economic satisfaction will depend on the actor's standard of living (and expectations), which can operate with a different causative structure. The calculation of institutional goal fulfillment for each actor should weigh each issue or social control according to its relevance.

The final satisfaction of each actor depends on the combined effects of its economic satisfaction and its institutional satisfaction or goal fulfillment. The more ideologist an actor is, the more weight it will give to institutional goal fulfillment by contrast to mere economic satisfaction (pp. 68–71).

Closely allied to the concept of satisfaction is that of legitimacy. Legitimacy measures the degree to which society is run according to principles the population feels just or acceptable. It is thus the result of a general averaging out of the institutional satisfaction or goal fulfillment of all actors, which can be accomplished in several ways. Each actor could be considered in proportion to its political weight, which would disregard the opinions of large but weak social sectors. This may be too "undemocratic" an accounting, although it is not possible to argue for a totally "democratic" form of calculating legitimacy, where actors would be considered in proportion to their numbers. Probably, some intermediate form would be accurate, for example, taking into account mobilizational rather than organizational weights, or some value resulting from combining political weight and population. It should be noted that in the calculation of legitimacy only institutional satisfaction, or goal fulfillment, not economic satisfaction, is taken into account, although a prolonged period of well being may end up making people's attitudes change and thereby facilitate legitimacy and consensus (pp. 78–79).

The predisposition to violence is a function of the actor's frustration, or relative deprivation (the opposite of satisfaction). Some actors may convert frustration into aggression at a higher rate than others, depending on their psychological authoritarianism and their anomie. On the other hand, if the actor is subject to menace (a concept to be discussed later in this section), its tendency to violence will be greater than would be predicted by looking only at the deprivation, both institutional and economic, that the actor is suffering at the moment. By contrast, if social legitimacy is high, the conversion of frustration into aggression will be blocked, not only for satisfied actors but also for those who, being dissatisfied (frustrated) have not contributed much to the general level of legitimacy.

On the basis of the violent predispositions of actors, the concept of menace can be developed. The menace to an actor comes from all those actors (including noninvolved ones) that are at the same time antagonistic to it and violent, or very highly antagonistic if not violent. From these enemies a force of attack is felt, proportional to their combined political weight and to the level of antagonism and violence. Against that attack a defense is provided by the political weight of the front to which the actor belongs. The relationship between "attack" and "defense" is the menace felt by the actor. This menace can be subdivided into components, according to origin. Thus, if only popular menacing actors are taken into account, a popular menace can be constructed; similarly, it is possible to define a menace coming from upper-status actors or a regional or foreign menace. It is also useful to consider the concept of potential menace, which results from the supposition that all antagonistic actors are fully mobilized and members of mobilizational coalitions, thus increasing considerably their political weights.

As can be seen, there is a vicious circle operating between predisposition to violence and menace. Violence was stated to be influenced partially by the existence of a menace hanging over the head of an actor. Now menace is itself defined as depending on the violence of some actors that are antagonistic to the one being considered (pp. 79–81, 87–90).

Table 6 outlines the main relationship in the cycle of violence.

Military Interventions and Repression

The military is one of the few actors, like the church and, in some instances, foreign interests, that in modern societies are not expected to engage directly in

Table 6. The Cycle of Violence

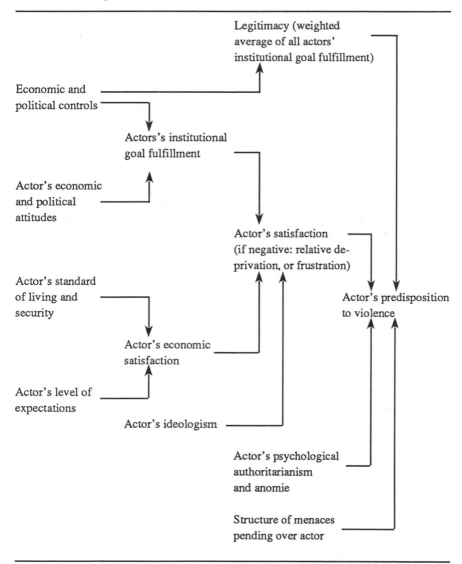

politics, although they do have economic interests, ideologies, and attitudes toward social controls. Even in such marginal areas—from the point of view of the consolidation of democracy—as Latin America, such actors can also be considered as potentially noninvolved, although in fact they are often engaged in government or influence it very directly. In these cases, they are still considered potentially noninvolved, although actually involved, that is, participating in politics and forming fronts with other actors. What pushes them into involvement is the feeling of being menaced, which is present when there is a strong coalition of antagonistic and violent actors set against them.[6] Even when noninvolved, however, their influence on the political scene is ever-present, because other actors avoid antagonizing them too much.

The involvement of the military in politics is not tantamount to a coup, although it does signify a situation of generalized praetorianism. The military actor, once activated into politics, needs to form a front with other actors before it can become a direct part of government. If the military's political weight were much greater than that of any other actor or coalition of actors, the armed forces would not need any allies to get to power. In fact, and contrary to a widespread belief held in countries affected by chronic military intervention, the military does not have such overpowering weight in comparison to other actors. A consequence of this supposition about relative weights is that the military, if totally isolated from other civilian groups, would scarcely be able to intervene in politics, much less stage a coup. But, of course, when coup conditions have materialized, there are often more than a few civilian groups willing to ally themselves with the military for their own purposes. The etiology of military intervention does not resolve itself, at any rate, into a study of the attitudes (democratic or otherwise) predominant among the military. Rather, it consists in an examination of the relationships of civilian groups between themselves and toward the military (pp. 35–37, 84–96).

If the front (incorporating the military) that accedes to power has a high predisposition to violence, the change of government will be violent and take the form of a coup. If violence is not present, the change of government may take more legal forms. But when the structure of menace is high enough to have stirred the armed forces from their noninvolvement, the likelihood is that they will also have become violent.

Connected to the subject of military involvement and dictatorship, the attitude toward repression should be analyzed. This is an attitude toward a political control, and it is important to know its values for all actors, not only the military. Coercive governments need not be only military, and even in dictatorships in general the military governs in association with other civilian groups.

The attitude toward repression (by the existing authorities) depends, of course, on the position of the actor vis-à-vis the government. This position can be that of supporter, neutral, internal opponent (member of a disgruntled faction of the ruling coalition), or external opponent (member of nongovernment coalitions that are antagonistic to the ruling group). For a supporter or a neutral, favorability to repression will depend mostly on its predisposition to violence, especially if the actor has high psychological authoritarianism and low pluralism. Opponents will oppose repression in relation to how antagonistic they are toward the government. If they come to power as a result of a rearrangement of coalitions, they may change their attitude to this issue in the next period.

It is necessary to make some distinctions in the field of repression and violence.

A governing actor's favorability to repression is not the same as the actual level of repression exerted. The latter depends on the average attitudes of all members of the governing coalition and on their ability to impose repression, which in turn is a function of the relative strength of government and opposition (see next section). For similar reasons, the predisposition to violence of an actor is not the same as the general level of violence prevailing in a society. However, this general level is not simply an average of all actors' violence, because experience shows that one or two small but extremely violent actors can affect the whole population even if it is not sympathetic to their aims and methods. The mechanism involved is too complex to formulate at this stage of development of the model (see pp. 70–83).

Attitudes toward Participation in Power

Economic attitudes (subjective economic interests) are considered exogenous in this model. Some political attitudes are also exogenous; others have been included as endogenous, that is, ruled by sociological hypotheses incorporated into the model. They are favorability to repression (already discussed) and a group related to the concentration and fragmentation of power and popular participation in it: level of participation, mode of participation, competitive elections, geographical concentration of power, and functional concentration of power in the executive.

The attitude toward level of participation refers to a favorability to extending the number of people involved, through elections or otherwise, in influencing the government. We can hypothesize that there are three types of causes of an actor's favorability to an increase in the level of participation: stratificational, ideological, and the structure of menace. The lower the status of an actor, the greater its tendency to favor extension of participation. Populism or egalitarianism also have a strong influence in the same direction, whereas pluralism has a slight association. If the actor registers perception of great menace of popular origin, it will tend to favor a reduction in the level of participation; the contrary holds if the menace comes from other high-status (or foreign) actors. In the latter case, even an upper middle or upper-class actor may consider itself part of the "people" against an oligarchic or foreign menace and react accordingly, seeking to occupy a position as popular leader.

The mode of participation can range from mobilizationism to associationism. The favorability to mobilizationism is closely associated to the populist ideology, but it can also depend on other factors, like economic insecurity, status incongruence, anomie, or the degree to which the actor's mobilization exceeds its own autonomous organization. The structure of menace also tends to increase the tendency to mobilizationism if it is mostly of upper-class or foreign origin, and to decrease it if it is of popular origin. A high level of populism favors mobilizationism, whereas conservatism and pluralism tend to diminish it (pp. 22–29, 62–67).

Favorability to competitive elections is almost identical to support for democracy in its present form, but it can derive from ideological conviction or from a tactical stance while in opposition. Thus, we will assume that pluralist actors will favor competitive elections, unless for some reason they favor repression. This applies to governmental or neutral actors, because those in opposition, if they favor an extension of participation and mobilizationism, will also support competitive elections while in opposition, whatever their values regarding pluralism or violence. Once in power, however, their attitude toward further competitive elections may shift, depending on their ideological pluralism and (with contrary effects) on their eventually newly acquired favorability to repression, which after accession to power is a function of their predisposition to violence.

Next we come to two closely connected attitudes relating to geographical and functional concentration of power. Geographical concentration of power ranges from centralism to federalism, the latter having extremes of autonomism and separatism. An actor will be sensitized to the subject of centralism versus federalism if the total amount of conflict from a different region is very high. The amount of conflict is a function of the political weight of extraregional actors and of their antagonism to the actor under consideration. Given this sensitization, the actor will tend to favor centralism if it is part of a powerful coalition (fusion), that is, one whose political weight forms a high percentage of the political weights of all coalitions. This favorability will be stronger if there is also a regional menace. If, however, the actor belongs to a weak coalition, it will tend toward federalism, veering toward more extreme forms (autonomism or separatism) if the degree of conflict is very intense and accompanied by menace (pp. 60–62).

Functional concentration of power can range from favoring a strong executive (executivism) to its opposite, the extreme power of sectional interests and lobbies (*frondisme*). In an intermediate position are forms of presidentialism or parliamentarism, whose actual functional concentration of power depends not only on constitutional arrangements but on the structure of political parties and political custom. Thus, the British system, although formally parliamentarian, is highly executivistic, whereas the American one is less executivistic than its presidentialist constitution would lead one to believe.

The etiology of the functional concentration of power bears some resemblance to that of geographical concentration of power, although there is no sensitizing threshold like that associated with regional conflict. Actors that are a part of very powerful coalitions (fusions) will tend toward executivism, the more if they feel menaced from whatever source. Actors belonging to weak fusions will prefer the opposite position, approaching *frondisme* if their coalition is very weak and if they feel threatened. When fusions are strong but balanced in political weight, members will favor a mixed form of government, in line with classical balance of powers theory.

Executivism need not be associated with centralism, although a highly executivistic regime or attitude is not easily compatible with intense federalism. Neither is executivism necessarily accompanied by repression. Caesarism, a typical form of government in a consolidating nationality, does imply, though, a convergence of geographical and functional concentration of power and repression (pp. 49–60).

Change of Government and of Social Controls

For a change of government to occur, an opposition front must have greater political weight than the incumbents. Of course, it is not necessarily true that the front with the most votes will come to power, but in some cases there is an approximate coincidence between political weight and votes (as in practicing democracies), and thus political alterations follow both the dictates of the constitution and of this model. If votes do not even approximately reflect political weight, they are illusory and incapable of bringing a coalition to power. In some instances, as in the limited democracies of nineteenth-century Europe, the restricted vote did to some extent represent power and was therefore instrumental in bringing about changes of government. In societies not run by voting standards, like preconstitutional monarchies or bureaucratic-collectivist regimes, changes of government should follow changes in coalition making or in relative weights, without necessarily involving violence or military coups (as in several post-Stalin changes in the Soviet Union).

Once a new coalition (front) is established in government, or the existing one is maintained (probably with changed attitudes, weights, and other variables), controls are adjusted to reflect the opinions of the actors, both those in and out of office. For each social control, there are actors' attitudes. They are averaged, weighted in proportion to political weights, and those of governing actors are adjusted by a coefficient that is a function of the existing degree of repression. Thus, in all cases, the opinions of the opposition and of neutral or noninvolved actors must be taken into account, but in inverse relation to the repressive nature of the government (pp. 148–156).

At this point the cycle is concluded and a new one must be prepared by giving values to the exogenous variables of the new period.

Final Considerations

Practically no hypotheses in this model are derived from other more general ones. According to some interpretations of the building of sociological theory, a mere array of sociological hypotheses may be accurate in stating relationships between variables, but it does not explain the reasons for the stated relationships. The "reason" for the relationships would lie in a few higher-level generalizations or laws, from which the various low-level hypotheses should be deducible. This is not done here simply because I have not been able to find that hierarchical system of hypotheses. I suspect, though, that at the present stage of development of sociological theory, the attempt would be unrewarding.

Although this model can be used to make excursions into the future (conditional on the existence of certain series of values for the exogenous variables in the future), a safer use is for exploring the past to better understand it. This task requires the following steps:

(1) selection of a process occurring over a certain time span, say, two decades, subdivided into periods;

(2) differentiation between exogenous and endogenous variables, all of which are known within the limits of confidence of our research capabilities or intrepidity in making assumptions for non-fully ascertained data;

(3) numerical experimentation, which can take several forms. Given the structure of the formulas and the full array of exogenous and endogenous data for all periods considered, one might, in an ideal case, calculate the coefficients and some other details of the formulas. This is not always possible, though, as there may be instances of overdetermination or underdetermination. It is necessary, then, to assign alternative values to the coefficients until there is a fit between known historical facts and the calculated endogenous variables. In the process, it may be necessary to change the structure of some formulas to fit the facts. Worse still, one may discover that some variable, which had been estimated as having a certain value, really must have had another magnitude more compatible with the data (assuming the validity of the formulas). Of course, the more information there is, and the more cases considered, the less possible it becomes to tinker with the coefficients and the values of the variables.

All of this, given the gross nature of measurement in this field, is mostly science fiction at the present time, although it can be an important intellectual exercise. The attempt to fill in the values for the variables can serve as a systematic method of data collection, helping comparisons and pointing to lacunae of theoretical thinking or research.

No concrete examples of how this model is applied are given here, as the formulas adopted would be excessively arbitrary, the measurements unreliable, and the mathematical paraphernalia necessary to describe even one simple process would seriously jeopardize the communicability of the results.[7] Further efforts at formalization and numerical experimentation must wait until there is a greater consensus about the type of model that is useful in the study of political process. This appendix is intended as a contribution toward that consensus.

Notes

1. The Study of Latin American Politics

1. Juan Bautista Alberdi, *Cartas sobre la prensa y la política militante en la República Argentina*, known as "Cartas Quillotanas," IV: 5–94. Original emphasis.

2. Gino Germani, *Política y sociedad en una época de transición: De la sociedad tradicional a la sociedad de masas*; revised English version, *Authoritarianism, Fascism, and National Populism*. See also his *The Sociology of Modernization: Studies on Its Historical and Theoretical Aspects with Special Regard to the Latin American Case.*

3. Celso Furtado, *Subdesenvolvimento e estagnação na América Latina*, and *Diagnosis of the Brazilian Crisis*; Fernando Henrique Cardoso and Enzo Faletto, *Dependency and Development in Latin America*; Hélio Jaguaribe, *Political Development: A General Theory and a Latin American Case Study*; Osvaldo Sunkel with Pedro Paz, *El subdesarrollo latinoamericano y la teoría del desarrollo*; André Gunder Frank, *Latin America: Underdevelopment or Revolution*. Richard N. Adams has emphasized the differences between "secondary" evolution in peripheral countries and "primary" evolution in path-breaking, industrially and technologically advanced societies. See his *The Second Sowing: Power and Secondary Development in Latin America*

4. Gabriel Almond and James S. Coleman, eds., *The Politics of Developing Areas*; Samuel Huntington, *Political Order in Changing Societies.*

5. Guillermo O'Donnell, *Modernization and Bureaucratic-Authoritarianism: Studies in South American Politics*; David Collier, ed., *The New Authoritarianism*; James Malloy, ed, *Authoritarianism and Corporatism in Latin America.*

6. Guillermo O'Donnell, Philippe Schmitter, and Lawrence Whitehead, eds., *Transitions from Authoritarian Rule: Prospects for Democracy*. This type of approach was already evident in Juan Linz, "Crisis, Breakdown, and Reequilibration."

7. See Carl Hempel, "The Function of General Laws in History"; Ernest Nagel, "The Logic of Historical Analysis"; idem, *The Structure of Science: Problems in the Logic of Scientific Research*; Karl Popper, *The Poverty of Historicism*; Richard Braithwaite, *Scientific Explanation*; George Murphy, "The New History"; Quentin Gibson, *The Logic of Social Explanation.* For a different approach, see Dorothy Emmet and Alasdair MacIntyre, eds., *Sociological Theory and Philosophical Analysis*, which has two articles by Alfred Schutz criticizing the "behaviorism" of Hempel and Nagel.

8. See Robert Brown, *Explanation in Social Sciences*, chapter 5, dedicated to what he calls the genetic method; Patrick Gardiner, ed., *Theories of History*, especially the articles by Alan Dogan, "Explanation in History," and Michael Scriven, "Truisms as the Grounds for

Historical Explanation"; Lawrence Stone, "The Revival of Narrative: Reflections on a New Old History."

9. In *El Tiempo* (January 1846). Mentioned in Jesús Reyes Heroles, *Historia del liberalismo mexicano* I: 10.

10. Ian Christie, *Crisis of Empire: Great Britain and the American Colonies, 1754–1783*, pp. 105–106.

11. For the difference bertween sociological laws relating variables to each other and historical laws, which purport to predict sequences of events, see Popper, *The Poverty of Historicism*.

12. Tulio Halperín Donghi, "El surgimiento de los caudillos en el marco de la sociedad rioplatense postrevolucionaria." The same type of analysis is found in his *Politics, Economy and Society in Argentina during the Revolutionary Period*.

13. See Theda Skocpol, *States and Social Revolutions: A Comparative Analysis of France, Russia, and China*, pp. 35–40, for a comment on this type of comparative research strategy, which, however, she calls "historical analysis" rather than sociological analysis. See also Adam Przeworsky and Henry Teune, *The Logic of Comparative Social Enquiry*.

14. E. Nagel, P. Suppes, and A. Tarski, eds., *Logic, Methodology and Philosophy of Science*; Herbert Simon, *Models of Man, Social and Rational: Mathematical Essays on Rational Human Behavior in a Social Setting*; Raymond Boudon, *L'Analyse mathématique des faits sociaux*; Max Weber, *Economy and Society*, vol. I, pt. 1, ch. 1, sec. 1; idem, *The Methodology of the Social Sciences*; Pierre Bourdieu et al., *Le métier de sociologue*, vol. I, chaps. 2-4, 2-5.

15. For some attempts in formalization, see Hubert Blalock, *Theory Construction: From Verbal to Mathematical Formulations*; Peter C. Ordeshook, *Game Theory and Political Theory: An Introduction*; José A. Silva Michelena, *A Strategy for Research in Social Policy*; Harold Guetzkow, ed., *Simulation in Social Science*; J. A. Laponce and Paul Smoker, eds., *Experimentation and Simulation in Political Science*; Hans Zetterberg, *Theory and Verification in Sociology*; Arthur Stinchcombe, *Constructing Social Theories*; Oscar Varsavsky and Alfredo Eric Calcagno, eds., *América Latina: Modelos Matemáticos*; Alfredo Eric Calcagno, Padro Sáinz, and Juan de Barbieri, *Estilos políticos latinoamericanos*; Oscar Cornblit, Torcuato Di Tella, and Ezequiel Gallo, "A Model of Political Change for Latin America"; Oscar Cornblit, "Political Coalitions and Political Behaviour: A Simulation Model"; Torcuato Di Tella, "Un modelo de análisis de procesos históricos."

16. Endogenous variables are those that can be calculated using the theoretical system incorporated in a model. Exogenous variables cannot be calculated and therefore must be provided by the observer. If the model is applied to a past historical situation, the calculated endogenous variables must be contrasted with the actual events. If the model is applied to the future, it can only give conditional outcomes; if certain facts, events, or changes take place, then certain other outcomes are predicted. See Appendix.

2. Tensions in the Class Structure

1. The central role of the hierarchical division of labor in the formation of class society can be seen in many of Karl Marx's and Friedrich Engels' works, notably in Engels, *Socialism, Utopian and Scientific*, and Marx, *Capital: A Critique of Political Economy*, vol. I, pt. 4, chaps. 13, 14, 15. In the latter, the role of modern technology in making possible the elimination of the division of labor is stated.

2. Alain Touraine, *The Post-industrial Society: Tomorrow's Social History. Classes,*

Conflicts, and Culture in the Programmed Society; André Gorz, *Farewell to the Working Class: An Essay in Post-industrial Socialism.*

3. During his last years, Marx revised his scheme about the conditions that could trigger a socialist revolution in the more developed parts of Europe. He admitted the possibility of the revolt (not necessarily socialist in its first stages) being ignited in Russia. The revolt, however, could only be successful if it acted as a detonating element for a general European conflagration. See Marx's letter to Vera Zasulitch and the preface to the Russian translation of the Manifesto of 1882. Quoted in Umberto Melotti, *Marx and the Third World*, p. 125. In German in Karl Marx and Friedrich Engels, *Werke* IV: 576.

4. The organizational experience of recent migrants to the cities of Latin America is considered in a growing body of literature, which often finds elements of spontaneous organization under extremely adverse conditions. However, those organizations seldom acquire national extension and are generally channeled, co-opted, or actually started by middle- and upper-class groups. See Bryan Roberts, *Organizing Strangers: Poor Families in Guatemala City*; Mario Margulis, *Migración y marginalidad en América Latina*; Germani, *Sociology of Modernization.*

5. Ernest Mandel, *From Class Society to Communism*, judges it very important to consider the bureaucracy in "workers' states" as a stratum and not as a class. The consequence is that the revolution destined to bring its downfall is political, not social. Karol Modzelewski and Jacek Juron, *Lettre ouverte au Parti Ouvrier Polonais*, consider the bureaucracy a class because it acts in practice as though it were the owner of the means of production; they therefore dismiss the role of the division of labor. In this they share Milovan Djilas' approach. Djilas accepts the current view according to which in Marxist theory the origin of classes lies in property. Michele Salvati and Bianca Becalli, in their article "Divisione del lavoro—Capitalismo, socialismo, utopía," study the division of labor as a source of class formation, but they do not admit that under present conditions technology has effects more like what Marx called "manufacture" than what he called "modern industry." They consider the present-day Soviet Union a "historical system of production," avoiding the words "mode of production," and thereby confusing their otherwise quite suggestive analysis. Official or semiofficial analyses from the Communist countries are of course very weak in this aspect. One exception is András N. Hegedüs, *Socialism and Bureaucracy*, and *The Structure of Socialist Society*. Alvin Gouldner, *The Future of Intellectuals and the Rise of the New Class*, and George Konrad and Ivan Szelenyi, *The Intellectuals on the Road to Class Power*, are very insightful but fail to put the connection between division of labor and class development in the center of the picture, where it belongs. I have commented at greater length on this subject in "La división del trabajo y el concepto marxista de clase social."

6. See Karl Deutsch, *Nationalism and Social Communication: An Enquiry into the Foundations of Nationality*, and "Social Mobilization and Political Development"; and Gino Germani, *La integración política de las masas y el totalitarismo*, and idem, *Authoritarianism, Fascism and National Populism*, chap. 6, who use the concept of social mobilization in the same way as in this volume, that is, as indicating a degree of availability for political action. J. P. Nettl, *Political Mobilization: A Sociological Analysis of Methods and Concepts*, and Charles Tilly, *From Mobilization to Revolution*, use the concept of mobilization (by itself or with "political" added) to indicate a capacity for voluntary and organized political action.

7. Torcuato S. Di Tella, "The Dangerous Classes in Early XIXth Century Mexico"; Moisés González Navarro, *Anatomía del poder en México, 1848–1853*; John Tutino, *From Insurrection to Revolution in Mexico.*.

8. Pietro Colletta, *Storia del reame di Napoli dal 1734 sino al 1825* II: 100; Mario Battaglini, ed., *La rivoluzione giacobina del 1799 a Napoli*; Michelangelo Schipa, *Masaniello*; Rosario Villari, *La rivolta antispagnola a Napoli. Le origini, 1585–1647.* See bibliography in Torcuato S. Di Tella, "Mafia y estructura social en el sur de Italia," and an analysis of a similar situation in Carlo G. Rossetti, "Banditismo político: Terre e guerra civile nella Sardegna del XIX secolo."

9. Mikhail Bakunin, "Cartas a un francés," pp. 142–149.

10. C. L. R. James, *Black Jacobins*; Thomas Ott, *The Haitian Revolution, 1789–1804*, Jean Casimir, *La cultura oprimida*; Torcuato S. Di Tella, *La rebelión de esclavos en Haití.*

11. Juan Uslar Pietri, *Historia de la rebelión popular en 1814: Contribución al estudio de la historia de Venezuela*, p. 83. The somewhat simplistic fashion in which Uslar Peitri characterizes Boves as a popular democratic chief is criticized by Germán Carrera Damas, *Boves, aspectos socioeconómicos de su acción histórica.* Uslar Pietri, as a conservative, is generous in granting "democratic" credentials to an authoritarian leader with mass support; Carrera Damas, a Marxist, rejects this.

12. Quoted in Carrera Damas, *Boves*, p. 35.

13. Letter to the Foreign Office secretary, Great Britain, 17 June 1814, Simón Bolívar, *Obras completas* I: 98. See also Indalecio Liévano Aguirre, *Los grandes conflictos sociales y económicos de nuestra historia*, and idem, "Bolívar y Santander."

14. José María Luis Mora, "Sobre la necesidad de fijar el derecho de ciudadanía en la república y hacerlo esencialmente afecto a la propiedad," pp. 630–639.

15. José Pedro Barrán and Benjamín Nahum, *Bases económicas de la revolución artiguista*; Tulio Halperín Donghi, "El surgimiento de los caudillos en el marco de la sociedad rioplatense postrevolucionaria." In Mexico the "yorkino" sector of liberalism, with chiefs like Vicente Gómez Farías and Lorenzo de Zavala, represents this tendency. See Charles Hale, *Mexican Liberalism in the Age of Mora, 1821–1853.* About the regime of Juan Manuel de Rosas, see Tulio Halperín Donghi, *De la revolución de la independencia a la confederación rosista*; and John Lynch, *Argentine Dictator: Juan Manuel de Rosas, 1829–1852*, who put different emphases on its mobilizationist nature.

16. Esteban Echeverría, "Ojeada retrospectiva sobre el movimiento intelectual en el Plata desde el año 37," p. 93. See idem, *Dogma socialista*, pp. 199–209, about the difference between the "people's reason" and the actual will of that same people at a given moment, on which sovereignty cannot be based.

17. The world *federalist* has opposite connotations in the United States and in Latin America. Given the previous separate institutional status of each one of the thirteen colonies and the confederate nature of their first common efforts, the project of forming a federation implied stronger bonds between the parts. The much more centralized nature of the Latin American colonial units left a legacy of centralism, a name maintained by those who wished to keep as much as possible of the previously existing geographical concentration of power (in Argentina they were called *unitarios*). By contrast, the federalists (*federales*) were those who fought for greater autonomy of the parts.

18. José Manuel Estrada, *La política liberal bajo la tiranía de Rosas*, pp. 13–14, 26–27, 47–48.

19. Bartolomé Mitre, *Historia de Belgrano y de la independencia argentina* III: 83–92.

20. Iturbide succeeded in mixing from the extreme Right, which opposed the reforms coming from Spain, to the Left of Lorenzo de Zavala and Vicente Gómez Farías, not only at the time of independence but also after the coup d'état and the proclamation of the Empire.

See Lorenzo de Zavala, *Ensayo histórico de las revoluciones de México desde 1808 hasta 1830*; Elizabeth Hoel Mills, *Don Valentín Gómez Farías y el desarrollo de su ideología política*; Torcuato S. Di Tella, *Iturbide y el cesarismo popular*.

3. Actors and Coalitions

1. Actors such as the church, which is normally noninvolved in modern Western societies, were not so in the times of Gregory VII. The church's Muslim equivalents continue to be involved, especially in the Iran of the ayatollahs. However, even in that case it may be argued that the clerics were thrust into intervention as a result of the aggression from the secularizing policy of the shah, which also eroded their economic bases, a part of the impact of modern capitalism on the bazaar and the mosque. See Theda Skocpol, "Rentier State and Shi'a Islam in the Iranian Revolution."

2. For various works that coincide in giving to the state more autonomy than posited in classical Marxist or liberal approaches, see Skocpol, *States and Social Revolutions*; Alfred Stepan, *State and Society: Peru in Comparative Perspective*; FLACSO-UNESCO, *Teoría, metodología y política del desarrollo en América Latina*; Richard Fagen, ed., *Capitalism and the State in U.S.–Latin American Relations*; Julio Cotler and Richard Fagen, eds., *Latin America and the United States: The Changing Political Realities*; and Oscar Oszlak, *La formación del estado argentino*.

3. Antonio Gramsci, *Gli intellettuali e l' organizzazione della cultura*. More common is the definition given by Seymour M. Lipset, *Political Man: The Social Bases of Politics*, chap. 10.

4. V. I. Lenin, *What Is to Be Done: Burning Questions of the Moment*, chap. 1, sec. C.

5. This interpretation contrasts with that of Gideon Sjoberg, for whom traditional societies, even in their urban sectors are constituted of only the extremes of wealth and poverty. See his *The Preindustrial City: Past and Present*. A greater differentiation of preindustrial social strata can be found in Clifford Gertz, *Peddlers and Princes: Social Change and Economic Modernization in Two Indonesian Towns*; and Bryan Roberts, *Cities of Peasants: The Political Economy of Urbanization in the Third World*.

6. About the problem of an actor's perception of its own interests, see Theodor Adorno and Max Horkheimer, *La sociedad: lecciones de sociología*, p. 173; Claus Offe and Helmut Wiesenthal, "Two Logics of Collective Action: Theoretical Notes on Social Class and Organizational Form, " I: 88.

7. José Ingenieros, *Sociología argentina*, chap. 2, polemicizes with Juan A. García, Juan B. Justo, and José M. Ramos Mejía, who considered the Federal party as representing in some way the proletariat and the Unitario party, the bourgeoisie (p. 63). See José M. Ramos Mejía, *Las multitudes argentinas*; Juan A. García, *La ciudad indiana*; Juan Alvarez, *Estudio sobre las guerras civiles argentinas*; Lucas Ayarragaray, *La anarquía argentina y el caudillismo: estudio psicológico de los orígines nacionales, hasta el año XXIX*; Joaquín Castellanos, *Labor dispersa*; Juan B. Justo, *Teoría y práctica de la historia*.

8. For the concept of populism and a study of several cases in Europe, the United States, and the Third World, see Ghita Ionescu and Ernest Gellner, eds., *Populism, Its Meaning and National Characteristics*. Populism in the sense in which it is generally employed today must be differentiated from the Russian variety, more akin to anarchism, and from the North American one, to which, however, it is more similar. See Franco Venturi, *Roots of Revolution: A History of the Populist and Socialist Movements in XIXth Century Russia*; Richard Hofstadter, *The Age of Reform: From Bryan to FDR*; Lawrence Goodwin,

Democratic Promise: The Populist Moment in America; Michael Conniff, *Latin American Populism in Comparative Perspective.* In "Populism and Reform in Latin America" I attempted a definition and classification of populism, which I still believe valid in its general outlines, as can be seen in chapter 7, where, however, I present the subject in a slightly different manner. Basically, I do not now consider it useful to refer to the "multiclass integrationist parties" (like the PRI or the right-wing Varguista PSD) as populist, nor do I reserve a special category for "military reform parties," which in the Latin American case have been frustrated attempts at reproducing the Peronista pattern. In chapter 7, on the other hand, I include in the comparative analysis socialist labor parties, which are not populist but express more autonomously the political opinions of the lower strata, with different kinds of allies drawn from other sectors of society.

9. Ignacio Llorente, "Alianzas políticas en el surgimiento del peronismo: el caso de la provincia de Buenos Aires."

10. Manuel Mora y Araujo, "Populismo, laborismo y clases medias: política y estructura social en la Argentina," and "Procesos electorales y fuerzas políticas: una perspectiva analítica."

4. Authority and the Fragmentation of Power

1. Quoted in Germán Carrera Damas, Carlos Salazar, and Manuel Caballero, El concepto de la historia en Laureano Vallenilla Lanz, taken from *Cesarismo democrático, Disgregación e integración,* and *Críticas de sinceridad y exactitud.* See also Francisco García Calderón, *Les democraties latines de l'Amerique.*

2. Howard Wiarda, ed., *Politics and Social Change in Latin America: The Distinct Tradition*; Claudio Véliz, *The Centralist Tradition of Latin America*; Magalí Sarfatti, *Spanish Bureaucratic Patrimonialism in America*; Fredrick Pike and Thomas Stritch, eds., *The New Corporatism: Social-Political Structures in the Iberian World.*

3. There is a line of reasoning that in recent years seeks to redefine democracy as necessarily being based on intense participatory activity by popular majorities, rather than in power fragmentation. Though no one would deny the importance of participation, the almost single-handed insistence on this component distorts the perception of the problem and does not help establish adequate strategies for the democratization of Latin American countries. See Lawrence B. Joseph, "Democratic Revisionism Revisited"; John F. Manley, "Neopluralism: A Class Analysis of Pluralism I and Pluralism II"; and S. M. Barnes and M. Kaase, *Political Action: Mass Participation in Five Western Democracies.* Fernando Henrique Cardoso criticizes very acutely this "mixture of lay anarchism and catholic solidarism" in "Dependência o democracia."

4. Simón Bolívar, "Memoria dirigida a los ciudadanos de la Nueva Granada por un caraqueño," in *Simón Bolívar: discursos, proclames y epistolario político,* pp. 39–50. See José Gil Fortoul, *Historia constitucional de Venezuela* I: 178–179.

5. Nicolás Sánchez Albornoz, *The Population of Latin America: A History*; Herbert Klein, *Slavery in the Americas: A Comparative Study of Cuba and Virginia*; idem, *African Slavery in Latin America and the Caribbean*; Carl Degler, *Neither Black nor White: Slavery and Race Relations in Brazil and the United States*; Richard Morse, *The Urban Development of Latin America, 1750–1920*; Jorge E. Hardoy, ed., *Urbanization in Latin America: Approaches and Issues*; José Luis Romero, *Latinoamérica: Las ciudades y las ideas.*

6. Gordon S. Wood, *The Creation of the American Republic, 1776–1787*; Jackson Turner Main, *The Antifederalists: Critics of the Constitution, 1781–1788*; J. Franklin Jameson, *The*

American Revolution Considered as a Social Movement; Joseph Charles, *The Origins of the American Party System, Three Essays*; William Nisbet Chambers, *Political Parties in a New Nation: The American Experience, 1776–1809.*

7. See Charles Beard, *An Economic Interpretation of the Constitution*, and *Economic Origins of Jeffersonian Democracy*; Richard Hofstadter, *The Idea of a Party System: The Rise of Legitimate Opposition in the United States, 1780–1840*; Frank Otto Gatell, ed., *Essays in Jacksonian America.*

8. "Contestación de un americano meridional a un caballero de esta isla," in Bolívar, *Discursos*, pp. 148–172.

9. "Discurso ante el Congreso de Angostura, 15 febrero 1819," in ibid., pp. 216–247.

10. José Joaquín Guerra, *La convención de Ocaña*; Simón Bolívar, *Proyecto de Constitución para la República de Bolivia y discurso del Libertador.*

11. "A los representantes del pueblo en la Convención Nacional," in Bolívar, *Discursos*, p. 327.

12. Chilton Williamson, *American Suffrage from Property to Democracy 1760–1860*; Peter G. Pulzer, *Political Representation and Elections in Britain*; Jean Lhomme, *La grande bourgeoisie au pouvoir, 1830–1880.*

13. Tobías Monteiro, *Historia do império: o primeiro reinado*; Francisco A. de Varnhagen, *História da independência do Brasil*; Agenor de Roure, *Formação constitucional do Brasil*; J. M. Pereira da Silva, *História da fundação do império brasileiro*; Manuel de Oliveira Lima, *O império brasileiro, 1822–1889*; José Murilo de Carvalho, *A construção da ordem: a elite política imperial.*

14. Alipio Bandeira, *O Brasil heroico em 1817*; Rodrigo Otávio, *A balaiada, 1839*; Luiz Vianna Filho, *A Sabinada: a república bahiana de 1837*; H. Canabarro Reichardt, *Idéias de liberdade no Rio Grande do Sul*; Izabel Andrade Marson, *Movimento praieiro, 1842–1849: imprensa, ideologia e poder político*; Alfredo Varela, *Revoluções cisplatinas: a república riograndense.*

15. José Honório Rodrigues, *Conciliação e reforma no Brasil: um desafio histórico cultural*; Hélio Jaguaribe, *Brasil: Crise e alternativas*; Wanderley Guilherme dos Santos, *Poder e política: crónica do autoritarismo brasileiro.*

16. Francisco A. Encina, *Portales: Introducción a la historia de la época de Diego Portales, 1830–1891*; Benjamín Vicuña Mackenna, *D. Diego Portales*; Simon Collier, *Ideas and Politics of Chilean Independence, 1808–1833*; Benjamín Vicuña Mackenna, *Vida de O'Higgins, la corona del héroe*; Alberto Edwards Vives, *La fronda aristocrática en Chile*; Julio Heise González, *Años de formación y aprendizaje políticos, 1810–1833.*

17. Manuel Montt was president between 1851 and 1861. He confronted liberal resistance, expressed in the unsuccessful revolt in 1851. Some traditional sectors of "Peluconismo" ("Tory" conservatism) opposed him because of his secularizing measures and regalist reaffirmation of rights vis-à-vis Rome. These groups formed the Conservative party, "ultramontane," according to the terminology of the times.

18. Edwards, *Fronda*, pp. 11–12. In 1859 the accumulation of resistance against Montt stimulated a Liberal revolution centered on the mining North, which also had the support of leaders later involved in the Radical party. The common opposition of ultramontane conservatives, on the Right, and liberals and radicals on the Left, kept Montt's government in constant tension. The same happened later to Balmaceda's modernizing and developmentalist regime, overthrown in the civil war of 1891. See Ismael Valdés Vergara, *La revolución de 1891*; Hernán Ramírez Necochea, *Balmaceda y la contrarrevolución de 1891*; Oscar

Bermúdez, *Historia del salitre desde sus orígenes hasta la Guerra del Pacífico*; Harold Blakemore, *British Nitrates and Chilean Politics, 1886–1896: Balmaceda and North.*

19. Julio Heise González, *150 años de evolución institucional, Chile, 1810–1960*; Fernando Campos Harriet, *Historia constitucional de Chile: las instituciones políticas y sociales*; J. Samuel Valenzuela, *Democratización por reforma: los conservadores y la expansión del sufragio en el siglo diecinueve chileno.*

20. Julio Heise González, *El período parlamentario, 1861–1925*; Jaime Eyzaguirre, *Chile durante el gobierno de Errázuriz Echaurren, 1896–1901.*

21. The old Chilean "*pipiolos*" were a radical or populist ("*exaltado*") liberal party, of the type of the Argentine Federals, headed by Dorrego in Buenos Aires, or the Yorkinos in Mexico, and differentiated, therefore, from the moderate liberals, who were nearer to the Argentine Unitarios or the Mexican Escoceses.

22. Juan Linz "Crisis, Breakdown and Reequilibration"; Guillermo O'Donnell, "Notas para el estudio de procesos de democratización política a partir del estado burocrático-autoritario."

23. Luis A. Romero, *La sociedad de la igualdad.*

24. Letter to Antonio Garfias, 10 December 1831, in *Epistolario de Don Diego Portales, 1821–1837. Recopilación y notas de Ernesto de la Cruz, con un prólogo y nuevas cartas, por Gilllermo Feliú Cruz* I: 352–353.

25. About the origin of English political parties in old factions, see Frank O. 'Gorman, "The Problem of Party in Modern British History: 1725–1832."

26. John Stuart Mill, *Representative Government*, pp. 342–343, 382–386.

27. Ibid., p. 347.

28. Ibid., p. 267.

29. In his work, which was very influential in liberal circles despite the little attention it paid to elections and political parties, Herbert Spencer referred tangentially to a possible corporatist organization of society. See *Principles of Sociology*, vol. 2, pt. 5, para. 578, pp. 648–656 of 1902 reedition.

30. Emile Durkheim, *The Division of Labor*, pp. 5, 25n, 27.

31. Víctor R. Haya de la Torre, *Treinta años de aprismo*, pp. 78, 129 n.

32. Mill, *Representative Government*, p. 442.

5. Violence and Revolution

1. John Dollard et al., *Frustration and Aggression*; Ted R. Gurr, *Why Men Rebel*; idem, ed., *Handbook of Political Conflict: Theory and Research*; Ivo Feierabend, Rosalind Feierabend, and Ted R. Gurr, eds., *Anger, Violence, and Politics: Theories and Research*; Louis H. Masotti and Don Bowen, eds., *Riots and Rebellion*; Ernest Duff and John MacCamant, with W. Morales, *Violence and Repression in Latin America: A Quantitative and Historical Analysis.*

2. James Davies, "Toward a Theory of Revolution."

3. Chalmers Johnson, *Revolutionary Change*; Shmuel N. Eisenstadt, *Modernization, Protest, and Change*; Harry Eckstein, ed., *Internal War: Problems and Approaches*; Jack A. Goldstone, "Theories of Revolution: The Third Generation."

4. The new class system based on bureaucratic domination should be designated, if one wishes to follow Marx's thinking, as a mode of production, leaving aside elaborations like "degenerated workers' state," "socialism with bureaucratic degenerations," and the like. See Umberto Melotti, *Marx and the Third World*, who uses the concept "bureaucratic collectiv-

ism." For a different outlook, Cesare Luperini et al., *El concepto de formación económica-social.*

5. For various approaches along these lines, see Nicos Poulantzas, ed., *La crise de l' état*; Norbert Lechner, ed., *Estado y política en América Latina*; and references in chap. 3, n. 2.

6. Theda Skocpol, *States and Social Revolutions: A Comparative Analysis of France, Russia, and China.*

7. Ibid., pp. 291–292.

8. Karl Mannheim, *Man and Society in an Age of Reconstruction: Studies in Modern Social Structure*; idem, *Diagnosis of Our Time*; Franz L. Neumann, *Behemoth: The Structure and Practice of National Socialism*; William Kornhauser, *The Politics of Mass Society*; Theodor Adorno et al., *The Authoritarian Personality*; Leo Lowenthal and Norbert Guterman, *Prophets of Deceit: A Study of the Techniques of the American Agitator*; Theodor Adorno and Max Horkheimer, *La sociedad: Lecciones de Sociología*, especially chap. 5; Seymour M. Lipset and Ernest Raab, *The Politics of Unreason: Right Wing Extremism in America, 1790–1970.*

9. Charles Tilly, *From Mobilization to Revolution.*

10. Bryan Roberts has argued that the recent origin of many migrants renders them more distrustful of each other than would be the case in a long-established urban working-class neighborhood. The lack of clear cleavages in the urban social structure often makes it less easy for the poorer sectors of the population to identify with a collective "we" against the "them" of the rest of society. If the migrants, or the poorer strata in general, share a common work experience, as in a large factory or an isolated mass (mining, agribusiness), it is easier for them to act collectively. See Roberts, *Organizing Strangers*; Luis Millones, *La cultura colonial urbana: una hipótesis de trabajo para el estudio de las poblaciones tugurizadas.* When a homogeneous ethnic group settles in a certain delimited area, however, solidarity structures emerge more naturally. See Teófilo Altamirano, *Presencia andina en Lima metropolitana: estudio sobre migrantes y clubes de provincianos.*

11. Gerhard Lenski, "Status Crystallization: A Non Vertical Dimension of Social Status"; E. F. Jackson and R. F. Curtis, "Effects of Vertical Mobility and Status Inconsistency: A Body of Negative Evidence"; Carlton Hornung, "Social Status, Status Inconsistency and Psychological Stress"; Everett Hagen, *On the Theory of Social Change.*

12. Antonio Henrique de Oliveira Marques, *History of Portugal*; Hugh Kay, *Salazar and Modern Portugal*; Herminio Martins, "Opposition in Portugal"; Howard Wiarda, *Corporatism and Development: The Portuguese Experience*; Philippe Schmitter, *Corporatism and Public Policy in Authoritarian Portugal.*

13. Natalio Botana, Rafael Braun, and Carlos Floria, *El régimen militar, 1966–1973*; Guillermo O'Donnell, *El estado burocrático autoritario, 1966–1973*; Rubén M. Perina, *Onganía, Levingston, Lanuse: los militares en la política argentina*; Beba Balvé et al., *Lucha de calles, lucha de clases: elementos para su análisis*; Francisco Delich, *Crisis y protesta social: Córdoba 1969–1973*; Juan Carlos Agulla, *Diagnóstico social de una crisis: Córdoba, mayo de 1969.*

14. In 1966 the aim of the coup was to prevent a very likely Peronist electoral victory. To avoid a repetition of the 1962 events, the intervention was planned to take place before and not after the elections, and the supposed inefficiency of President Illia was used as justification. The cover was so thin that very few were fooled. The appearance of some trade union chiefs (Vandor and Alonso) in General Onganía's assumption of office must be understood as an attempt to protect themselves from the effects of the coup, rather than as

support for it. The search for dialogue, admittedly, implied mutual distribution of areas of power and little affection for democratic principles. However, these had been continually violated by omission or commission by most Argentine political groups.

15. About the concept of legitimacy, Max Weber, *Economy and Society*, vol. I, pt. 1, chap. 3; Lipset, *Political Man*; Juan Linz, "Crisis, Breakdown and Reequilibration."

16. José L. Moreno, "La estructura social y demográfica de la ciudad de Buenos Aires en el año 1778." About the gaucho, see Richard Slatta, *Gauchos and the Vanishing Frontier*.

17. See Jorge I. Domínguez, *Insurrection or Loyalty: The Breakdown of the Spanish American Empire*; Hugh M. Hamill, Jr., *The Hidalgo Revolt: Prelude to Mexican Independence*; José Ramírez Flores, *El gobierno insurgente en Guadalajara, 1810–1811*.

18. Germán Guzmán, Orlando Fals Borda, and Eduardo Umaña Luna, *La violencia en Colombia: estudio de un proceso social*; John Booth, "Rural Violence in Colombia."

19. David Goodman and Michael Redclift, *From Peasant to Proletarian: Capitalist Development and Agrarian Transitons*; Alain de Janvry, *The Agrarian Question and Reformism in Latin America*; Kenneth Duncan and Ian Rutledge, eds., *Essays on the Development of Agrarian Capitalism in the Nineteenth and Twentieth Centuries*; Enrique Florescano, ed., *Haciendas, latifundios y plantaciones en América Latina*; Norman Long and Bryan Roberts, eds., *Peasant Cooperation and Capitalist Expansion in Central Peru*; Charles Erasmus et al., *Contemporary Change in Traditional Communities of Mexico and Peru*; Francisco Ferrara, *¿Qué son las ligas agrarias?*; Leopoldo Bartolomé, "Colonos, plantadores y agroindustrias"; Eduardo Archetti and Kristinne Stolen, *Explotación familiar y acumulación de capital en el campo argentino* ; Torcuato S. Di Tella, *La teoría del primer impacto del crecimiento económico*; Glaucio Dillon Soares, "The Politics of Uneven Development." For a classical analysis of the impact of capitalism on traditional economic structures, see Rosa Luxemburg, *The Accumulation of Capital*, chaps. 27–29.

20. Cases of rural violence hovering between what is commonly defined as criminal and what may become political in Maria Sylvia de Carvalho Franco, *Homens livres na ordem escravocrata*; Billy Jaynes Chandler, *Lampião, o rei dos cangaceiros*; Estácio de Lima, *O mundo estranho dos cangaceiros*; Linda Lewin, "The Oligarchical Limitations of Social Banditry in Brazil: The Case of the 'Good' Thief Antonio Silvino."

21. For Mexico, Wayne Cornelius, *Politics and the Migrant Poor in Mexico City*, and idem, "The Cityward Movement: Some Political Implications." For Chile, Glaucio Dillon Soares and Robert Hamblin, "Socio-economic Variables and Voting for the Left: Chile, 1952"; Alejandro Portes, "Leftist Radicalism in Chile: A Test of Three Hypotheses"; idem, "Political Primitivism, Differential Socialization and Lower Class Leftist Radicalism"; Adam Przeworski and Glaucio Soares, "Theories in Search of a Curve: A Contextual Interpretation of Left Vote." Two studies on Brazil are Eli Diniz, *Voto e máquina política: patronagem e clientelismo no Rio de Janeiro*, and José Arlindo Soares, *A frente do Recife e o governo do Arraes*. Some authors, among them Samuel Huntington and Joan Nelson, *No Easy Choice: Political Participation in Developing Countries*, pp. 108–110, argue that migrants from the countryside are rather conservative because they feel that they have bettered their condition by coming to the city and they orient themselves toward social mobility. However, this attitude is compatible with a connection to mass movements of the most diverse ideological character. Ideology is supplied by the elites that lead those movements; the connection between elites and masses is usually of the charismatic kind and through the mobilizational mode. In popular urban political movements moderation cannot come as a result of the supposed social conservatism of their bases, but from solid economic

or welfare achievements by strong organization with internal participation. Alain Touraine revises the literature on the subject in "Urban Marginality."

6. Military Interventionism

1. See Michel Crozier, Samuel Huntington, and Joji Watanuki, *The Crisis of Democracy: Report on the Governability of Democracies to the Trilateral Commission*, about the "ungovernability" of societies in certain stages of development; Gino Germani, "Democracia y autoritarismo en la sociedad moderna"; and for a critique of this kind of analysis, Claus Offe, *Contradictions of the Welfare State*, and Adam Przeworski, "Institutionalization of Voting Patterns, or Is Mobilization the Source of Decay?"

2. David Apter, *The Politics of Modernization*, and idem, *Choice and the Politics of Allocation: A Developmental Theory*.

3. According to Guillermo O'Donnell, *Modernization and Bureaucratic-Authoritarianism*, "Authoritarianism and not democracy is the most likely concomitant of the higher levels of modernization in the contemporary South American context. . . . [The] reemergence of populism [is] very unlikely and its maintenance in power for more than a very brief stretch of time almost an impossibility" (in Spanish edition, pp. 22, 110). See also his *Tensiones en el estado burocrático autoritario y la cuestión de la democracia* and various comments on this thesis in David Collier, ed., *The New Authoritarianism*; and E. Kvaternik, "Sobre partidos y democracia en la Argentina entre 1955 y 1966." A recent revision of the literature on the subject is found in Helgio Trindade, "La cuestión del fascismo en América Latina."

4. Carlos Waisman, *Reversal of Development in Argentina: Postwar Counterrevolutionary Policies and Their Structural Consequences*.

5. Guillermo O'Donnell, Philippe Schmitter, and Lawrence Whitehead, eds., *Transitions from Authoritarian Rule: Prospects for Democracy*; Guillermo O'Donnell, "Notas para el estudio de procesos de democratización política a partir del estado burocrático-autoritario; Linz, "Crisis, Breakdown, and Reequilibration." Jaguaribe's approach, though compatible with those analyses, puts more emphasis on economic decision making and on the organization of multiclass "neobismarckian" parties, necessary to make national capitalist projects viable. Hélio Jaguaribe, *Political Development: A General Theory and a Latin American Case Study*.

6. For the Peruvian experience, Alfred Stepan, *State and Society: Peru in Comparative Perspective*; Víctor Villanueva, *Nueva Mentalidad Militar en Perú?*; Vivián Trías, *Perú: Fuerzas armadas y revolución*; James Petras and Robert La Porte, *Perú: transformación revolucionaria o modernización?*; Fernando Fuenzalida et al., *Perú , hoy*; and Liisa North and Tanya Korovkin, *The Peruvian Revolution and the Officers in Power, 1967–1976*. To contrast with Argentina, see Alain Rouquié, *Poder militar y sociedad política en la Argentina*; Robert Potash, *El ejército y la política en la Argentina*; and Eugenio Kvaternik, *Crisis sin salvataje: la crisis político militar de 1962–63*.

7. Paula Beiguelman, *Formação política do Brasil*, vol. I; R. Magalhães Júnior, *Deodoro: a espada contra o império*; Francolino Cameu and Artur Vieira Peixoto, *Floriano Peixoto: vida e governo*; Richard Graham, "Causes for the Abolition of Negro Slavery in Brazil: An Interpretative Essay"; idem, *Britain and the Onset of Modernization in Brazil (1850–1914)*.

8. Edgar Carone, *O tenentismo: acontecimentos, personagens, programas*; Boris Fausto, *A revolução de trinta: historiografia e historia*; Nelson Werneck Sodré, *História militar do Brasil*; Eurico de Lima Figueiredo, ed., *Os militares e a revolução de trinta*; Maria Cecília Spina Forjaz, *Tenentismo e aliança liberal, 1927–1930*.

9. Samuel Huntington, *Political Order in Changing Societies*; Alfred Stepan, *State and Society: Peru in Comparative Perspective*, esp. chap. 3.

10. Hélio Silva, *O ciclo de Vargas*; Michael Conniff, *Urban Politics in Brazil: The Rise of Populism, 1925–1945*; Simón Schwartzman, *Bases do autoritarismo brasileiro*; Leôncio Martins Rodríguez, *Conflito industrial e sindicalismo em Brasil*.

11. Alain Joxe, *Las fuerzas armadas en el sistema político de Chile*; Frederick Nunn, *Chilean Politics, 1920–31: The Honorable Mission of the Armed Forces*; René Montero Moreno, *La verdad sobre Ibáñez*, Ernesto Wurth Rojas, *Ibáñez, caudillo enigmático*.

12. Waisman, *Reversal of Development*, chaps. 6 and 7, tends to emphasize the unwarranted nature of the fears of social revolution entertained by the Argentine upper classes during the thirties and forties. He does agree that, however unfounded, those fears did have social effects in determining their behavior.

13. José María Sarobe, *Política económica argentina*, pp. 16–17, 31. This publication is part of a series of brochures published by the Unión Industrial Argentina (UIA) and based on conferences given at its Instituto de Estudios y Conferencias Industriales. Lt. Col. Mariano Abarca in a conference on 31 May 1944 also visualized the formation of great economic groups, including a Europe under the hegemony "of the East or the West," and stated that it was not possible to maintain a country with Argentina's capacity as a colony (*La industrialización de la Argentina*). Later in the same year navy lieutenant Horacio J. Gómez, introduced by Rear Admiral Pedro S. Casal, reminded his audience that "nations are always potentially in conflict" and that in present-day wars all the population takes part, because it is "Gen. Industry" that wins them (*La industria nacional y los problemas de la marina*, pp. 12, 16).

14. On 30 September 1943, Col. Carlos J. Martínez, director of the Fábrica Nacional de Aceros, founded in 1935, pointed to the need to prepare for the eventuality of a war and to strengthen the role of the state, which had to cover the minimum needs of national defense (*La industria siderúrgica nacional*, pp. 42, 45, 47). In the same line, retired major Juan Rawson Bustamante, a professor of aeronautical organization and mobilization at the Escuela Superior de Guerra, emphasized the role the state had played during the First World War (*Las posibilidades aeronáuticas de postguerra*). In a conference on 15 June 1944, inaugurating a series of radio programs sponsored by the UIA, Lt. Col. Alejandro G. Unsain commented on the "magisterial" conference Colonel Perón had given recently at the University of La Plata about the relationship between industrialization and national defense (*Un ciclo de 22 conferencias radiotelefónicas*).

15. Carlos Díaz Alejandro, *Essays on the Economic History of the Argentine Republic*, denies that the war meant particularly intensive growth for Argentine industry. This statement, based on an analysis of global statistical data, must be confronted with the perception of contemporaries, probably based on a greater concern for some sectors that depended particularly on protection. For economist Ricardo Ortiz, consultant to the UIA, there was no doubt that "the present war . . . has been a powerful stimulus for our manufacturing capacity" (*Un ciclo de 16 conferencias radiotelefónicas*, p. 15). In the same broadcasting cycle, Luis Colombo, president of the UIA, boasted that "industry has prevented a major labor crisis" (p. 12), and the following year industrialist Rolando Lagomarsino referred to "the extraordinary development attained by Argentine industry during the last decennium, especially since the beginning of the present war" (p. 37). A member of the Instituto Bunge de Investigaciones Económicas y Sociales, in a collective work based on articles published in the Catholic newspaper *El Pueblo* between June 1943 and

December 1944, argued that "the preaching of a few pioneers and the efforts of a few intelligent industrialists . . . would have come to nothing if the war had not cut the flow of imported manufactures" (Instituto Alejandro E. Bunge de Investigaciones Económicas y Sociales, *Soluciones argentinas a los problemas económicos y sociales del presente*, p. 112).

16. Conference by Col. Manuel N. Savio, 10 November 1942 (*Política de la producción metalúrgica argentina*, p. 33).

17. Leopoldo Melo, *La postguerra y algunos de los planes sobre el nuevo orden económico*, p. 15; Luis Colombo et al., *Discursos pronunciados con motivo del banquete con que se celebró la clausura del Primer Ciclo de Conferencias*, p. 13; and Ricardo Gutiérrez, address in the first cycle of radio broadcasts, 1943.

18. Instituto Alejandro E. Bunge, *Soluciones argentinas*, pp. 37, 200–204, 154–176.

19. Intervención Federal en la Provincia de Tucumán, *Causas y fines de la revolución libertadora del 4 de junio: nueve meses de gobierno en la provincia de Tucumán*, pp. 72, 145. Dr. Alfredo Labougle, vice-rector of the University of Buenos Aires and soon afterward director of the UIA's instituto, in his conference of 14 July 1943, a month after the miltary coup, took the opportunity to support de facto president Gen. Pedro Pablo Ramírez, who as early as 1930 believed the Sáenz Peña law (granting a secret ballot) was not applicable to a country "with 40 percent illiterates." Labougle added that it was not likely that many people would come from Europe after the war, because over there they wanted to retain the honest ones, and "we have had enough of bad elements who have infiltrated" (Alfredo Labougle, *Las industrias argentinas en el pasado, presente y porvenir*, pp. 3–4, 62.

20. Mario Rapaport, *Gran Bretaña, Estados Unidos y las clases dirigentes agentinas: 1940–1945*; Carlos Escudé, *Gran Bretaña, Estados Unidos y la declinación argentina, 1942–1949*.

21. For the subject of entrepreneurial support to Peronism, see Judith Teichman, "Interest Conflict and Entrepreneurial Support of Perón"; Eduardo Jorge, *Industria y concentración económica*; Mónica Peralta Ramos, *Etapas de acumulación y alianzas de clases en la Argentina, 1930–1970*.

22. Alain Rouquié, *Poder militar* II: 16.

23. Fernando Henrique Cardoso, *Ideologías de la burguesía industrial en sociedades dependientes: Argentina y Brasil*.

24. Alfred Stepan, *The Military in Politics: Changing Patterns in Brazil*.

25. José Nun, "The Middle Class Military Coup."

26. William Riker, *The Theory of Political Coalitions*. See also Robert Dahl, ed., *Regimes and Oppositions*, and a reference in that book by R. Dix about a hypothesis by Carl Lande, according to whom in societies not divided by intense class or religious antagonism, competition among elites tends to produce factions with a parity of force. This parity also can be observed under conditions of class, ethnic, or religious conflict. In some cases where electorally dominant structures exist, as in Mexico with its ruling party, the PRI, or in India with its Congress party, or in many single-party Asian or African regimes, it is necessary to consider foreign interests as a very strong actor partaking of the internal political game. In these cases, parity, if it exists, is not reflected in votes.

7. The Organization of the Popular Classes

1. Friedrich Engels, *The German Revolutions*, p. 129.

2. Friedrich Engels, *The Condition of the Working Class in England in 1844*, p. 266.

3. Friedrich Engels, "Los bakuninistas en acción. Informe sobre la sublevación española

del verano de 1873," p. 195.

4. Lenin is very explicit about the fact that the revolution in Russia would be capitalist. See *The Development of Capitalism in Russia: The Process of the Formation of a Home Market for Large Scale Industry*, and *Two Tactics of Social Democracy in the Democratic Revolution*. See also Boris Sapir, "The Conception of the Bourgeois Revolution."

5. If the revolution was going to be capitalist, the Mensheviks deduced that its leadership corresponded to the bourgeoisie, the working-class party giving temporary support as long as the revolution remained progressive. Others thought that from the beginning it was necessary to be in the opposition against a capitalist government, however "progressive." Lenin brought in a new argument, stressing that as the bourgeoisie was incapable of providing leadership to the revolution, this became the worker's task. However, Lenin accepted the belief that economic and technological considerations made a socialist regime impossible. See *Two Tactics*.

6. Víctor Raúl Haya de la Torre, *Treinta años de aprismo*, pp. 54, 29.

7. Karl Kautsky, *La defensa de los trabajadores y la jornada de ocho horas*, p. 50. For Kautsky, one of the main objectives of the reduction of the working day was to free workers for "attending adequately the development of the associations. . . . Free time can and should be employed not in frivolous or unhealthy pleasures but in the service of civilization and social progress" (pp. 141–144).

8. M. Bakunin, *Selected Writings*, p. 170. See also his letter to Sergei Nekaev, 2 June 1870, in ibid.

9. *La Anarquía*, an anarchist newspaper published in La Plata, commenting on a trade union–sponsored meeting where socialists had been harassed, and some not allowed to speak, said that in the future "instead of catcalls and protests we should go against them with a dagger, already stained with bourgeois blood, so as not to let any one of those scoundrels alive" (26 October 1895). After an unsuccessful bakers' strike in 1902, the anarchist paper *El Rebelde* argued that the defeat had been due to the legalitarian character of the movement (in spite of the fact that the leaders of the union were anarchists also). According to its report, strikers just gathered at the Casa del Pueblo (an anarchist union and cultural center) playing games and idling, rather than "employing violence and destroying the interests of the bourgeois." The paper went on to argue that the numerical superiority of strikers over policemen guarding the bakeries made a resort to violence practical (13 September 1902). After the defeat of a previous strike, the anarchist-controlled bakery union newspaper ridiculed the more radical *La Nuova Civiltá*, which had published an editorial under the self-explanatory title, "O tutto o niente" ("All or Nothing"). The bakers argued that this motto was easy for "those who have ample private means. . . . If the writers of *Nuova Civiltá* had blisters on their hands they would soon change their way of thinking" (*El Obrero*, formerly *El Obrero Panadero*, 13 April 1901).

10. Enrique Dickman, *Recuerdos de un militante socialista*, p. 68.

11. *El Obrero*, 6 October 1901.

12. *El Obrero* published extensive reappraisals of trade union tactics after the defeat of the 1902 strike. An editorial argued that though it was true that "energetic and revolutionary strikes" are necessary, they must be backed by organization. The authors admitted that they "had also had those [more violent] beliefs, but the frustrations [they had] undergone had served them as an experience." They added that "the charlatans who say that the sort of people who are usually found in 'fondas,' in plazas, in the marketplace, in other words, the nonmembers, are as good fighters as those who are organized, are telling a solemn lie. We

do not think that a fighter is one who rises when he listens that there is a strike, maybe only because of fear of getting a thrashing" (3 July 1902). See also the number of 5 August 1902.

13. Juan B. Justo, *Teoría y práctica de la historia*, pp. 347–354. For a description of more recent similar events, see Branco Pribicevic, *The Shop Stewards' Movement and Workers' Control, 1910–1922*; Victor L. Allen, *Trade Union Leadership*.

14. In T. Di Tella et al., *Sindicato y comunidad: dos tipos de estructura sindical latinoamericana*, chaps. 6 and 7, an attempt is made to study the operation of these factors in two Chilean union settings. See for a comparative overview Rubén Kaztman and José Luis Reyna, eds., *Fuerza de trabajo y movimientos laborales en América Latina*.

15. Chilean trade unions have had a weak bureaucratic structure partly due to President Alessandri's law of 1924, forbidding payments to union officials and forcing the formation of autonomous "industrial" unions in factories employing over fifty workers. See Alan Angell, *Politics and the Labor Movement in Chile*; Dale Johnson, ed., *The Chilean Road to Socialism*; James Petras, *Politics and Social Forces in Chilean Development*; Arturo Valenzuela, "Chile"; and Joan Garcés, *El estado y los problemas tácticos en el gobierno de Allende*.

16. Jaime Castillo Velasco, *Los caminos de la revolución*; Edward J. Williams, *Latin American Christian Democratic Parties*; Peter Snow, *El radicalismo chileno*; David Rock, *Politics in Argentina, 1890–1930*; François Bourricaud, *Power and Society in Contemporary Peru*; and John D. Martz and David Myers, *Venezuela: The Democratic Experience*.

17. For various interpretations of populism in Latin America, see Gino Germani, *Authoritarianism, Fascism, and National Populism*; Torcuato S. Di Tella, "Populism and Reform in Latin America"; Ernesto Laclau, *Politics and Ideology in Marxist Theory*; Francisco Weffort, *O populismo na política brasileira*.

18. Hernán Ramírez Necochea, *Historia del movimiento obrero en Chile: antecedentes, siglo XIX*; Julio César Jobet, *Luis Emilio Recabarren: los orígenes del movimiento obrero y del socialismo chilenos*; Elías Lafertte, *Vida de un comunista: páginas autobiográficas*; Paul Drake, *Socialism and Populism in Chile, 1932–1952*.

19. See Julio Godio, *La semana trágica de enero 1919*; David Rock, "Lucha civil en la Argentina: La semana trágica de enero de 1919"; and Rock's comments on Godio in *Desarrollo Económico* 12, no. 45 (April–June 1972).

20. See *Acción Socialista* (16 April 1906) for a description of the breakaway by the official organ of the new group.

21. Syndicalists, according to railway worker José Domenech, "deep down in their hearts were Radicales, all Radicales." He believed the majority of union members—not to speak of the working class as a whole—were Radicales, particularly in the Unión Ferroviaria, with its many locals in the interior of the country (Oral History Program, Instituto Torcuato Di Tella, Buenos Aires [OHP], interview with José Domenech, box 1, cuaderno 11, pp. 75, 166).

22. Luis Gay, syndicalist leader of the telephone workers, estimates that in the early thirties some fourteen thousand people worked in his industry, of which fewer than thirty-five hundred were affiliated with unions; there were no more than two hundred militants. Even so, he thinks that "at this time [1970] in the labor movement there are fewer activists than in those days" (OHP box 1, cuaderno 4, pp. 41–42). According to Mateo Fossa, craft unions allowed a greater participation of members, both because of their smaller size and because problems that had to be considered affected the everyday work experience of their members more directly (OHP box 1, cuaderno 1, p. 27).

23. *La Unión Obrera* (February–March 1906). Luis Lotito, a syndicalist leader, wrote a

series of articles on the "Proletariado tucumano" in *Acción Socialista*, nos. 58–62 (1907–1908).

24. *Acción Socialista* (29 January 1910).

25. *Revista Socialista Internacional* 1, no. 7 (25 May 1909), p. 451.

26. Philip B. Taylor, *Government and Politics of Uruguay*; Milton Vanger, *José Battle y Ordóñez of Uruguay*; Luis Benvenuto et al., *Uruguay hoy*.

27. Thomas Skidmore, *Politics in Brazil, 1930–64: An Experiment in Democracy*; Ronald Schneider, *The Political System of Brazil: Emergence of an Authoritarian "Modernizing" Regime*; Alfred Stepan, *The Military in Politics: Changing Patterns in Brazil*; John W. F. Dulles, *Vargas of Brazil: A Political Biography*; Hélio Jaguaribe, "Las elecciones de 1962 en el Brasil"; and Fernando H. Cardoso and Bolívar Lamounier, eds., *Os partidos e as eleições no Brasil*.

28. Leôncio Martins Rodrigues, *Trabalhadores, sindicatos e industrialização*; Angelina Figueiredo, "Intervenções sindicais e o novo sindicalismo"; José A. Moises, "La huelga de los trescientos mil y las comisiones de empresa."

29. Peru, although it has low mass education levels, has very high proportions of its population in high schools and universities, which helps explain the spread of the leftist political orientation among sectors of the middle class.

30. James Malloy, *Bolivia, the Uncompleted Revolution*; Herbert Klein, *Parties and Political Change in Bolivia, 1880–1952*.

31. Guillermo Lora, *A History of the Bolivian Labor Movement*; Juan Combo, *Bolivia bajo el modelo de Banzer*; Christopher Mitchell, *The Legacy of Populism in Bolivia: From the MNR to Military Rule*.

32. For internal currents within the populist and leftist parties, see Guillermo Bedregal, "Bolivia: la apertura democrática y las tareas de los partidos políticos"; Edwin Moller, "La apertura democrática y el PRIN/Bolivia"; Fernando Arauco, "La lucha del pueblo boliviano."

33. Alan Knight, *The Mexican Revolution*; Charles Cumberland, *The Mexican Revolution: Genesis under Madero*; Peter Calvert, *The Mexican Revolution, 1910–14: The Diplomacy of Anglo American Conflict*; and Jesús Silva Herzog, *Breve historia de la revolución mexicana*. Silva Herzog, in his analyses of the class bases of the Mexican Revolution, repeatedly ignores the middle classes, ranging on one side the large landowners, capitalists, and foreign interests, and on the other, the workers, peasants, and some intellectuals. He only tangentially includes sectors of the middle classes among the revolutionary coalition. John Tutino, *From Rebellion to Revolution in Mexico, 1750–1940*, also underemphasizes the role of the middle classes.

34. John Womack, *Zapata and the Mexican Revolution*; Jorge Basurto, *El proletariado industrial en México, 1850–1930*; Moisés González Navarro, *Las huelgas textiles en el porfiriato*. For an analysis of Mexican politics, Pablo González Casanova, *Democracy in Mexico*; and José L. Reyna and Richard Weinert, eds., *Authoritarianism in Mexico*.

35. Peter Klaren, *Modernization, Dislocation, and Aprismo: Origins of the Peruvian Aprista Party, 1870–1932*; James Payne, *Labor and Politics in Peru: The System of Political Bargaining*; Grant Hilliker, *The Politics of Reform in Peru: The Aprista and Other Mass Parties of Latin America*; Peter Blanchard, *The Origins of the Peruvian Labor Movement, 1883–1919*; David Collier, *Squatters and Oligarchs: Authoritarian Rule and Policy Change in Peru*.

36. Harry Kantor, *The Ideology and Program of the Peruvian Aprista Movement*; Víctor R. Haya de la Torre, *Treinta años de aprismo*.

37. John Martz, *Acción Democrática: Evolution of a Modern Political Party*; John Powell, *Political Mobilization of the Venezuelan Peasant*; Philip B. Taylor, *The Venezuelan "Golpe" of 1958*; Arturo Sosa and Eloi Lengrand, *Del garibaldismo estudiantil a la izquierda criolla: los orígenes marxistas del Proyecto A. D., 1928–1935*.

38. For other parties of this type, see Charles Ameringer, *Don Pepe: A Political Biography of José Figueres of Costa Rica*; Jacobo Schifter, *La fase oculta de la guerra civil en Costa Rica*; José Moreno, *Barrios in Arms: Revolution in Santo Domingo*; Robert William Anderson, *Party Politics in Puerto Rico*; Kalman Silvert, *A Study in Government: Guatemala*; Richard N. Adams, *Crucifixion by Power: Essays in Guatemalan National Social Structure, 1944–1966*.

39. For the prerevolutionary political situation, see Wyatt MacGaffey and Clifford R. Barnett, *Cuba: Its People, Its Culture*; Lowry Nelson, *Rural Cuba*; and Luis Aguilar, *Cuba 1933: Prologue to Revolution*.

40. Bert Hoselitz, "Desarrollo económico en América Latina," contrasts the rapid development of Mexico and Brazil during the 1925–1929 to 1950–1954 periods with Argentina's and Chile's much more reduced development and Cuba's almost null growth in per capita product during those same periods. See also Simon Kuznets, Wilbert Moore, and Joseph Spengler, eds., *Economic Growth: Brazil, India, Japan*; and Werner Baer, *Industrialization and Economic Development in Brazil*.

41. See Maurice Zeitlin, *Revolutionary Politics and the Cuban Working Class*; Hugh Thomas, *Cuba, the Pursuit of Freedom*; Jorge Domínguez, *Cuba: Order and Revolution*.

42. For various interpretations of the postrevolutioanry political structure, see Richard Fagen, *The Transformation of Political Culture in Cuba*; K. S. Karol, *Guerrillas in Power: The Course of the Cuban Revolution*; Irving L. Horowitz, ed., *Cuban Communism*.

43. See Richard Gott, *Guerrilla Movements in Latin America*; Teodoro Petkoff, *Proceso a la izquierda o la falsa conducta revolucionaria*.

44. The growth of cotton and cattle production in Nicaragua, replacing the previous importance of coffee, was apparently responsible for the displacement and proletarianization of many peasants associated with earlier forms of land management. Jaime Wheelock and Luis Carrión, *Apuntes sobre el desarrollo económico y social de Nicaragua;* Thomas W. Walker, ed., *Nicaragua: The First Five Years*; Eduardo Crawley, *Nicaragua in Perspective*; the chapters on Nicaragua in Pablo González Casanova, ed., *América Latina: historia de medio siglo*; and Colegio de México, *Centroamérica en crisis*.

45. See Manuel Mora y Araujo and Ignacio Llorente, eds., *El voto peronista*. The large vote Peronism got in the less-developed parts of the country was of course numerically mostly rural and peasant, but the support from insecure or downwardly mobile sectors of the middle classes of those areas was strategic. They acted as an intermediary to mobilize popular support via local *caudillista* structures of a more traditional type than the ones that could function in the more industrialized areas.

46. See Vamireh Chacón, *Historia dos partidos brasileiros*.

47. Marcos Pérez Jiménez, *Frente a la infamia*; Mario Briceño Iragorry, *Pérez Jiménez presidente: la autoelección de un déspota: 30 de noviembre de 1952*; Darío Parra, *Venezuela, "democracia" versus "dictadura" ;* Guillermo Feo Calcaño, *Democracia versus dictadura: artículos periodísticos*; Felipe Echavarría Olozaga, *Colombia, una democracia indefensa: la resurrección de Rojas Pinilla*; Elmo Valencia, *Libro rojo de Rojas*; Roberto Harker Valdivieso, *La rebelión de los curules: Boceto en negro para el ex-general Rojas Pinilla*; Percy MacLean y Estenós, *Historia de una revolución*; Tad Szulc, *Twilight of the*

Tyrants.

8. Early Socialist Organization: The Argentine Case

1. Seymour M. Lipset, using comparative data, shows that the resistance to mobility was no greater in Europe than in the United States. In the latter, however, the profile of the pyramid was wider and expanding, so that there was ever more space for the middle classes. From the point of view of the effects on the popular strata, what matters are the chances they had of climbing the social ladder, whatever the cause: widening of the pyramid, or low resistance to mobility. It can be said, then, that American society was as "rigid" as the European, only if rigidity is measured as the resistance of upper and middle strata against downward mobility. Lipset's data, then, do not contradict the fact that there were more possibilities for upward social mobility in the United States than in Europe. See S. M. Lipset and R. Bendix, *Social Mobility in Industrial Society*; S. M. Miller, "Comparative Social Mobility"; S. M. Lipset, *Revolution and Counterrevolution: Change and Persistence in Social Structure.*

2. Gordon Greenwood, ed., *Australia: A Social and Political History*, p. 84; John M. Ward, *Empire in the Antipodes: The British in Australasia, 1840–1868.*

3. Myron Burgin, *Aspectos económicos del federalismo argentino*, p. 157; Woodbine Parish, *Buenos Aires y las provincias del Río de la Plata desde su descubrimiento y conquista por los españoles*; John Fogarty, Ezequiel Gallo, and Héctor Diéguez, eds., *Argentina y Australia*; and Ezequiel Gallo and Gustavo Ferrari, eds., *La Argentina, del ochenta al centenario.*

4. Donald G. Creighton, *Dominion of the North: A History of Canada*; Arthur R. M. Lower, *Colony to Nation: A History of Canada*; W. T. Easterbrook and H. G. Aitken, *Canadian Economic History*; Christopher M. Platt and Guido Di Tella, eds., *Argentina, Australia and Canada: Studies in Comparative Development.*

5. The process of colonization was not so successful in other places, like South Africa, where there was no amalgam, and India, where results were disastrous in terms of destruction of life and property of the preexistent society.

6. Giovanni Preziosi, *Gli italiani negli Stati Uniti del Nord*, p. 48; Roberto Cortés Conde, *El progreso argentino*, pp. 240–274, for a comparison between the standards of living in Italy and Argentina; Herbert Klein, "La integración de italianos en Argentina y Estados Unidos: un análisis comparativo," to whom I owe the idea that the Italians, in certain periods, particularly at the beginning, found more opportunities in Argentina than in the United States; and Mario Nascimbene, "Aspectos demográficos y educacionales de la inmigración a la Argentina: el impacto de la corriente inmigratoria italiana entre 1876 y 1925."

7. Preziosi, *Gli italiani*; and Silvano Tomasi and Madeline H. Engel, eds., *The Italian Experience in the United States*, especially articles by Luciano Iorizio, "The Padrone and Immigrant Distribution," who furnishes data on popular violence against Italians, including several lynchings in the South (p. 50), and by Samuel Baily, "Italians and Organized Labor in the United States and Argentina, 1880–1910," for whom trade unions in Argentina performed functions similar to those of the political "machines" of North American cities. For more information, see Francesco Cordasco and Salvatore Lagumina, *Italians in the United States: A Bibliography of Reports, Texts, Critical Studies, and Related Materials.*

8. The first provincial census for Santa Fe listed 41 percent foreigners for the city of Rosario, but if only men between fifteen and forty were counted, the figure increased to 64 percent. In the first municipal census for Rosario, in 1900, there were more foreign than

Argentinian property holders (54 percent). See Miguel Angel de Marco and Oscar Ensinck, *Historia de Rosario*, p. 281 ff. The future president, Roque Sáenz Peña, in his campaign warned that within the next couple of decades, "the native element will remain in a minority" and that to nationalize the country three political measures would be necessary: expansion of primary education, compulsory military service, and compulsory voting. See Roque Sáenz Peña, *Escritos y discursos* II: 14–16; and Fernando Devoto and Gianfausto Rosoli, eds., *La inmigración italiana en la Argentina*.

9. It was considered dangerous to make citizenship too easy to attain, because of the extreme, or at least anticonservative, attitudes that it was supposed (with some reason) that foreigners would express in their electoral participation. Regarding the resistance of the leaders of the foreign communities to adopt Argentine nationality, see the newspaper *Eco delle Societá Italiane*, which staged a campaign against citizenship in 1899. Also Giuseppe Parisi, *Storia degli italiani nell'Argentina*. Some Italians were preoccupied with the "lack of security of life and property of those who work and produce, particularly if they are foreigners," in the words of Silvio Celletti, *Rapporto al Commissario di Emigrazione*. See Vittorio Falorsi, *Problemi di emigrazione*, p. 37; Paulo Brenna, *L'emigrazione italiana nel periodo antebellico*; Giuseppe Guadagnini, *In America: Repubblica Argentina*; and Emilio Zuccarini, *Il lavoro degli italiani nella Repubblica Argentina dal 1516 al 1900. Studi, leggende e ricerche*.

10. Joaquín V. González, "Estudio sobre la revolución" I: 250–254.

11. "What is the cause of today's deep troubles, if not the fact that the working classes have no representatives in Congress?" asked J. V. González in the 27 November 1902 session of the Chamber of Deputies. He added that one should not worry about the prospect of the incorporation of the believers in the "more extreme and strange theories of contemporary socialism [because] it is much more dangerous for them to be absent" (ibid., VI: 181–182).

12. See "Invitación-manifiesto para la formación de un partido nacional," ibid., XXIII: 25.

13. Roberto Campolietti, *La colonizzazione italiana nell'Argentina*; Klein, "Integración de italianos."

14. Ezequiel Gallo, *Farmers in Revolt*; Raúl Larra, *Lisandro de la Torre: vida y drama del solitario de Pinas*; Roberto Etchepareborda, *Tres revoluciones: 1890, 1893 y 1905*.

15. Garibaldi founded the Italian Legion in Montevideo and was commander of the Uruguayan Fleet. Among Mazzini's followers was Gian B. Cuneo, a journalist, later a biographer of Garibaldi and the Argentine government's colonization representative in Italy. In Montevideo he published *Il Legionario Italiano* (1844–1846) and established a solid political friendship with General Mitre. Mitre always maintained a strong backing from the liberal and republican Italian community, which started during the defense of Montevideo against Rosas. See Jorge Sergi, *Historia de los Italianos en la Argentina*, pp. 141–146; and Niccoló Cuneo, *Storia dell'Emigrazione italiana nell'Argentina 1810–1870*.

16. *L'Amico del Popolo* 2, no. 58 (15 February 1880). At a later stage, an editorial defined the paper as belonging to the "republican socialist party" (vol. 14, no. 122, 16 October 1892). In 1897 it entered into a polemic with the "scientific-positivist socialists," who dubbed the editor, Monacelli, a bourgeois because of his support for private property (vol. 18, no. 927, 20 September 1896).

17. The Socialist party was formed at the initiative of various groups, among them the Germans of Vorwaerts, the French of Les Egaux, and the Italians of the Fascio dei Lavoratori. Germán Ave Lallemant entered into a polemic with the *Amico del Popolo*, arguing that it was necessary to "refuse unity with the petty bourgeoisie, which hides its exploitative tendencies

under the mantle of free thought, republicanism, anti-Catholicism, etc." (*El Obrero* 2, no. 51, 9 January 1892). See also José Ratzer, *Los marxistas argentinos del noventa*. In the same issue of *El Obrero*, Lallemant criticized the Centro Político Extranjero (presided over by Schelky, who published the *Argentinisches Wochenblatt*. Schelky, after having opposed the Unión Cívica Radical, now supported their presidential candidate, Bernardo de Irigoyen, who promised votes for foreigners. See Richard J. Walter, *The Socialist Party of Argentina, 1890–1930*).

18. A great deal of Mitre's support came from foreigners, particularly Italians, who, in spite of not being citizens, could not help taking sides in times of acute conflict, even if only to defend themselves. In 1880, when the governor of Buenos Aires, Carlos Tejedor, decided to resist the national authorities bent on federalizing the city of Buenos Aires, the conflict was perceived as a confrontation between the modern and liberal society of that city and the backward and conservative one of the interior provinces, dominated by their oligarchies. When the conflict erupted, two Italian battalions, seven thousand strong, according to press reports, were formed under the command of an Italian, Larghi. They marched past Mitre's house and participated in the barricades on Tejedor's side (Parisi, *Storia degli Italiani nell'Argentina*, pp. 407–409). *L'Amico del Popolo*, earlier in the year, when elections were approaching, regretted that Tejedor had only a slim chance, due to the population's apathy (vol. 2, no. 58, 15 February 1880).

19. Mariano de Vedia y Mitre, *La revolución del noventa: origen y fundación de la Unión Cívica: Causas, desarrollo y consecuencias de la revolución de julio*; and José Landerberger and Francisco Conte, comps., *La Unión Cívica: origen, organización y tendencia*. At a meeting in Rosario the participants had "flags of all countries." See Demarco and Ensick, *Historia de Rosario*, p. 258. A Santa Fe provincial law of December 1890 took away from foreigners the right to vote in municipal elections (ibid., p. 259). See also César A. Cabral, *Alem: informe sobre la frustración argentina*, p. 432.

20. See Seymour M. Lipset and Stein Rokkan, eds., *Party Systems and Voter Alignments: Cross-National Perspectives*; and Natalio Botana, *El orden conservador: la política argentina entre 1880 y 1916*.

21. Tulio Halperín Donghi, ed., *Proyecto y construcción de una nación: Argentina, 1846–1880*, esp. pp. LXXXVII–CI, and idem, "Un nuevo clima de ideas."

22. Anarchist sectors of the so-called Partido Liberal Mexicano, under the direction of the Flores Magón brothers, and others in the Casa del Obrero Mundial participated actively in the revolution. The more doctrinaire members did not wish to cooperate directly with Francisco Madero's movement but formed armed groups anyway, many of which ended up joining the mainstream revolution more closely. See John Hart, *Anarchism and the Mexican Working Class, 1850–1900*; and Ciro Cardoso et al., *La clase obrera en la historia de México: de la dictadura porfirista a los tiempos libertarios*. The old Argentine anarchist militant Dr. Juan Creaghe migrated to Mexico to participate in the conflict (*Ideas y Figuras* 4, no. 75, 11 July 1912). The working-class Argentine press commented on Mexican events very assiduously. The official organ of the Confederación Obrera Regional Argentina (CORA), led by the revolutionary syndicalists, wanted to emulate "Mexican workers [who] have performed what we haven't even attempted: the defeat of armed forces supported by strong batteries" (*La Confederación* 2, no. 10, July 1911).

23. Plácido Grela, *El grito de Alcorta: historia de la rebelión campesina de 1912*. Juan Alvarez, *Estudio sobre las guerras civiles argentinas*, was concerned with the Pampean agricultural producers' instability, which might push them toward Buenos Aires, thereby

reproducing the *montoneras* of the last century.

24. Enrique del Valle Iberlucea, *Discursos parlamentarios*.

25. Carlos Payá and Eduardo Cárdenas, *El primer nacionalismo argentino en Gálvez y Ricardo Rojas*.

26. The classical Socialist party argument in favor of a separation between politics and trade unionism was that, otherwise, divisionism would set in. With regard to the manner of establishing connections between the party and trade unions, see Juan B. Justo, *La realización del socialismo* VII: 276–277, 280 ff, 301–303.

27. See Frederick F. Ridley, *Revolutionary Syndicalism in France*; Leo Valiani, "Le mouvement syndical ouvrier italien entre le fascisme et l'antifascisme"; Claudio Schwarzenberg, *Il sindacalismo fascista*; Renzo de Felice, *Mussolini*. Hubert Lagardelle, first editor of Sorel's *Reflexions on Violence*, ended up with life imprisonment, a victim not of the bourgeoisie but of the French liberation, after being Vichy's secretary of state for labor.

28. The syndicalist-controlled CGT of 1930 had to face the new military government with what Luis Gay, one of the leaders at the time, termed "a bit of *equilibrio*" (OHP book 1, cuaderno 4, p. 18). Tramonti's connections with Ortiz during his attempt to regain control of the Unión Ferroviaria are described in detail by José Domenech, according to whom, "in the union movement, in those days, something of what it is today was already there" (OHP, book 1, cuaderno 11, pp. 151, 109–114).

9. Mass Organization and the Rise of Peronism

1. For the problems of democracy in trade unions, see Seymour M. Lipset, Martin Trow, and James S. Coleman, *Union Democracy: The Internal Politics of the International Typographical Union*; David Edelstein and Malcolm Warner, *Comparative Union Democracy: Organization and Opposition in British and American Unions*. For the transition to mass unionism in Great Britain, see Hugh Clegg, *General Union: A Study of the National Union of General and Municipal Workers*; Henry Pelling, *A History of British Trade Unionism*; John Lovell, *Stevedores and Dockers: A Study of Trade Unionism in the Port of London, 1870–1914*.

2. Annie Kriegel, *La croissance de la C.G.T., 1918–21, essai statistique*; Antoine Prost, *La C.G.T. à l'époque du Front Populaire, 1934–1939: essai de description numérique*.

3. Affiliation figures are not very reliable, particularly after the consolidation of Perón's government, when they are obviously inflated and approximated. A detailed analysis can be found in Miguel Murmis and Juan Carlos Portantiero, *Estudios sobre los orígenes del peronismo*.

4. Yrigoyen, as leader of a popular movement, always had some labor following. There was no strong organized Radical sector among unionists, though. In this sense, Yrigoyenism is markedly different from other populist movements like Peronism or Aprismo. For Yrigoyen's alleged support of the Syndicalist Unión Sindical Argentina, see interview with socialist municipal worker Francisco Pérez Leirós (OHP book 3, cuaderno 12, p. 25).

5. See interviews with Pérez Leirós (OHP, book 3, cuaderno 12) and Domenech (OHP book 1, cuaderno 11).

6. Ibid. See also Félix Luna, *Ortiz: reportaje a la Argentina opulenta*, who refers to the good relations between Ortiz and Tramonti, although not in connection with the above episode.

7. To use their words, "The new elite that proposes a populist project finds an already organized working class, which also has a social project of its own, and to whom it expressly

offers an alliance" and therefore "there would not be a dissolution of labor's autonomy in favor of heteronomy in the initial moment of Peronism in Argentina but rather, if at all, at a later stage" (Murmis and Portantiero, *Estudios*, pp. 112, 123). This seems a better description of Roosevelt's than of Perón's tactics, if one takes into account the very strong repression to which many members of the old working-class movement in Argentina were subjected by the military government of 1943–1946, including interventions of unions and jailing of leaders.

8. Two of the latest statements by Germani on this subject are to be found in "El surgimiento del peronismo: el rol de los obreros y los migrantes internos, and *Authoritarianism, Fascism, and National Populism*, chap. 6. A polemic has developed on this subject in the pages of several journals, with various historians criticizing Germani's emphasis on internal migrants. See notes by Peter Smith, Eldon Kenworthy, and Tulio Halperín Donghi in *Desarrollo Económico*, nos. 54, 56; also Tulio Halperín Donghi, *La democracia de masas*, and Walter Little, "The Popular Origins of Peronism."

9. The Partido Laborista was certainly an innovator in political methods. Luis Gay, describing its electoral campaign, tells how "central mass meetings [were] transmitted to the whole country through the radio . . . in each locality where the radio network reaches another meeting is held . . . just before or after the transmission of the central meeting. . . . Those long, tiresome . . . electoral campaigns no longer exist; the Partido Laborista holds 3, 4, or 5 [central] meetings in total, but always with the same character" (OHP, book 1, cuaderno 4, p. 91). According to Mariano Tedesco (OHP book 5, cuaderno 7, p. 45), the idea of the Partido Laborista "was generated in the Consejo de Asesores . . . de Trabajo y Previsión" (secretaries of trade unions, who had been invited by Perón to become advisers to the ministry). For Rafael Ginocchio, "the C.G.T. was not an appendix of the government, it was the government itself" (OHP 5/5, p. 35). Some became Peronists after being called from jail to have an interview with Perón, as was the case with Cipriano Reyes (OHP 7/6)

10. See figures given by Germani in "El *surgimiento del peronismo*" (p. 448), based on a 1960 census sample. According to this sample, in greater Buenos Aires 76.9 percent of unskilled, 57.8 percent of semiskilled, and 44.5 percent of skilled workers were internal migrants. If we take into account statistical considerations explained in that article, it seems that the situation in 1945 was not too different. As for the participants in the events, of all shades of opinion, the impact of mass internal migration seemed quite obvious. For Mariano Tedesco, a young Peronist from the Textile Union, it was "a flood coming from the interior" (OHP book 5, cuaderno 7, p. 10); for Mateo Fossa, an independent leftist, it was based on "*cabecitas negras*" (blacks) and "people from the interior" (OHP book 1, cuaderno 1, pp. 33, 53, 61); for Socialist Lucio Bonilla it was "the famous landslide," made up of people "coming in flocks" (OHP book 1, cuaderno 2, pp. 56, 77); for Oscar Tabasco, a political friend of Luis Gay, "in 1945 it was a flood, no one remained without being organized" (OHP book 1, cuaderno 4, p. 42). Tedesco himself says that he was quite inexpert (he was only twenty-two at the time), and that so were most of the people who acted with him, and that Perón "had to rely on leaders, almost all of them *novatos*" (OHP book 5, cuaderno 7, pp. 30, 47, 76). On the other hand, José Domenech and Francisco Pérez Leirós, both very bitter anti-Peronists, comment on the great numbers of old unionists who joined the bandwagon (OHP book 1, cuaderno 11, p. 177, and book 3, cuaderno 2, p. 165).

11. In conservative circles there was some realization of the need for a modicum of protectionism and economic planning, as attempted during the thirties or in the Plan Pinedo of 1940 for import substitution (it was not approved because of systematic opposition to all governmental projects by the Radical party, which had a majority in the lower chamber). But

there is a great difference between moderate protection and the blanket protectionism needed by new industrialist interests.

12. For the ideology and "language" of Peronism, see Emilio de Ipola, *Ideología y discurso populista*; Oscar Landi, *Crisis y lenguajes políticos*; Eliseo Verón and Silvia Sigal, "Perón, discurso político e ideología." For the evolution of trade unionism in more recent years, after the end of Perón's first period, Marcelo Cavarozzi, *Sindicatos y política en Argentina, 1955–1958*; idem, *Consolidación del sindicalismo peronista y emergencia de la fórmula política argentina durante el gobierno frondizista*; Bernardo Gallitelli and Andrés A. Thompson, eds., *Sindicalismo y regímenes militares en Argentina y Chile*; Juan Carlos Torre, *El proceso político interno en los sindicatos en Argentina*; and idem, *Los sindicalistas en el poder: 1973–1976*; Guido Di Tella, *Argentina under Perón, 1973–1976: The Nation's Experience with a Labour-based Government*.

10. Reform and the Politics of Social Democracy

1. The word *intellectuals* is used by Gramsci to decribe those who "correctly " use their intelligence in political action. Antonio Gramsci, *Gli intellettuali e l'organizzazione della cultura*; Alessandro Pizzorno et al., *Gramsci y las ciencias sociales*; Juan Carlos Portantiero, *Los usos de Gramsci*. In Soviet sociology the word becomes equivalent to administrative, technical, and professional workers.

2. An important exception occurs in markedly underdeveloped Third World countries, where the military may opt for establishing a revolutionary anti-imperialist regime under their own control. This is not a common experience in Latin America.

3. Carl Landauer, *European Socialism: A History of Ideas and Movements from the Industrial Revolution to Hitler's Seizure of Power*; Massimo Salvadori, *Karl Kautsky and the Socialist Revolution, 1880–1938*; Georges Haupt et al., *Les marxistes et la question nationale*.

4. Eric Hobsbawm, *Labouring Men: Studies in the History of Labour*; Henry Pelling, *Popular Politics and Society in Late Victorian Britain: Essays*; Chris Cook and Ian Taylor, *The Labour Party: An Introduction to Its History, Structure, and Politics*; Robert Trelford McKenzie, *British Political Parties: The Distribution of Power within the Conservative and Labour Parties*.

5. Werner Sombart, *Why Is There No Socialism in the United States?*; S. M. Lipset, "Why No Socialism in the United States?"; John Laslett and S. M. Lipset, eds., *Failure of a Dream? Essays in the History of American Socialism*; David Montgomery, *The Fall of the House of Labor: The Workplace, the State, and Labor Activism, 1865–1925*.

6. Luis A Sánchez, *Haya de la Torre y el Apra: crónica de un hombre y un partido*; Felipe Cossio del Pomar, *Haya de la Torre el Indoamericano*; Eugenio Chang Rodríguez, *La literatura política de González Prada, Mariátegui y Haya de la Torre*.

7. Fernando Claudin, *L'Eurocommunisme*.

8. This argument has been put forth by Miguel Murmis and Juan Carlos Portantiero, *Estudios sobre los orígenes del peronismo*; and Juan Carlos Torre, *La vieja guardia sindical y Perón*.

9. Henry Pelling, *The Origins of the Labour Party, 1880–1900*; Frank Bealey and Henry Pelling, *Labour and Politics, 1900–1906: A History of the Labour Representation Committee*; Norman MacKenzie and Jeanne MacKenzie, *The First Fabians*; A. M. McBriar, *Fabian Socialism and English Politics*; G. B. Shaw et al., *Fabian Essays in Socialism*.

10. John R. Stevenson, *The Chilean Popular Front*; Arturo Valenzuela, *Political Brokers*

in Chile: Local Government in a Centralist Polity; Arturo Valenzuela and J. Samuel Valenzuela, eds., *Chile: Politics and Society*; Eduardo Ortiz, ed., *Temas socialistas*.

Appendix: A Theoretical Model of Political Processes

1. See Arthur Stinchcombe, *Constructing Social Theories*; W. G. Runciman, *A Treatise on Social Theory*, vol. 1: *The Methodology of Social Theory*; Peter Ordeshook, *Game Theory and Political Theory: An Introduction*; Cathy S. Greenblat and Richard D. Duke, *Gaming-Simulation: Rationale, Design, and Applications. A Text with Parallel Readings for Social Scientists, Educators, and Community Workers*; J. A. Laponce and Paul Smoker, eds., *Experimentation and Simulation in Political Science*.

2. Popper, *The Poverty of Historicism*.

3. In this model, violence is considered a social psychological variable, not an ideological dimension. Any concrete ideology consists not only of a certain set of values in the six standard ideological dimensions, but also includes some attitudes (like the previously mentioned favorability to repression) and some social-psychological traits, like predisposition to violence. The assumption behind this treatment of violence is that it responds more directly to the environment of the individual than do the standard six dimensions. Favorability to repression also responds more to situational conditions of the actor than to ideological influences.

4. In order not to complicate the exposition of the model, affinity is here supposed to depend only on differences in attitudes toward social controls. A more complete version of the model would have to take into account at least another fact: the difference in predisposition toward violence, which, of course, is an attitude, although it does not take the form of opinion about a social control. Experience with some of the runs of this model shows that it is also convenient to include differences in level of satisfaction. This helps break up ruling coalitions in which some actors, although sharing the attitudes of the government, feel dissatisfied because of lack of payoffs. In this case, the government actor may be considered—almost by definition—to be satisfied with its own record.

5. Treating the ideology of ideological specialists in this way is an illustration of the meaning of a variable's being exogenous. It does not mean that it is *external* to the social system under consideration, or that it is influenced from outside. It simply means that it is external to the theoretical system applied in the model, or, in other words, that we do not know which are the forces determining changes in that variable.

6. This formulation of the determinants of military intervention may seem to put too much of the responsibility for bringing in the military on the shoulders of aggressive anti–status quo actors. This is not so, because full social causation must take into account the interaction of variables, including the exogenous ones, whose movements and changes, although not predicted by this mode, are certainly under the influence of social forces. An alternative interpretation would have the military intervene simply as a result of its own predisposition to violence or favorability to repression, or as a result of its extremely conservative views. The latter is a realistic interpretation, but by itself is not enough to determine intervention. When the military (and the upper classes) is excessively rigid and conservative, it is likely to support policies such that widespread dissatisfaction will be typical of many low-status actors, thus generating a predisposition toward violence among them and the menace that activates the military according to the hypothesis in the text. If the system of domination is not seriously challenged by anyone, there is no need for the armed forces to intervene. The challenge, of course, need not come only from low-status actors; it may also come from other

middle- or even upper-status groups, including functional ones like the church or even sections of the military itself.

7. Apart from several unpublished experiments, the best example of the application of an earlier version of this model to a concrete case is Oscar Cornblit, *Cambio político en Cuzco y Oruro a fines del siglo XVIII: un estudio comparado en simulación* (internal document, Instituto Torcuato Di Tella, Buenos Aires, no date). The formulas applied can be seen in his article "Political Coalitions and Political Behavior: A Simulation Model."

Bibliography

Abarca, Mariano. *La industrialización de la Argentina*. Buenos Aires: Unión Industrial Argentina (UIA), 1944.

Adams, Richard N. *Crucifixion by Power: Essays in Guatemalan National Social Structure, 1944–1966*. Austin: University of Texas Press, 1970.

———. *The Second Sowing: Power and Secondary Development in Latin America*. San Francisco: Chandler, 1967.

Adorno, Theodor, and Max Horkheimer. *La sociedad: lecciones de sociología*. Buenos Aires: Proteo, 1969. (Originally published as *Soziologische Exkurse*. Frankfurt-on-Main: Europaische Verlagsanstalt, 1966.)

Adorno, Theodor, et al. *The Authoritarian Personality*. New York: Harper & Brothers, 1950.

Aguilar, Luis. *Cuba 1933: Prologue to Revolution*. Ithaca: Cornell University Press, 1972.

Agulla, Juan Carlos. *Diagnóstico social de una crisis: Córdoba, mayo de 1969*. Córdoba: EDITEL, 1969.

Alberdi, Juan Bautista. *Cartas sobre la prensa y la política militante en la República Argentina*. Vol. 4, pp. 5–94. In *Obras completas*. 8 vols. Buenos Aires: Imprenta de la Tribuna Nacional, 1886–1887.

Allen, Victor L. *Trade Union Leadership*. London: Longmans and Green, 1957.

Almond, Gabriel, and James S. Coleman, eds. *The Politics of Developing Areas*. Princeton, N.J.: Princeton University Press, 1960.

Altamirano, Teófilo. *Presencia andina en Lima metropolitana: estudio sobre migrantes y clubes de provincianos*. Lima: Pontificia Universidad Católica del Perú, 1984.

Alvarez, Juan. *Estudio sobre las guerras civiles argentinas*. Buenos Aires: J. Roldán, 1914.

Ameringer, Charles. *Don Pepe: A Political Biography of José Figueres of Costa Rica*. Albuquerque: University of New Mexico Press, 1978.

Anderson, Robert William. *Party Politics in Puerto Rico*. Stanford: Stanford University Press, 1965.

Angell, Alan. *Politics and the Labor Movement in Chile*. New York: Oxford University Press, 1972.

Apter, David. *Choice and the Politics of Allocation: A Developmental Theory*. New Haven, Conn.: Yale University Press, 1971.

———. *The Politics of Modernization*. Chicago: University of Chicago Press, 1965.

Arauco, Fernando. "La lucha del pueblo boliviano." *Revista Mexicana de Ciencias Políticas y Sociales* 21, no. 82 (October–December 1975): 57–69.

Archetti, Eduardo, and Kristinne Stolen. *Explotación familiar y acumulación de capital en el campo argentino*. Buenos Aires: Siglo Veintiuno, 1975.

Ayarragaray, Lucas. *La anarquía argentina y el caudillismo: estudio psicológico de los orígenes nacionales, hasta el año XXIX*. Buenos Aires: F. Lajouane, 1904.

Baer, Werner. *Industrialization and Economic Development in Brazil*. Homewood, Ill.: Irwin, 1965.

Bakunin, Mikhail. "Cartas a un francés." In *La revolución social en Francia*, pp. 142–149. Duonoo Airoo. La Protootu, 1901.

———. *Selected Writings*. London: Jonathan Cape, 1973.

Balvé, Beba, et al. *Lucha de calles, lucha de clases: elementos para su análisis (Córdoba, 1971–1969)*. Buenos Aires: Ediciones de la Rosa Blindada, 1973.

Bandeira, Alípio. *O Brasil heroico em 1817*. Rio de Janeiro: Imprensa Nacional, 1918.

Barnes, S. M., and M. Kaase. *Political Action: Mass Participation in Five Western Democracies*. Beverly Hills, Calif.: Sage, 1979.

Barrán, José Pedro, and Benjamín Nahum. *Bases económicas de la revolución artiguista*. Montevideo: Ediciones de la Banda Oriental, 1972.

Bartolomé, Leopoldo. "Colonos, plantadores y agroindustrias: la explotación agrícola familiar en el sudeste de Misiones." *Desarrollo Económico* 15, no. 58 (July–September 1975): 239–264.

Basurto, Jorge. *El proletariado industrial en México, 1850–1930*. Mexico City: UNAM, Instituto de Investigaciones Sociales, 1975.

Battaglini, Mario, ed. *La rivoluzione giacobina del 1799 a Napoli*. Messina: Casa Editrice G. D'Anna, 1973.

Bealey, Frank, and Henry Pelling. *Labour and Politics, 1900–1906: A History of the Labour Representation Committee*. London: Macmillan, 1958.

Beard, Charles. *An Economic Interpretation of the Constitution*. New York: Macmillan, 1913.

———. *Economic Origins of Jeffersonian Democracy*. New York: Macmillan, 1915.

Bedregal, Guillermo. "Bolivia: la apertura democrática y las tareas de los partidos políticos." *Nueva Sociedad*, no. 34 (January–February 1978): 101–114.

Beiguelman, Paula. *Formação política do Brasil*. 2 vols. São Paulo: Livraria Pioneira, 1967.

Benvenuto, Luis, et al. *Uruguay hoy*. Buenos Aires: Siglo Veintiuno, 1971.

Bermúdez, Oscar. *Historia del salitre desde sus orígenes hasta la Guerra del Pacífico*. Santiago: Editorial de la Universidad de Chile, 1963.

Blakemore, Harold. *British Nitrates and Chilean Politics, 1886–1896: Balmaceda and North*. London: Athlone Press, 1974.

Blalock, Hubert. *Theory Construction: From Verbal to Mathematical Formulations*. Englewood Cliffs, N.J.: Prentice-Hall, 1969.

Blanchard, Peter. *The Origins of the Peruvian Labor Movement, 1883–1919*. Pittsburgh: University of Pittsburgh Press, 1982.

Bolívar, Simón. *Discursos, proclamas y epistolario político*. Edited by M. Hernández Sánchez-Barba. Madrid: Editora Nacional, 1975.

———. *Discursos, proclamas y epistolario político*. Madrid: Editora Nacional, 1975.

———. *Obras completas*. 2 vols. Havana: Editorial Lex, 1948.

———. *Proyecto de constitución para la República de Bolivia y discurso del libertador*. Bogotá: S. S. Fox, 1826.

Bonilla, Frank, and José A. Silva Michelena. *A Strategy for Research in Social Policy*.

Cambridge, Mass.: MIT Press, 1967.

Booth, John. "Rural Violence in Colombia." *Western Political Quarterly* 27, no. 4 (December 1974): 657–679.

Botana, Natalio. *El orden conservador: la política argentina entre 1880 y 1916.* Buenos Aires: Sudamericana: 1977.

Botana, Natalio, Rafael Braun, and Carlos Floria. *El régimen militar, 1966–1973.* Buenos Aires: Ediciones de la Bastilla, 1974.

Boudon, Raymond. *Analyse mathématique des faits sociaux.* Paris: Plon, 1967.

Bourdieu, Pierre; Jean Claude Chamboredon, and Jean Claude Passeron. *Le métier de sociologue.* 2 vols. Paris: Mouton et Bordas, 1968.

Bourricaud, François. *Power and Society in Contemporary Peru.* New York: Praeger, 1970.

Braithwaite, Richard. *Scientific Explanation.* Cambridge: At the University Press, 1959.

Brenna, Paulo. *L'emigrazione italiana nel periodo antebellico.* Florence: Bemporat, 1918.

Briceño Iragorry, Mario. *Pérez Jiménez presidente: la autoelección de un déspota: 30 de noviembre de 1952.* Caracas: Centauro, 1971.

Brown, Robert. *Explanation in Social Sciences.* Chicago: Aldine, 1963.

Burgin, Myron. *Aspectos económicos del federalismo argentino.* Buenos Aires: Hachette, 1960.

Cabral, César A. *Além: informe sobre la frustración argentina.* Buenos Aires: A. Peña Lillo, 1967.

Calcagno, Alfredo Eric, Pedro Sáinz, and Juan De Barbieri. *Estilos políticos latinoamericanos.* Santiago: FLACSO, 1972.

Calvert, Peter. *The Mexican Revolution, 1910–14: The Diplomacy of Anglo American Conflict.* Cambridge: At the University Press,1968.

Cameu, Francolino, and Artur Vieira Peixoto. *Floriano Peixoto: vida e governo.* Brasília: Universidade de Brasília, 1983.

Campolietti, Roberto. *La colonizzazione italiana nell'Argentina.* Buenos Aires: A. Cantiello, 1902.

Campos Harriet, Fernando. *Historia constitucional de Chile: las instituciones políticas y sociales.* Santiago: Editorial Jurídica de Chile, 1977.

Cardoso, Ciro, et al. *La clase obrera en la historia de México: de la dictadura porfirista a los tiempos libertarios.* Mexico City: UNAM, Instituto de Investigaciones Sociales, 1980.

Cardoso, Fernando Henrique. *Autoritarismo e democratização.* Rio de Janeiro: Paz e Terra, 1975.

———. "Dependência o democracia." Paper presented to Seminar on Recent Changes in Social Structures and Stratification in Latin America, organized by ECLA (CEPAL), Santiago, Chile, 12–15 September 1983.

———. *Ideologías de la burguesía industrial en sociedades dependientes: Argentina y Brasil.* Mexico City: Siglo Veintiuno, 1971.

Cardoso, Fernando Henrique, and Bolívar Lamounier, eds. *Os partidos e as eleições no Brasil.* Rio de Janeiro: Paz e Terra, 1975.

Cardoso, Fernando Henrique, and Enzo Faletto. *Dependency and Development in Latin America.* Berkeley and Los Angeles: University of California Press, 1977.

Carone, Edgar. *O tenentismo: acontecimentos, personagens, programas.* São Paulo: DIFEL, 1975.

Carrera Damas, Germán. *Boves, aspectos socioeconómicos de su acción histórica.* 2d ed.

Colección Vigilia. Caracas: Ministerio de Educación, 1968.

Carrera Damas, Germán, Carlos Salazar, and Manuel Caballero. *El concepto de la historia en Laureano Valenilla Lanz*. Caracas: Universidad Nacional de Venezuela, Escuela de Historia, 1966.

Carvalho, José Murilo de. *A construção da ordem: a elite política imperial*. Brasília: Universidade de Brasília, 1980.

Casimir, Jean. *La cultura oprimida*. Mexico City: Nueva Imagen, 1980.

Castellanos, Joaquín. *Labor dispersa*. Lausanne: Imprenta Payot, 1000.

Castillo Velasco, Jaime. *Los caminos de la revolución*. Santiago: Editorial del Pacífico, 1972.

Cavarozzi, Marcelo. *Consolidación del sindicalismo peronista y emergencia de la fórmula política argentina durante el gobierno frondizista*. Buenos Aires: CEDES, 1979.

————. *Sindicatos y política en Argentina, 1955–1958*. Buenos Aires: CEDES, 1979.

Celletti, Silvio. *Rapporto al Commissario di Emigrazione*. Rome: n.p., 1914.

Chacón, Vamireh. *Historia dos partidos brasileiros*. Brasília: Universidade de Brasília, 1981.

Chambers, William Nisbet. *Political Parties in a New Nation: The American Experience, 1776–1809*. New York: Oxford University Press, 1963.

Chandler, Billy Jaynes. *The Bandit King: Lampião of Brazil*. College Station: Texas A&M University Press, 1978.

Chang Rodríguez, Eugenio. *La literatura política de González Prada, Mariátegui y Haya de la Torre*. Mexico City: Editorial De Andrea, 1957.

Charles, Joseph. *The Origins of the American Party System: Three Essays*. Williamsburg, Va.: Institute of Early American History and Culture, 1956.

Christie, Ian. *Crisis of Empire: Great Britain and the American Colonies, 1754–1783*. London: Edward Arnold, 1966.

Un ciclo de 16 conferencias radiotelefónicas. Buenos Aires: UIA, 1943.

Un ciclo de 22 conferencias radiotelefónicas. Buenos Aires: UIA, 1944.

Claudin, Fernando. *L'Eurocommunisme*. Paris: Maspero, 1977.

Clegg, Hugh. *General Union: A Study of the National Union of General and Municipal Workers*. Oxford: Blackwell, 1954.

Colegio de México. *Centroamérica en crisis*. Mexico City: Colegio de México, 1980.

Colletta, Pietro. *Storia del reame di Napoli dal 1734 al 1825*. 3 vols. 1834. Reprint. Naples: Libreria Scientifica Editrice, 1951–1957.

Collier, David, ed. *The New Authoritarianism*. Princeton, N.J.: Princeton University Press, 1979.

————. *Squatters and Oligarchs: Authoritarian Rule and Policy Change in Peru*. Baltimore, Md.: Johns Hopkins University Press, 1976.

Collier, Simon. *Ideas and Politics of Chilean Independence, 1801–1833*. Cambridge: At the University Press, 1967.

Colombo, Luis, et al. *Discursos pronunciados con motivo del banquete con que se celebró la clausura del primer ciclo de conferencias*. Buenos Aires: UIA, 1942.

Combo, Juan. *Bolivia bajo el modelo de Banzer*. Bogotá: n.p., 1977.

Conniff, Michael L. *Latin American Populism in Comparative Perspective*. Albuquerque: University of New Mexico Press, 1982.

————. *Urban Politics in Brazil: The Rise of Populism, 1925–1945*. Pittsburgh: University of Pittsburgh Press, 1981.

Cook, Chris, and Ian Taylor, eds. *The Labour Party: An Introduction to Its History, Structure, and Politics.* London: Longmans, 1980.

Cordasco, Francesco, and Salvatore Lagumina. *Italians in the United States: A Bibliography of Reports, Texts, Critical Studies, and Related Materials.* New York: Oriole Editions, 1978.

Cornblit, Oscar. "Political Coalitions and Political Behavior: A Simulation Model." In J. A. Laponce and Paul Smoker, eds., *Experimentation and Simulation in Political Science,* 225–258. Toronto: Toronto University Press, 1972.

Cornblit, Oscar, Torcuato S. Di Tella, and Ezequiel Gallo. "A Model of Political Change for Latin America." *Social Science Information* 7, no. 2 (April 1968): 13–48.

Cornelius, Wayne. "The Cityward Movement: Some Political Implications." In Douglas Chalmers, ed., *Changing Latin America: New Interpretations of Its Politics and Society,* pp. 27–41. New York: Academy of Political Science, 1972.

———. *Politics and the Migrant Poor in Mexico City.* Stanford, Calif.: Stanford University Press, 1975.

Cortés Conde, Roberto. *El progreso argentino.* Buenos Aires: Sudamericana, 1979.

Cossio del Pomar, Felipe. *Haya de la Torre el Indoamericano.* Mexico City: Editorial América, 1939.

Cotler, Julio, and Richard Fagen, eds. *Latin America and the United States: The Changing Political Realities.* Stanford, Calif.: Stanford University Press, 1974.

Crawley, Eduardo. *Nicaragua in Perspective.* New York: St. Martin's, 1984.

Creighton, Donald G. *Dominion of the North: A History of Canada.* Toronto: Macmillan, 1962.

Crozier, Michel, Samuel Huntington, and Joji Watanuki. *The Crisis of Democracy: Report on the Governability of Democracies to the Trilateral Commission.* New York: New York University Press, 1975.

Cumberland, Charles. *The Mexican Revolution: Genesis under Madero.* Austin: University of Texas Press, 1952.

Cuneo, Niccoló. *Storia dell' emigrazione italiana nell'Argentina 1810–1870.* Milan: Garzanti, 1940.

Dahl, Robert, ed. *Regimes and Oppositions.* New Haven, Conn.: Yale University Press, 1973.

Davies, James. "Toward a Theory of Revolution." *American Sociological Review* 27, no. 1 (February 1962): 5–19.

Degler, Carl. *Neither Black nor White: Slavery and Race Relations in Brazil and the United States.* New York: Macmillan, 1971.

Delich, Francisco. *Crisis y protesta social: Córdoba 1969–1973.* 2d ed. Mexico City: Siglo Veintiuno, 1974.

Deutsch, Karl. *Nationalism and Social Communication: An Enquiry into the Foundations of Nationality.* New York: Wiley: 1953.

———. "Social Mobilization and Political Development." *American Political Science Review* 55, no. 3 (September 1961): 493–514.

Devoto, Fernando, and Gianfausto Rosoli, eds. *La inmigración italiana en la Argentina.* Buenos Aires: Biblos, 1985.

Díaz Alejandro, Carlos. *Essays on the Economic History of the Argentine Republic.* New Haven, Conn.: Yale University Press, 1970.

Dickman, Enrique. *Recuerdos de un militante socialista.* Buenos Aires: Editorial La

Vanguardia, 1949.

Diniz, Eli. *Voto e máquina política: patronagem e clientelismo no Rio de Janeiro*. Rio de Janeiro: Paz e Terra, 1982.

Di Tella, Guido. *Argentina under Perón, 1973–1976: The Nation's Experience with a Labour-based Government*. New York: St. Martin's, 1983.

Di Tella, Torcuato S. "The Dangerous Classes in Early Nineteenth-Century Mexico." *Journal of Latin American Studies* 5, no. 1 (1973): 79–105.

―――. La división del trabajo y el concepto marxista de clase social. *Revista Latinoamericana de Ciencias Sociales*. New Series, no. 2 (1975): 7–36.

―――. *Iturbide y el cesarismo popular*. Cuadernos Simón Rodríguez, no. 9. Buenos Aires: Fundación Simón Rodríguez, 1987.

―――. "Mafia y estructura social en el sur de Italia." *Desarrollo Económico* 18, no. 69 (April–June 1978): 121–130.

―――. *Un modelo de análisis de procesos históricos*. Documento de Trabajo, no. 90. Buenos Aires: Instituto Torcuato Di Tella, 1976.

―――. "Populism and Reform in Latin America." In Claudio Véliz, ed., *Obstacles to Change in Latin America*, 47–74. New York: Oxford University Press, 1965.

―――. *La rebelión de esclavos en Haití*. Buenos Aires: IDES, 1984.

―――. *La teoría del primer impacto del crecimiento económico*. Rosario: Universidad del Litoral, 1966.

Di Tella, Torcuato S., et al. *Sindicato y comunidad: dos tipos de estructura sindical latinoamericana*. Buenos Aires: Editorial del Instituto, 1967.

Dix, Robert H. *Colombia: The Political Dimensions of Change*. New Haven, Conn.: Yale University Press, 1967.

Dollard, John, et al. *Frustration and Aggression*. New Haven, Conn.: Yale University Press, 1939.

Domínguez, Jorge. *Cuba, Order and Revolution*. Cambridge, Mass.: Belknap Press of Harvard University Press, 1978.

―――. *Insurrection or Loyalty: The Breakdown of the Spanish American Empire*. Cambridge, Mass.: Harvard University Press, 1980.

Donoso, Ricardo. *Las ideas políticas en Chile*. Mexico City: Fondo de Cultura Económica, 1946.

Drake, Paul. *Socialism and Populism in Chile, 1932–1952*. Urbana: University of Illinois Press, 1978.

Duff, Ernest, and John MacCamant, with W. Morales. *Violence and Repression in Latin America: A Quantitative and Historical Analysis*. New York: Free Press, 1976.

Dulles, John W. F. *Vargas of Brazil: A Political Biography*. Austin: University of Texas Press, 1967.

Duncan, Kenneth, and Ian Rutledge, eds. *Land and Labour in Latin America: Essays on the Development of Agrarian Capitalism in the Nineteenth and Twentieth Centuries*. Cambridge: At the University Press, 1977.

Durkheim, Emile. *The Division of Labor*. Glencoe, Ill.: Free Press, 1949.

Easterbrook, W. T., and H. G. Aitken. *Canadian Economic History*. Toronto: Macmillan, 1956.

Echavarría Olozaga, Felipe. *Colombia, una democracia indefensa: la resurrección de Rojas Pinilla*. Rome: n.p., 1965.

Echeverría, Esteban. "Ojeada retrospectiva sobre el movimiento intelectual en el Plata desde el año 37." In *Dogma socialista*. 1838. Reprint. La Plata: Universidad Nacional de la Plata, 1940.

Eckstein, Harry, ed. *Internal War: Problems and Approaches*. New York: Free Press of Glencoe, 1964.

Edelstein, David, and Malcolm Warner. *Comparative Union Democracy: Organization and Opposition in British and American Unions*. London: Allen & Unwin, 1975.

Edwards Vives, Alberto. 2d ed. *La fronda aristocrática*. Santiago: Ercilla, 1936.

Eisenstadt, Shmuel N. *Modernization, Protest, and Change*. Englewood Cliffs, N.J.: Prentice-Hall, 1966.

Emmet, Dorothy, and Alasdair MacIntyre, eds. *Sociological Theory and Philosophical Analysis*. New York: Macmillan, 1970.

Encina, Francisco A. *Introducción a la historia de la época de Diego Portales, 1830–1891*. Santiago: Nascimento, 1934.

Engels, Friedrich. "Los bakuninistas en acción. Informe sobre la sublevación española de 1873." In Karl Marx and Friedrich Engels, *Revolución en España*, 191–214. 4th ed. Barcelona: Ariel, 1973.

Engels, Friedrich. *The Condition of the Working Class in England in 1844*. Oxford: Blackwell, 1958.

———. *The Peasant War in Germany: Revolution and Counterrevolution*. Chicago: University of Chicago Press, 1967.

———. *Socialism, Utopian and Scientific*. New York: Scribner's, 1892.

Erasmus, Charles, Solomon Miller, and Louis C. Faron. *Contemporary Change in Traditional Communities of Mexico and Peru*. Urbana: University of Illinois Press, 1967.

Escudé, Carlos. *Gran Bretaña, Estados Unidos y la declinación argentina, 1942–1949*. Buenos Aires: Editorial de Belgrano, 1983.

Estrada, José Manuel. *La política liberal bajo la tiranía de Rosas*. 1873. Reprint. Buenos Aires: Ediciones Estrada, 1947.

Etchepareborda, Roberto. *Tres revoluciones: 1890, 1893, y 1905*. Buenos Aires: Pleamar, 1968.

Eyzaguirre, Jaime. *Chile durante el gobierno de Errázuriz Echaurren, 1896–1901*. Santiago: Zig-Zag, 1956.

Fagen, Richard. *The Transformation of Political Culture in Cuba*. Stanford, Calif.: Stanford University Press, 1969.

———, ed. *Capitalism and the State in U.S.–Latin American Relations*. Stanford, Calif.: Stanford University Press, 1979.

Falorsi, Vittorio. *Problemi di emigrazione*. Bologna: Zanichelli, 1924.

Fals Borda, Orlando. *Campesinos de los Andes: estudio sociológico de Saucío*. Bogotá: Iqueima, 1961.

Fausto, Boris. *A revolução de trinta: historigrafia e história*. São Paulo: Brasiliense, 1970.

Feierabend, Ivo, Rosalind Feierabend, and Ted R. Gurr, eds. *Anger, Violence, and Politics: Theories and Research*. Englewood Cliffs, N.J.: Prentice-Hall, 1972.

Felice, Renzo de. *Mussolini*. Turin: Einaudi, 1974 .

Feo Calcaño, Guillermo. *Democracia versus dictadura: artículos periodísticos*. Caracas: n.p., 1963.

Ferrara, F. *¿Qué son las ligas agrarias?* Buenos Aires: Siglo Veintiuno, 1973.

Ferrari, Gustavo, and Ezequiel Gallo, eds. *La Argentina del ochenta al centenario*. Buenos Aires: Sudamericana, 1980.

Figueiredo, Argelina. "Intervenções sindicais e o novo sindicalismo." *Dados*, no. 17 (1978): 135–155.

Figueiredo, Eurico de Lima, ed. *Os militares e a revolução de trinta*. Rio de Janeiro: Paz e Terra, 1979.

FLACSO-UNESCO, ed. *Teoría, metodología y política del desarrollo en América Latina*. Buenos Aires and Santiago: FLACSO, 1972.

Florescano, Enrique, ed. *Haciendas, latifundios y plantaciones en América Latina*. Mexico City: Siglo Veintiuno, 1975.

Fogarty, John, Ezequiel Gallo, and Héctor Diéguez, eds. *Argentina y Australia*. Buenos Aires: Instituto Torcuato Di Tella, 1979.

Folino, Norberto. *Barceló, Ruggierito y el populismo oligárquico*. Buenos Aires: Falbo, 1966.

Forjaz, Maria Cecília Spina. *Tenentismo e aliança liberal, 1927–1930*. São Paulo: Livraria Editorial Polis, 1978.

Franco, Sylvia de Carvalho. *Homens livres na ordem escravocrata*. São Paulo: Instituto de Estudos Brasileiros, 1969.

Frank, André Gunder. *Latin America: Underdevelopment or Revolution*. New York: Monthly Review Press, 1969.

Fuenzalida, Fernando, et al. *Perú, hoy*. Mexico City: Siglo Veintiuno, 1971.

Furtado, Celso. *Diagnosis of the Brazilian Crisis*. Berkeley and Los Angeles: University of California Press, 1965.

———. *Subdesenvolvimento e estagnação na América Latina*. Rio de Janeiro: Civilização Brasileira, 1966.

Gallitelli, Bernardo, and Andrés A. Thompson, eds. *Sindicalismo y regímenes militares en Argentina y Chile*. Amsterdam: CEDLA, 1982.

Gallo, Ezequiel. *Farmers in Revolt*. London: Athlone Press, 1976.

Garcés, Joan. *El estado y los problemas tácticos en el gobierno de Allende*. Mexico City: Siglo Veintiuno, 1974.

García, Juan A. *La ciudad indiana: Buenos Aires desde 1600 hasta mediados del siglo XVIII*. Buenos Aires: A. Zamora, 1955.

García Calderón, Francisco. *Les démocraties latines de l'Amérique*. Paris: Flammarion, 1912.

Gardiner, Patrick, ed. *Theories of History*. Glencoe, Ill.: Free Press, 1959.

Gatell, Frank Otto, ed. *Essays in Jacksonian America*. New York: Holt, Rinehart & Winston, 1970.

Geertz, Clifford. *Peddlers and Princes: Social Change and Economic Modernization in Two Indonesian Towns*. Chicago: University of Chicago Press, 1963.

Germani, Gino. *Authoritarianism, Fascism, and National Populism*. New Brunswick, N.J.: Transaction Books, 1978.

———. "Democracia y autoritarismo en la sociedad moderna." *Crítica y Utopía*, no. 1 (1979): 25–67.

———. *La integración política de las masas y el totalitarismo*. Buenos Aires: Colegio Libre de Estudios Superiores, 1956.

———. *Política y sociedad en una época de transición: de la sociedad tradicional a la sociedad de masas*.. Buenos Aires: Paidós, 1962.

———. *The Sociology of Modernization: Studies on Its Historical and Theoretical Aspects with Special Regard to the Latin American Case*. New Brunswick, N.J.: Transaction

Books, 1981.

―――. "El surgimiento del peronismo: el rol de los obreros y los migrantes internos." *Desarrollo Económico* 13, no. 51 (October–December 1973): 435–488.

Gibson, Quentin. *The Logic of Social Explanation.* London: Routledge & Kegan Paul, 1966.

Gil Fortoul, José. *Historia constitucional de Venezuela.* 2d ed. 2 vols. Caracas: Parra León Hermanos, 1930.

Godio, Julio. *La Semana Trágica de enero 1919.* Buenos Aires: Granica, 1972.

Goldstone, Jack A. "Theories of Revolution: The Third Generation." *World Politics* 32, no. 3 (April 1980): 425–453.

Gómez, Horacio J. *La industria nacional y los problemas de la marina.* Buenos Aires: UIA, 1944.

González, Joaquín V. *Obras completas.* 25 vols. Buenos Aires: Imprenta Neratali, 1935–1937.

González Casanova, Pablo. *Democracy in Mexico.* New York: Oxford University Press 1970.

―――, ed. *América Latina: historia de medio siglo.* 2 vols. Mexico City: Siglo Veintiuno, 1981.

González Navarro, Moisés. *Anatomía del poder en México, 1848–1853.* Mexico City: Colegio de México, 1977.

―――. *Las huelgas textiles en el Porfiriato.* Puebla: Editorial J. M. Cajica, 1970.

González y González, Luis. *Pueblo en vilo. Microhistoria de San José de Gracia.* Mexico City: Colegio de México, 1968.

Goodman, David, and Michael Redclift. *From Peasant to Proletarian: Capitalist Development and Agrarian Transitions.* New York: St. Martin's Press, 1982.

Goodwin, Lawrence. *Democratic Promise: The Populist Moment in America.* New York: Oxford University Press, 1976.

Gorz, André. *Farewell to the Working Class: An Essay in Postindustrial Socialism.* London: Pluto Press, 1982.

Gott, Richard. *Guerrilla Movements in Latin America.* Garden City, N.Y.: Doubleday, 1971.

Gouldner, Alvin. *The Future of Intellectuals and the Rise of the New Class.* New York: Seabury, 1979.

Graham, Richard. "Causes for the Abolition of Negro Slavery in Brazil: An Interpretative Essay." *Hispanic American Historical Review* 46, no. 2 (May 1966): 123–137.

Gramsci, Antonio. *Gli intellettuali e l'organizzazione della cultura.* 6th ed. Turin: Einaudi, 1955.

Greenwood, Gordon, ed. *Australia: A Social and Political History.* Sydney: Angus & Robertson, 1955.

Grela, Plácido. *El grito de Alcorta: historia de la rebelión campesina de 1912.* Rosario: Ediciones Tierra Nuestra, 1958.

Guadagnini, Giuseppe. *In America: Repubblica Argentina.* Milan: Cumolart, 1892.

Guerra, José Joaquín. *La convención de Ocaña.* Bogotá: Biblioteca de Historia Nacional, 1908.

Guetzkow, Harold, ed. *Simulation in Social Science.* Englewood Cliffs, N.J.: Prentice-Hall, 1962.

Gurr, Ted R. *Why Men Rebel.* Princeton, N.J.: Princeton University Press, 1970.

―――, ed. *Handbook of Political Conflict: Theory and Research.* New York: Free Press,

1980.

Guzmán, Germán, Orlando Fals Borda, and Eduardo Umaña Luna. *La violencia en Colombia: estudio de un proceso social.* 2 vols. Bogotá: Ediciones Tercer Mundo, 1962.

Hagen, Everett. *On the Theory of Social Change.* Homewood, Ill.: Dorsey, 1962.

Hale, Charles. *Mexican Liberalism in the Age of Mora, 1821–1853.* New Haven, Conn.: Yale University Press, 1968.

Halperin Donghi, Tulio. *De la revolución de la independencia a la confederación rosista.* Buenos Aires: Paidós, 1972.

———. *La democracia de masas.* Buenos Aires: Paidós, 1972.

———. "Un nuevo clima de ideas." In Gustavo Ferrari and Ezequiel Gallo, eds., *La Argentina del ochenta al centenario.* Buenos Aires: Sudamericana, 1980.

———. *Politics, Economy and Society during the Revolutionary Period.* Cambridge: At the University Press, 1975.

———. "El surgimiento de los caudillos en el marco de la sociedad rioplatense postrevolucionaria." *Estudios de Historia Social* 1, no. 1 (October 1965): 121–149.

———, ed. *Proyecto y construcción de una nación: Argentina, 1846–1880.* Caracas: Biblioteca Ayacucho, 1980.

Hamill, Hugh M., Jr. *The Hidalgo Revolt: Prelude to Mexican Independence.* Gainesville: University of Florida Press, 1966.

Hardoy, Jorge E., ed. *Urbanization in Latin America: Approaches and Issues.* Garden City, N.Y.: Anchor Books, 1975.

Harker Valdivieso, Roberto. *La rebelión de los curules: boceto en negro para el ex-general Rojas Pinilla.* Santander, Colombia: n.p., 1968.

Hart, John. *Anarchism and the Mexican Working Class, 1850–1900.* Austin: University of Texas Press, 1978.

Haupt, Georges, Michael Lowy, and Claudie Weill. *Les marxistes et la question nationale.* Paris: Maspero, 1974.

Haya de la Torre, Víctor R. *Treinta años de aprismo.* Mexico City: Fondo de Cultura Económica, 1956.

Hegedüs, András N. *Socialism and Bureaucracy.* London: L. Allison & Busby, 1976.

———. *The Structure of Socialist Society.* New York: St. Martin's, 1977.

Heise González, Julio. *Años de formación y aprendizaje políticos, 1810–1833.* Santiago: Editorial Universitaria, 1978.

———. *150 años de evolución institucional: Chile, 1810–1960.* Santiago: Editorial Andrés Bello, 1960.

———. *El período parlamentario, 1861–1925.* Santiago: Editorial Universitaria, 1982.

Hempel, Carl. *Aspects of Scientific Explanation and Other Essays in the Philosophy of Science.* New York: Free Press, 1965.

———. "The Function of General Laws in History." *Journal of Philosophy* 39 (1942): 35–48.

Hilliker, Grant. *The Politics of Reform in Peru: The Aprista and Other Mass Parties of Latin America.* Baltimore, Md.: Johns Hopkins University Press, 1971.

Hirschman, Albert. *Essays in Trespassing: Economics to Politics and Beyond.* Cambridge: At the University Press, 1981.

———. *Journeys towards Progress: Studies of Economic Policy-Making in Latin America.* New York: Twentieth Century Fund, 1963.

Hobsbawn, Eric. *Labouring Men: Studies in the History of Labour*. London: Weidenfeld & Nicholson, 1964.

Hofstadter, Richard. *The Age of Reform: From Bryan to FDR*. New York: Knopf, 1955.

———. *The Idea of a Party System: The Rise of Legitimate Opposition in the United States, 1780–1840*. Berkeley & Los Angeles: University of California Press, 1969.

Hornung, Carlton. "Social Status, Status Inconsistency, and Psychological Stress." *American Sociological Review* 42, no. 4 (August 1977): 623–638.

Horowitz, Irving L., ed. *Cuban Communism*. Chicago: Aldine, 1970.

Hoselitz, Bert. "Desarrollo económico en América Latina." *Desarrollo Económico* 2, no. 3 (October–December 1962): 49–65.

Huntington, Samuel. *Political Order in Changing Societies*. New Haven, Conn.: Yale University Press, 1968.

Huntington, Samuel, and Joan Nelson. *No Easy Choice: Political Participation in Developing Countries*. Cambridge, Mass.: Harvard University Press, 1976.

Ingenieros, José. *Sociología argentina*. Buenos Aires: Editorial Losada, 1962.

Instituto Alejandro E. Bunge de Investigaciones Económicas y Sociales. *Soluciones argentinas a los problemas económicos y sociales del presente*. Buenos Aires: Guillermo Kraft, 1945.

Intervención Federal en la Provincia de Tucumán. *Causas y fines de la revolución libertadora del 4 de junio: nueve meses de gobierno en la Provincia de Tucumán*. Tucumán: Publicación Oficial, 1944.

Ionescu, Ghita, and Ernest Gellner, eds. *Populism: Its Meaning and National Characteristics*. New York: Macmillan 1969.

Ipola, Emilio de. *Ideología y discurso populista*. Mexico City: Folios, 1982.

Jackson, Elton F., and Richard F. Curtis. "Effects of Vertical Mobility and Status Inconsistency: A Body of Negative Evidence." *American Sociological Review* 37, no. 6 (December 1972): 701–713.

Jaguaribe, Hélio. *Brasil: crise e alternativas*. Rio de Janeiro: Zahar, 1974.

———. "Las elecciones de 1962 en el Brasil." *Desarrollo Económico* 3, no. 4 (January–March 1964): 607–630.

———. *Political Development: A General Theory and a Latin American Case Study*. New York: Harper & Row, 1973.

James, C. L. R. *Black Jacobins*. London: Secker & Warburg, 1938.

Jameson, J. Franklin. *The American Revolution Considered as a Social Movement*. Princeton, N.J.: Princeton University Press, 1926.

Janvry, Alain de. *The Agrarian Question and Reformism in Latin America*. Baltimore, Md.: Johns Hopkins University Press, 1982.

Jobet, Julio César. *Luis Emilio Recabarren: los orígenes del movimiento obrero y del socialismo chilenos*. Santiago de Chile: Prensa Latinoamericana, 1955.

Johnson, Chalmers. *Revolutionary Change*. Boston: Little, Brown, 1966.

Johnson, Dale, ed. *The Chilean Road to Socialism*. Garden City, N.Y.: Anchor Press, 1979.

Jorge, Eduardo. *Industria y concentración económica*. Buenos Aires: Siglo Veintiuno, 1971.

Joseph, Lawrence B. "Democratic Revisionism Revisited." *American Journal of Political Science* 25, no. 1 (February 1981): 160–184.

Joxe, Alain. *Las fuerzas armadas en el sistema político de Chile*. Santiago: Editorial Universitaria, 1970.

Justo, Juan B. *La realización del socialismo.* In *Obras completas,* vol. I. 7 vols. Buenos Aires: Editorial La Vanguardia, 1947.

—————. *Teoría y práctica de la historia.* 1909. Reprint. Buenos Aires: Lotito y Barberis, 1915.

Kantor, Harry. *The Ideology and Program of the Peruvian Aprista Movement.* Berkeley and Los Angeles: University of California Press, 1966.

Karol, K. S. *Guerrillas in Power: The Course of the Cuban Revolution.* New York: Hill & Wang, 1970.

Kautsky, Karl. *La defensa de los trabajadores y la jornada de ocho horas.* Barcelona: Imprenta de Henrich y Cía, 1904.

Kay, Hugh. *Salazar and Modern Portugal.* London: Hawthorne Books, 1970.

Kaztman, Rubén, and José Luis Reyna, eds. *Fuerza de trabajo y movimientos laborales en América Latina.* Mexico City: Colegio de México, 1968.

Klaren, Peter. *Modernization, Dislocation, and Aprismo: Origins of the Peruvian Aprista Party, 1870–1932.* Austin: University of Texas Press, 1972.

Klein, Herbert. *African Slavery in Latin America and the Caribbean.* New York: Oxford University Press, 1986.

—————. "La integración de italianos en Argentina y Estados Unidos: un análisis comparativo." *Desarrollo Económico* 21, no. 81 (April–June 1981): 3–27.

—————. *Parties and Political Change in Bolivia, 1880–1952.* Cambridge: At the University Press, 1969.

—————. *Slavery in the Americas: A Comparative Study of Cuba and Virginia.* Chicago: University of Chicago Press, 1967.

Knight, Alan. *The Mexican Revolution.* 2 vols. Cambridge: At the University Press, 1986.

Konrad, George, and Ivan Szelenyi. *The Intellectuals on the Road to Class Power.* New York: Harcourt, Brace & Jovanovich, 1979.

Kornhauser, William. *The Politics of Mass Society.* Glencoe, Ill.: Free Press, 1959.

Kriegel, Annie. *La croissance de la C.G.T., 1918–21: essai statistique.* The Hague: Mouton, 1966.

Kuron, Jacek, and Karol Modzleweski. *Lettre ouverte au Parti Ouvrier Polonais.* Paris: Maspero, 1969.

Kuznets, Simon, Wilbert Moore, and Joseph Spengler, eds. *Economic Growth: Brazil, India, Japan.* Durham, N.C.: Duke University Press, 1955.

Kvaternik, Eugenio. *Crisis sin salvaje: la crisis político militar de 1962–63.* Buenos Aires: IDES, 1987.

—————. "Sobre partidos y democracia en la Argentina entre 1955 y 1966." *Desarrollo Económico* 18, no. 71 (October–December 1978): 409–431.

Labougle, Alfredo. *Las industrias argentinas en el pasado, presente y porvenir.* Buenos Aires: UIA, 1943.

Laclau, Ernesto. *Politics and Ideology in Marxist Theory: Capitalism, Fascism and Populism.* London: Verso, 1977.

Lafertte, Elías. *Vida de un comunista: páginas autobiográficas.* Santiago: n.p., 1961.

Landauer, Carl. *European Socialism: A History of Ideas and Movements from the Industrial Revolution to Hitler's Seizure of Power.* Berkeley and Los Angeles: University of California Press, 1959.

Landerberger, José, and Francisco Conte, comps. *La Unión Cívica: origen, organización y tendencia.* Buenos Aires, 1890.

Landi, Oscar. *Crisis y lenguajes políticos.* Buenos Aires: CEDES, 1981.

Laponce, J. A., and Paul Smoker, eds. *Experimentation and Simulation in Political Science.* Toronto: University of Toronto Press, 1972.

Larra, Raúl. *Lisandro de la Torre: vida y drama del solitario de Pinas.* Buenos Aires: Editorial Hemisferio, 1942.

Laslett, John, and Seymour M. Lipset, eds. *Failure of a Dream? Essays in the History of American Socialism.* Berkeley and Los Angeles: University of California Press, 1984.

Lechner, Norbert, ed. *Estado y política en América Latina.* Mexico City: Siglo Veintiuno, 1981.

Lenin, V. I. *The Development of Capitalism in Russia: The Process of the Formation of a Home Market for Large Scale Industry.* Moscow: Foreign Languages Publishing House, 1956.

———. *Two Tactics of Social Democracy in the Democratic Revolution.* New York: International Publishers, 1935.

———. *What Is to Be Done: Burning Questions of the Moment.* New York: International Publishers, 1929.

Lenski, Gerhard. "Status Crystallization: A Nonvertical Dimension of Social Status." *American Sociological Review* 19, no. 4 (August 1954): 405–413.

Lewin, Linda. "The Oligarchical Limitations of Social Banditry in Brazil: The Case of the 'Good' Thief Antonio Silvino." *Past and Present,* no. 82 (February 1979): 116–146.

Lhomme, Jean. *La grande bourgeoisie au pouvoir, 1830–1880: essai sur l'histoire sociale de la France.* Paris: Presses Universitaires de France, 1960.

Liévano Aguirre, Indalecio. "Bolívar y Santander." In Academia Colombiana de la Historia, *Curso superior de historia de Colombia.* Vol. 3, pp. 241–279. 6 vols. Bogotá: Editorial ABC, 1950.

———. *Los grandes conflictos sociales y económicos de nuestra historia.* 2d ed. Bogotá: Ediciones Tercer Mundo, 1966.

Lima, Estácio de. *O mundo estranho dos cangaceiros: ensaio bio-sociológico.* Salvador: Editora Itapoa, 1965.

Lima, Manuel de Oliveira. *O império brasileiro, 1822–1889.* São Paulo: Companhia Melhoramentos, 1927.

Linz, Juan. "Crisis, Breakdown and Reequilibration." In Juan Linz and Alfred Stepan, eds., *The Breakdown of Democratic Regimes,* Part I, pp. 3–124. Baltimore, Md.: Johns Hopkins University Press, 1978.

Linz, Juan, and Alfred Stepan, eds. *The Breakdown of Democratic Regimes.* Baltimore, Md.: Johns Hopkins University Press, 1978.

Lipset, Seymour M. *Political Man: The Social Bases of Politics.* Garden City, N.Y.: Doubleday, 1960.

———. *Revolution and Counterrevolution: Change and Persistence in Social Structure.* New York: Basic Books, 1968.

———. "Why No Socialism in the United States?" In Seweryn Bialer and Sofia Sluzar, eds., *Sources of Contemporary Radicalism,* pp. 31–149. Boulder, Colo.: Westview, 1977.

Lipset, Seymour M., and R. Bendix. *Social Mobility in Industrial Society.* Berkeley and Los Angeles: University of California Press, 1958.

Lipset, Seymour M., and James S. Coleman. *Union Democracy: The Internal Politics of the International Typographical Union.* Glencoe, Ill.: Free Press, 1956.

Lipset, Seymour M., and Ernest Raab. *The Politics of Unreason: Right Wing Extremism in*

America, 1790–1970. New York: Harper & Row, 1970.

Lipset, Seymour M., and Stein Rokkan, eds. *Party Systems and Voter Alignments: Cross-National Perspectives*. New York: Free Press, 1967.

Little, Walter. "The Popular Origins of Peronism." In David Rock, ed., *Argentina in the Twentieth Century*, 162–178. London: Duckworth, 1975.

Llorente, Ignacio. "Alianzas políticas en el surgimiento del peronismo: el caso de la provincia de Buenos Aires." In Manuel Mora y Araujo and Ignacio Llorente, eds., *El voto peronista*, pp. 269–317. Buenos Aires: Sudamericana, 1980.

Long, Norman, and Bryan Roberts, eds. *Peasant Cooperation and Capitalist Expansion in Central Peru*. Austin: University of Texas Press, 1978.

Lora, Guillermo. *A History of the Bolivian Labor Movement*. Cambridge: At the University Press, 1977.

Lovell, John. *Stevedores and Dockers: A Study of Trade Unionism in the Port of London, 1870–1914*. New York: Kelley, 1969.

Lowenthal, Leo, and Norbert Guterman. *Prophets of Deceit: A Study of the Techniques of the American Agitator*. New York: Harper and Brothers, 1950.

Lower, Arthur R. M. *Colony to Nation: A History of Canada*. Toronto: Longmans Green, 1946.

Luna, Félix. *Ortiz: reportaje a la Argentina opulenta*. Buenos Aires: Sudamericana, 1978.

Luperini, Cesare, et al. *El concepto de formación económica-social*. Córdoba: Pasado y Presente, 1973.

Luxemburg, Rosa. *The Accumulation of Capital*. New Haven, Conn.: Yale University Press, 1951.

Lynch, John. *Argentine Dictator: Juan Manuel de Rosas, 1829–1852*. New York: Oxford University Press, 1981.

McBriar, A. M. *Fabian Socialism and English Politics*. Cambridge: At the University Press, 1962.

MacGaffey, Wyatt, and Clifford R. Barnett. *Cuba: Its People, Its Culture*. New Haven, Conn.: HRAF Press, 1962.

MacKenzie, Norman, and Jeanne MacKenzie. *The First Fabians*. London: Quartet Books, 1977.

McKenzie, Robert Trelford. *British Political Parties: The Distribution of Power within the Conservative and Labour Parties*. New York: St. Martin's, 1955.

MacLean y Estenós, Percy. *Historia de una revolución*. Buenos Aires: EAPAL, 1953.

Magalhães Júnior, R. *Deodoro: a espada contra o império*. 2 vols. São Paulo: Companhia Editora Nacional, 1957.

Main, Jackson Turner. *The Antifederalists: Critics of the Constitution, 1781–1788*. Chapel Hill: University of North Carolina Press, 1961.

Malloy, James. *Bolivia, the Uncompleted Revolution*. Pittsburgh: University of Pittsburgh Press, 1970.

———, ed. *Authoritarianism and Corporatism in Latin America*. Pittsburgh: University of Pittsburgh Press, 1977.

Mandel, Ernest. *From Class Society to Communism*. London: Ink Links, 1972.

Manley, John F. "Neopluralism: A Class Analysis of Pluralism I and Pluralism II." *American Political Science Review* 77, no. 2 (June 1983): 368–383.

Mannheim, Karl. *Diagnosis of Our Time*. New York: Oxford University Press, 1944.

———. *Man and Society in an Age of Reconstruction: Studies in Modern Social Structure*.

New York: Kegan Paul, Trench, Trubner, 1940.

Marco, Miguel Angel de, and Oscar Ensinck. *Historia de Rosario*. Rosario: Museo Histórico Provincial de Rosario Dr. Julio Marc, 1978.

Margulis, Mario. *Migración y marginalidad en América Latina*. Buenos Aires: Paidós, 1967.

Marques, Antonio Henrique de Oliveira. *History of Portugal*. New York: Columbia University Press, 1972.

Marson, Izabel Andrade. *Movimento praieiro, 1842–1849: imprensa, ideologia e poder político*. São Paulo: Editora Moderna, 1980.

Martínez, Carlos J. *La industria siderúrgica nacional*. Buenos Aires: UIA, 1943.

Martins, Hermínio. "Opposition in Portugal." *Government and Opposition* 4, no. 2 (Spring 1969): 250–263.

Martz, John D. *Acción Democrática: Evolution of a Modern Political Party*. Princeton, N.J.: Princeton University Press, 1966.

Martz, John D., and David Myers, eds. *Venezuela: The Democratic Experience*. New York: Praeger, 1977.

Marx, Karl. *Capital: A Critique of Political Economy*. 3 vols. New York: International Publishers, 1967.

Marx, Karl, and Friedrich Engels. *Werke*. 39 vols., supplement, appendix. Berlin: Dietz Verlag, 1964–1971.

Masotti, Louis H., and Dan Bowen, eds. *Riots and Rebellion*. Beverly Hills, Calif.: Sage, 1968.

Melo, Leopoldo. *La postguerra y algunos de los planes sobre el nuevo orden económico*. Buenos Aires: UIA, 1942.

Melotti, Umberto. *Marx and the Third World*. London: Macmillan, 1977.

Mill, John Stuart. *Utilitarianism. On Liberty. Representative Government*. New York: E. P. Dutton, 1951.

Miller, S. M. "Comparative Social Mobility." *Current Sociology* 9, no. 1 (1960): 1–89.

Millones, Luis. *La cultura colonial urbana: una hipótesis de trabajo para el estudio de las poblaciones tugurizadas*. Lima: Universidad Católica, 1975.

Mills, Elizabeth Hoel. "Don Valentín Gómez Farías y el desarrollo de su ideología política." MA thesis, UNAM, 1957.

Mitchell, Christopher. *The Legacy of Populism in Bolivia: From the MNR to Military Rule*. New York: Praeger, 1977.

Mitre, Bartolomé. *Historia de Belgrano y de la independencia argentina*. 5 vols. Reprint. Buenos Aires: Editorial Jackson, n.d.

Moisés, José A. "La huelga de los trescientos mil y las comisiones de empresa." *Revista Mexicana de Sociología* 40, no. 2 (April–June 1978): 493–514.

Moller, Edwin, et al. "La apertura democrática y el PRIN/Bolivia." *Nueva Sociedad*, no. 37 (July–August 1978): 166–170.

Monteiro, Tobías. *Historia do império: o primeiro reinado*. 2 vols. Rio de Janeiro: F. Briguiet e Cia, 1939.

Montero Moreno, René. *La verdad sobre Ibáñez*. Buenos Aires: n.p., 1953.

Montgomery. *The Fall of the House of Labor: The Workplace, the State, and American Labor Activism, 1865–1925*. New York: Cambridge University Press, 1987.

Mora, José María Luis. *Obras sueltas*. 2d ed. Mexico City: Editorial Porrúa, 1963.

Mora y Araujo, Manuel. "Populismo, laborismo y clases medias: política y estructura social en la Argentina." *Criterio* 1755–1756 (1977): 9–12.

———. "Procesos electorales y fuerzas políticas: una perspectiva analítica." In Virgilio Beltrán, ed., *Futuro político de la Argentina*, pp. 83–108. Buenos Aires: Instituto Torcuato Di Tella, 1978.

Moreno, José Antonio. *Barrios in Arms: Revolution in Santo Domingo*. Pittsburgh: University of Pittsburgh Press, 1970.

Moreno, José Luis. "La estructura social y demográfica de la ciudad de Buenos Aires en el año 1770." *Anales del Instituto de Investigaciones Históricas, Universidad del Litoral*, no. 8 (1965): 151–170.

Morse, Richard. *The Urban Development of Latin America, 1750–1920*. Stanford: Center for Latin American Studies, Stanford University, 1971.

Murmis, Miguel, and Juan Carlos Portantiero. *Estudios sobre los orígenes del peronismo*. Buenos Aires: Siglo Veintiuno, 1971.

Murphy, George. "The New History." In Ralph Andreano, ed., *The New Economic History: Recent Papers on Methodology*, pp. 1–16. New York: Wiley, 1970.

Nagel, Ernest. "Some Issues in the Logic of Historical Analysis." *Scientific Monthly* 74, no. 3 (March 1952): 162–169.

———. *The Structure of Science: Problems in the Logic of Scientific Research*. New York: Harcourt, Brace & World, 1961.

Nagel, E., P. Suppes, and A. Tarski, eds. *Logic, Methodology, and Philosophy of Science*. Stanford, Calif.: Stanford University Press, 1962.

Nascimbene, Mario. "Aspectos demográficos y educacionales de la inmigración a la Argentina: el impacto de la corriente inmigratoria italiana entre 1876 y 1925." *Cuadernos de la Facultad de Ciencias Sociales y Económicas*, no. 4 (1978): 63–120.

Nelson, Lowry. *Rural Cuba*. Minneapolis: University of Minnesota Press, 1950.

Nettl, J. P. *Political Mobilization: A Sociological Analysis of Methods and Concepts*. New York: Basic Books, 1967.

Neumann, Franz L. *Behemoth: The Structure and Practice of National Socialism*. New York: Oxford University Press, 1942.

North, Liisa, and Tanya Korovkin. *The Peruvian Revolution and the Officers in Power, 1967–1976*. Montreal: Centre for Developing Area Studies, McGill University, 1981.

Nun, José. "The Middle Class Military Coup." In Claudio Véliz, ed., *The Politics of Conformity in Latin America*, pp. 66–118. New York: Oxford University Press, 1967.

Nunn, Frederick. *Chilean Politics, 1920–31: The Honorable Mission of the Armed Forces*. Albuquerque, University of New Mexico Press, 1976.

O'Donnell, Guillermo. *El estado burocrático autoritario 1966–1973*. Buenos Aires: Editorial de Belgrano, 1982.

———. *Modernización y autoritarismo*. Buenos Aires: Paidos, 1972.

———. *Modernization and Bureaucratic-Authoritarianism: Studies in South American Politics*. Berkeley: Institute of International Studies, University of California, 1973.

———. "Notas para el estudio de procesos de democratización política a partir del estado burocrático-autoritario." *Desarrollo Económico* 22, no. 86 (July–September 1982): 231–248.

———. *Tensiones en el estado burocrático autoritario y la cuestión de la democracia*. Buenos Aires: CEDES, 1978.

O'Donnell, Guillermo, Philippe Schmitter, and Lawrence Whitehead, eds. *Transitions from Authoritarian Rule: Prospects for Democracy*. Baltimore, Md.: Johns Hopkins

University Press, 1986.

Offe, Claus. *Contradictions of the Welfare State.* London: Hutchinson, 1984.

Offe, Claus, and Helmut Wiesenthal. "Two Logics of Collective Action: Theoretical Notes on Social Class and Organizational Form." In Vol. 1 (1980) of Maurice Zeitlin, ed., *Political Power and Social Theory.* 6 vols. Greenwich, Conn.: Jai Press, 1980–1987, I: 67–115.

O'Gorman, Frank. "The Problem of Party in Modern British History: 1725–1832." *Government and Opposition* 16, no. 4 (Autumn 1981): 447–470.

Ordeshook, Peter C. *Game Theory and Political Theory: An Introduction.* Cambridge: At the University Press, 1986.

Ortiz, Eduardo, ed. *Temas socialistas.* Santiago: Vector, Centro de Estudios Económicos y Sociales, 1983.

Oszlak, Oscar. *La formación del estado argentino.* Buenos Aires: Editorial de Belgrano, 1982.

Otávio, Rodrigo. *A balaiada, 1839.* Rio de Janeiro: n.p., 1942.

Ott, Thomas. *The Haitian Revolution, 1789–1804.* Knoxville: University of Tennessee Press, 1973.

Panzeri, R., et al. *La división capitalista del trabajo.* Córdoba: Pasado y Presente, 1972.

Parish, Woodbine. *Buenos Aires y las provincias del Río de la Plata desde su descubrimiento y conquista por los españoles.* 1852. Reprint. Buenos Aires: Hachette, 1958.

Parisi, Giuseppe. *Storia degli italiani nell'Argentina.* Rome: Voghera, 1907.

Parra, Darío. *Venezuela, "democracia" versus "dictadura."* Madrid: n.p., 1961.

Payá, Carlos, and Eduardo Cárdenas. *El primer nacionalismo argentino en Gálvez y Ricardo Rojas.* Buenos Aires: Peña Lillo, 1978.

Payne, James. *Labor and Politics in Peru: The System of Political Bargaining.* New Haven, Conn.: Yale University Press, 1965.

Pelling, Henry. *A History of British Trade Unionism.* London: Macmillan, 1963.

———. *The Origins of the Labour Party, 1880–1900.* London: Macmillan, 1954.

———. *Popular Politics and Society in Late Victorian Britain: Essays.* London: Macmillan, 1968.

Peralta Ramos, Mónica. *Etapas de acumulación y alianzas de clases en la Argentina, 1930–1970.* Buenos Aires: Siglo Veintiuno, 1972.

Pérez Jiménez, Marcos. *Frente a la infamia.* Caracas: Ediciones Garrido, 1968.

Perina, Rubén M. *Onganía, Levingston, Lanusse: los militares en la política argentina.* Editorial de Belgrano, 1983.

Petkoff, Teodoro. *Proceso a la izquierda o la falsa conducta revolucionaria.* Barcelona: Planeta, 1976.

Petras, James. *Politics and Social Forces in Chilean Development.* Berkeley and Los Angeles: University of California Press, 1969.

Petras, James, and Robert La Porte. *Perú: transformación revolucionaria o modernización?* Buenos Aires: Amorrortu, 1971.

Pike, Fredrick, and Thomas Stritch, eds. *The New Corporatism: Social-Political Structures in the Iberian World.* Notre Dame, Ind.: University of Notre Dame Press, 1974.

Pizzorno, Alessandro, et al. *Gramsci y las ciencias sociales.* Córdoba: Pasado y Presente, 1974.

Platt, Christopher M., and Guido Di Tella, eds. *Argentina, Australia and Canada: Studies in Comparative Development.* Oxford: St. Antony's Macmillan Series, 1985.

Popper, Karl. *The Poverty of Historicism.* 2d ed. London: Routledge & Kegan Paul, 1961.

Portales, Diego. *Epistolario de Don Diego Portales, 1821–1837.* Edited by Ernesto de la Cruz, with prologue and new letters added by Guillermo Feliú Cruz. 3 vols. Santiago: Ministerio de Justicia, 1937.

Portantiero, Juan Carlos. *Los usos de Gramsci.* Mexico City: Pasado y Presente, 1981.

Portes, Alejandro. "Leftist Radicalism in Chile: A Test of Three Hypotheses." *Comparative Politics* 2, no. 2 (June 1970): 251–274.

———. "Political Pluralism, Differential Socialization, and Lower Class Leftist Radicalism." *American Sociological Review* 36, no. 5 (October 1971): 820–835.

Potash, Robert. *El ejército y la política en la Argentina.* 2 vols. Buenos Aires: Sudamericana, 1971–1981.

Poulantzas, Nicos, ed. *La crise de l' état.* Paris: Presses Universitaires de France, 1976.

Powell, John. *Political Mobilization of the Venezuelan Peasant.* Cambridge, Mass.: Harvard University Press, 1971.

Preziosi, Giovanni. *Gli italiani negli Stati Uniti del Nord.* Milan: Libreria Editrice Milanese, 1909.

Pribicevic, Branco. *The Shop Stewards' Movement and Workers' Control, 1910–1922.* Oxford: Blackwell, 1959.

Prost, Antoine. *La C.G.T. à l' époque du Front Populaire, 1934–1939: essai de description numérique.* Paris: Armand Colin, 1964.

Przeworski, Adam. "Institutionalization of Voting Patterns, or Is Mobilization the Source of Decay?" *American Political Science Review* 69, no. 1 (March 1975): 49–67.

Przeworski, Adam, and Glaucio Soares. "Theories in Search of a Curve: A Contextual Interpretation of Left Vote." *American Political Science Review* 65 (1971): 51–68.

Przeworski, Adam, and Henry Teune. *The Logic of Comparative Social Enquiry.* New York: Wiley, 1970.

Pulzer, Peter G. *Political Representation and Elections in Britain.* London: Allen & Unwin, 1972.

Ramírez Flores, José. *El gobierno insurgente en Guadalajara, 1810–1811.* Guadalajara: Gobierno de Jalisco, Secretaría General, Unidad Editorial, 1980.

Ramírez Necochea, Hernán. *Balmaceda y la contrarrevolución de 1891.* Santiago: Editorial Universitaria, 1958.

———. *Historia del movimiento obrero en Chile: antecedentes, siglo XIX.* Santiago: Austral, 1956.

Ramos Mejía, José M. *Las multitudes argentinas.* Buenos Aires: Editorial de Belgrano, 1977.

Rapaport, Mario. *Gran Bretaña, Estados Unidos y las clases dirigentes argentinas: 1940–1945.* Buenos Aires: Editorial de Belgrano, 1981.

Ratzer, José. *Los marxistas argentinos del noventa.* Córdoba: Pasado y Presente, 1969.

Rawson Bustamante, Juan. *Las posibilidades aeronáuticas de postguerra.* Buenos Aires: UIA, 1944.

Reichardt, H. Canabarro. *Idéias de liberdade no Rio Grande do Sul.* Rio de Janeiro: Jornal do Commercio, 1928.

Reyes Heroles, Jesús. *Historia del liberalismo mexicano.* 3 vols. Mexico City: Universidad Nacional Autónoma de México (UNAM), Facultad de Derecho, 1957–1961.

Reyna, José L., and Richard Weinert, eds. *Authoritarianism in Mexico.* Philadelphia: Institute for the Study of Human Issues, 1977.

Ridley, Frederick F. *Revolutionary Syndicalism in France.* Cambridge: At the University Press, 1970.

Riker, William. *The Theory of Political Coalitions.* New Haven, Conn.: Yale University Press, 1962.

Roberts, Bryan. *Cities of Peasants: The Political Economy of Urbanization in the Third World.* 2d ed. Beverly Hills, Calif.: Sage, 1979.

———. *Organizing Strangers: Poor Families in Guatemala City.* Austin: University of Texas Press, 1973.

Rock, David, ed., *Argentina in the Twentieth Century.* London: Duckworth, 1975.

———. "Lucha civil en la Argentina. La semana trágica de enero de 1919." *Desarrollo Económico* 11, nos. 42–44 (July 1971–March 1972): 165–215.

———. *Politics in Argentina, 1890–1930: The Rise and Fall of Radicalism.* Cambridge: At the University Press, 1975.

Rodrigues, José Honório. *Conciliação e reforma no Brasil: um desafio histórico cultural.* Rio de Janeiro: Civilização Brasileira, 1965.

Rodríguez, Leôncio Martins. *Conflito industrial e sindicalismo em Brasil.* São Paulo: DIFEL, 1966.

———. *Trabalhadores, sindicatos e industrialização.* São Paulo: Brasiliense, 1974.

Romero, José Luis. *Latinoamérica: las ciudades y las ideas.* Mexico City: Siglo Veintiuno, 1976.

Romero, Luis A. *La sociedad de la igualdad.* Buenos Aires: Instituto Torcuato Di Tella, 1978.

Rossetti, Carlo G. "Banditismo político: terre e guerra civile nella Sardegna del XIX secolo." *Review, Fernand Braudel Center* 5, no. 4 (1982): 643–693.

Rouquié, Alain. *Poder militar y sociedad política en la Argentina.* 2 vols. Buenos Aires: Emecé, 1981–1982.

Roure, Agenor de. *Formação constitucional do Brasil.* Rio de Janeiro: Typografia do Jornal do Commercio, 1914.

Sáenz Peña, Roque. *Escritos y discursos.* 2 vols. Buenos Aires: Jacobo Peuser, 1914–1915.

Salvadori, Massimo. *Karl Kautsky and the Socialist Revolution, 1880–1938.* London: New Left Books, 1979.

Salvati, Michele, and Bianca Becalli. "La divisione del lavoro: capitalismo, socialismo, utopía." *Quaderni Piacentini,* no. 40 (1970).

Sánchez, Luis A. *Haya de la Torre y el Apra: crónica de un hombre y un partido.* Santiago: Editorial del Pacífico, 1955.

Sánchez Albornoz, Nicolás. *The Population of Latin America: A History.* Berkeley and Los Angeles: University of California Press, 1974.

Santos, Wanderley Guilherme dos. *Poder e política: crónica do autoritarismo brasileiro.* Rio de Janeiro: Forense Universitaria, 1978.

Sapir, Boris. "The Conception of the Bourgeois Revolution." In Leopold Haimson, ed., *The Mensheviks: From the Revolution of 1917 to the Second World War,* pp. 364–388. Chicago: University of Chicago Press, 1974.

Sarfatti, Magalí. *Spanish Bureaucratic Patrimonialism in America.* Berkeley: Institute of International Studies, University of California, 1966.

Sarobe, José María. *Política económica argentina.* Buenos Aires: UIA, 1942.

Savio, Manuel N. *Política de la producción metalúrgica argentina.* Buenos Aires: UIA, 1942.

Schifter, Jacobo. *La fase oculta de la guerra civil en Costa Rica.* San José: EDUCA, 1979.

Schipa, Michelangelo. *Masaniello.* Bari: Laterza, 1925.

Schmitter, Philippe. *Corporatism and Public Policy in Authoritarian Portugal.* London: Sage, 1975.

Schneider, Ronald. *The Political System of Brazil: Emergence of an Authoritarian "Modernizing" Regime, 1964–70.* New York: Columbia University Press, 1971.

Schwartzman, Simón. *Bases do autoritarismo brasileiro.* Brasília: Universidade de Dranília, 1900.

Schwarzenberg, Claudio. *Il sindacalismo fascista.* Milan: Mursia, 1975.

Sergi, Jorge. *Historia de las italianos en la Argentina.* Buenos Aires: Editora Italo Argentina, 1940.

Shaw, George B., et al. *Fabian Essays in Socialism.* London: W. Scott, 1889.

Sigal, Silvia, and Eliseo Verón. "Perón, discurso político e ideología." In Alain Rouquié, ed., *Argentina, Hoy,* pp. 151–205. Mexico City: Siglo Veintiuno, 1981.

Silva, Hélio. *O ciclo de Vargas.* Rio de Janeiro: Civilização Brasileira, 1964 .

Silva, J. M. Pereira da. *Historia da fundação do império brasileiro.* Rio de Janeiro: E. Belmatte; Paris: B. L. Barnier, 1877.

Silva Herzog, Jesús. *Breve historia de la revolución mexicana.* 2 vols. Mexico City: Fondo de Cultura Económica, 1960.

Silvert, Kalman. *A Study in Government: Guatemala.* New Orleans: Middle America Research Institute, 1954.

Simon, Herbert. *Models of Man, Social and Rational: Mathematical Essays on Rational Human Behavior in a Social Setting.* New York: Wiley, 1957.

Sjoberg, Gideon. *The Preindustrial City, Past and Present.* Glencoe, Ill.: Free Press, 1960.

Skidmore, Thomas. *Politics in Brazil, 1930–64: An Experiment in Democracy.* New York: Oxford University Press, 1967.

Skocpol, Theda. "Rentier State and Shi'a Islam in the Iranian Revolution." *Theory and Society* 11, no. 3 (May 1982): 265–283.

———. *States and Social Revolutions: A Comparative Analysis of France, Russia, and China.* Cambridge: At the University Press, 1979.

Slatta, Richard. *Gauchos and the Vanishing Frontier.* Lincoln: University of Nebraska Press, 1983.

Snow, Peter. *El radicalismo chileno: historia y doctrina del Partido Radical.* Buenos Aires: Editorial Francisco de Aguirre, 1972.

Soares, Glaucio Dillon. "The Politics of Uneven Development: The Case of Brazil." In Seymour M. Lipset and Stein Rokkan, eds., *Party Systems and Voter Alignments: Cross National Perspectives,* pp. 467–496. New York: Free Press, 1967.

Soares, Glaucio Dillon, and Robert Hamblin. "Socio-economic Variables and Voting for the Radical Left: Chile 1952." *American Political Science Review* 61, no. 4 (December 1967): 1053–1065.

Soares, José Arlindo. *A frente de Recife e o governo do Arraes.* Rio de Janeiro: Paz e Terra, 1982.

Sodré, Nelson Werneck. *História militar do Brasil.* Rio de Janeiro: Civilização Brasileira, 1965.

Sombart, Werner. *Why Is There No Socialism in the United States?* 1906. Reprint. London: Macmillan, 1976.

Sorel, Georges. *Reflexions on Violence.* London: Allen & Unwin, 1925.

Sosa, Arturo, and Eloi Lengrand. *Del garibaldismo estudiantil a la izquierda criolla: los orígenes marxistas del Proyecto A. D., 1928–1935*. Caracas: Centauro, 1981.

Spencer, Herbert. *Principles of Sociology*. 3 vols. New York: Appleton, 1900–1905.

Stepan, Alfred. *The Military in Politics: Changing Patterns in Brazil*. Princeton, N.J.: Princeton University Press, 1971.

————. *State and Society: Peru in Comparative Perspective*. Princeton, N.J.: Princeton University Press, 1968.

Stevenson, John R. *The Chilean Popular Front*. Philadelphia: University of Pennsylvania Press, 1942.

Stinchcombe, Arthur. *Constructing Social Theories*. New York: Harcourt, Brace & World, 1968.

Stone, Lawrence. "The Revival of Narrative: Reflections on a New Old History." *Past and Present* 85 (November 1979): 3–24.

Sunkel, Osvaldo, and Pedro Paz. *El subdesarrollo latinoamericano y la teoría del desarrollo*. Mexico City: Siglo Veintiuno, 1969.

Szulc, Tad. *Twilight of the Tyrants*. New York: Holt, 1959.

Taylor, Philip B. *Government and Politics of Uruguay*. New Orleans: Tulane University Press, 1960.

————. *The Venezuelan Golpe de Estado of 1958: The Fall of Marcos Pérez Jiménez*. Washington, D.C.: Institute for the Comparative Study of Political Systems, 1968.

Teichman, Judith. "Interest Conflict and Entrepreneurial Support for Perón." *Latin American Research Review* 16, no. 1 (1981): 144–155.

Thomas, Hugh. *Cuba, the Pursuit of Freedom*. New York: Harper & Row, 1971.

Tilly, Charles. *From Mobilization to Revolution*. Reading, Mass.: Addison-Wesley, 1978.

Tomasi, Silvano, and Madeline H. Engel, eds. *The Italian Experience in the United States*. Staten Island, N.Y.: Center for Migration Studies, 1970.

Torre, Juan Carlos. *El proceso político interno en los sindicatos en Argentina*. Documento de Trabajo, no. 89. Buenos Aires: Instituto Torcuato Di Tella, 1974.

————. *La vieja guardia sindical y Perón*. Buenos Aires: Sudamericana, forthcoming.

————. *Los sindicalistas en el poder: 1973–1976*. Buenos Aires: Centro Editor de América Latina, 1983.

Touraine, Alain. "La marginalidad urbana." *Revista Mexicana de Sociología* 39, no. 4 (October–December 1977): 1105–1142.

————. *The Post-Industrial Society: Tomorrow's Social History. Classes, Conflicts, and Culture in the Programmed Society*. New York: Random House, 1971.

Trías, Vivián. *Perú: fuerzas armadas y revolución*. Montevideo: Ediciones de la Banda Oriental, 1971.

Trindade, Helgio. "La cuestión del fascismo en América Latina." *Desarrollo Económico* 23, no. 91 (October–December 1983): 429–447.

Tutino, John. *From Insurrection to Revolution in Mexico. Social Bases of Agrarian Violence, 1750–1940*. Princeton: Princeton University Press, 1986.

Uslar Pietri, Juan. *Historia de la rebelión popular en 1814: contribución al estudio de la historia de Venezuela*. Caracas: Edime, 1962.

Valdés Vergara, Ismael. *La revolución de 1891*. Buenos Aires: Editorial Francisco de Aguirre, 1970.

Valencia, Elmo. *Libro rojo de Rojas*. Bogotá: Ediciones Culturales, 1970.

Valenzuela, Arturo. "Chile." In Juan Linz and Alfred Stepan, eds., *The Breakdown of*

Democratic Regimes, Part 4, pp. 3–168. Baltimore, Md.: Johns Hopkins University Press, 1976.

————. *Political Brokers in Chile: Local Government in a Centralized Polity*. Durham, N.C.: Duke University Press, 1977.

Valenzuela, Arturo, and J. Samuel Valenzuela, eds. *Chile: Politics and Society*. New Brunswick, N.J.: Transaction Books, 1976.

Valenzuela, J. Samuel. *Democratización por reforma: los conservadores y la expansión del sufragio en el siglo diecinueve chileno*. Buenos Aires: IDES, 1984.

Valiani, Leo. "Le mouvement syndical ouvrier italien entre le fascisme et l'antifascisme." In International Institute for Social History, *Mouvements ouvriers et depression economique de 1929 a 1939*. Assen, the Netherlands, 1966.

Valle Iberlucea, Enrique del. *Duscursos parlamentarios*. Valencia: F. Sempere y Cía., 1914.

Vanger, Milton. *José Battle y Ordóñez of Uruguay*. Cambridge, Mass.: Harvard University Press, 1963.

Varela, Alfredo. *Revoluções cisplatinas: a República Riograndense*. 2 vols. Porto: Chardron, 1915.

Varnhagen, Francisco A. de, visconde de Porto Seguro. *História da independência do Brasil*. Rio de Janeiro: Imprensa Nacional, 1919.

Varsavsky, Oscar, and Alfredo Eric Calcagno, eds. *América Latina: modelos matemáticos*. Santiago: Editorial Universitario, 1971.

Vedia y Mitre, Mariano de. *La revolución del Noventa: Origen y fundación de la Unión Cívica. Causas, desarrollo y consecuencias de la revolución de julio*. Buenos Aires: Talleres Gráficos Argentinos de L. J. Rosso, 1929.

Véliz, Claudio. *The Centralist Tradition of Latin America*. Princeton, N.J.: Princeton University Press, 1980.

————, ed. *Obstacles to Change in Latin America*. New York: Oxford University Press, 1965.

————, ed. *The Politics of Conformity in Latin America*. New York: Oxford University Press, 1967.

Venturi, Franco. *Roots of Revolution: A History of the Populist and Socialist Movements in Nineteenth-Century Russia*. London: Weidenfeld & Nicholson, 1960.

Vianna Filho, Luiz. *A sabinada: a república bahiana de 1837*. Rio de Janeiro: J. Olympio, 1938.

Vicuña Mackenna, Benjamín. *D. Diego Portales*. Santiago: Editorial del Pacífico, 1974.

————. *Vida de O'Higgins. La corona del héroe*. Santiago: Editorial Universitaria, 1978.

Villanueva, Víctor. *Nueva mentalidad militar en Perú?* Buenos Aires: Replanteo, 1969.

Villari, Rosario. *La rivolta antispagnola a Napoli. Origini, 1585–1647*. Bari: Laterza, 1967.

Waisman, Carlos. *Reversal of Development in Argentina: Postwar Counterrevolutionary Policies and Their Structural Consequences*. Princeton, N.J.: Princeton University Press, 1987.

Walker, Thomas W., ed. *Nicaragua: The First Five Years*. New York: Praeger, 1985.

Walter, Richard J. *The Socialist Party of Argentina, 1890–1930*. Austin: University of Texas Press, 1977.

Ward, John M. *Empire in the Antipodes: The British in Australasia, 1840–1868*. London: Edmund Arnold, 1966.

Weber, Max. *Economy and Society*. 3 vols. New York: Bedminster, 1968.

————. *The Methodology of the Social Sciences*. New York: Free Press of Glencoe, 1949.

Weffort, Francisco. *O populismo na política brasileira*. Rio de Janeiro: Paz e Terra, 1978.

Wheelock, Jaime, and Luis Carrión. *Apuntes sobre el desarrollo económico y social de Nicaragua*. Managua: N.p., n.d.

Wiarda, Howard. *Corporatism and Development: The Portuguese Experience*. Amherst: University of Massachusetts Press, 1977.

————, ed. *Politics and Social Change in Latin America: The Distinct Tradition*. Amherst: University of Massachusetts Press, 1974.

Williams, Edward J. *Latin American Christian Democratic Parties*. Knoxville: University of Tennessee Press, 1967.

Williamson, Chilton. *American Suffrage from Property to Democracy, 1760–1860*. Princeton, N.J.: Princeton University Press, 1960.

Womack, John. *Zapata and the Mexican Revolution*. New York: Knopf, 1969.

Wood, Gordon S. *The Creation of the American Republic, 1776–1787*. Chapel Hill: University of North Carolina Press, 1969.

Wurth Rojas, Ernesto. *Ibáñez, caudillo enigmático*. Santiago: Editorial del Pacífico, 1958.

Zavala, Lorenzo de. *Ensayo histórico de las revoluciones de México desde 1808 hasta 1830*. 2 vols. Paris: Imprenta de P. Dupont y G. Laguionie, 1831.

Zeitlin, Maurice. *Revolutionary Politics and the Cuban Working Class*. Princeton, N.J.: Princeton University Press, 1967.

Zetterberg, Hans. *Theory and Verification in Sociology*. 3d ed. Totowa, N.J.: Bedminster, 1965.

Zuccarini, Emilio. *Il lavoro degli italiani nella Repubblica Argentina del 1516 al 1910. Studi, leggende e ricerche*. Buenos Aires: La Patria degli Italiani, 1910.

Periodicals

Acción Socialista, Buenos Aires, Argentina

L'Amico del Popolo, Buenos Aires, Argentina

La Anarquía, La Plata, Argentina

La Confederación, Buenos Aires, Argentina

Eco delle Società Italiane, Buenos Aires, Argentina

Ideas y Figuras, Buenos Aires, Argentina

La Nuova Civiltà, Buenos Aires, Argentina

El Obrero, Buenos Aires, Argentina

El Obrero (formerly *El Obrero Panadero*), Buenos Aires, Argentina

El Rebelde, Buenos Aires, Argentina

Revista Socialista Internacional, Buenos Aires, Argentina

La Unión Socialista, Buenos Aires, Argentina

Interviews (Oral History Program [OHP], Instituto Torcuato Di Tella, Buenos Aires, Argentina)

Lucio Bonilla	Rafael Ginocchio
José Domenech	Ernesto Janin
Manuel Fosa	Francisco Pérez Leirós
Mateo Fossa	Cipriano Reyes
Luis Gay	Mariano Tedesco

Index

WHITMAN COLLEGE LIBRAR